Relational Theory

for Computer Professionals

What Relational Databases

Are Really All About

C. J. Date

Relational Theory for Computer Professionals

by C. J. Date

Copyright © 2013 C. J. Date. All rights reserved.
Printed in the United States of America.

Published by O'Reilly Media, Inc.
1005 Gravenstein Highway North, Sebastopol, CA 95472

O'Reilly books may be purchased for educational, business, or sales promotional use. Online editions are also available for most titles (*http://my.safaribooksonline.com*). For more information, contact our corporate/institutional sales department: (800) 998-9938 or *corporate@oreilly.com*.

Printing History:
May 2013:   First Edition.

Revision History:
  2013-05-07   First release
See *http://oreilly.com/catalog/errata.csp?isbn=0636920029649* for release details.

ISBN: 978-1-449-36943-9
[LSI]

Mathematical science shows what is.
It is the language of unseen relations between things.
—Ada, Countess of Lovelace,
quoted in Dorothy Stein (ed.):
Ada: A Life and a Legacy (1985)

That is the essence of science:
Ask an impertinent question, and you are on the way to a pertinent answer.
—Jacob Bronowski:
The Ascent of Man (1973)

Hofstadter's Law: *It always takes longer than you expect,*
even when you take into account Hofstadter's Law.
—Douglas R. Hofstadter:
Gödel, Escher, Bach: An Eternal Golden Braid (1979)

———— ◆◆◆◆◆ ————

To my wife Lindy
and my daughters Sarah and Jennie
with all my love

About the Author

C. J. Date is an independent author, lecturer, researcher, and consultant, specializing in relational database technology. He is best known for his book *An Introduction to Database Systems* (8th edition, Addison-Wesley, 2004), which has sold nearly 900,000 copies at the time of writing and is used by several hundred colleges and universities worldwide. He is also the author of numerous other books on database management, including most recently:

- From Ventus: *Go Faster! The TransRelational^{TM} Approach to DBMS Implementation* (2002, 2011)

- From Addison-Wesley: *Databases, Types, and the Relational Model: The Third Manifesto* (3rd edition, coauthored with Hugh Darwen, 2007)

- From Trafford: *Logic and Databases: The Roots of Relational Theory* (2007) and *Database Explorations: Essays on The Third Manifesto and Related Topics* (coauthored with Hugh Darwen, 2010)

- From Apress: *Date on Database: Writings 2000–2006* (2007) and *The Relational Database Dictionary, Extended Edition* (2008)

- From O'Reilly: *SQL and Relational Theory: How to Write Accurate SQL Code* (2nd edition, 2012); *Database Design and Relational Theory: Normal Forms and All That Jazz* (2012); and *View Updating and Relational Theory: Solving the View Update Problem* (2013)

Mr. Date was inducted into the Computing Industry Hall of Fame in 2004. He enjoys a reputation that is second to none for his ability to explain complex technical subjects in a clear and understandable fashion.

C o n t e n t s

Preface

The relational model of data is one of the great technical inventions of the last hundred years. It's the foundation of everything we do in the database field; indeed, it's what made database management a science, instead of what it was formerly, viz., little more than an ad hoc collection of tricks, techniques, and rules of thumb. Thus, everyone professionally involved in database management, even to the smallest degree, owes it to himself or herself to acquire a reasonable knowledge and understanding of the relational model—for without it, fully effective and productive job performance is impossible.

Unfortunately, it isn't as easy as it should be to come by the aforesaid "reasonable knowledge and understanding." There are several reasons for this state of affairs, but one of the biggest is the language SQL, which is the official standard "relational" language[1] and is supported in some shape or form by just about every database product on the market today. It's widely recognized—at least, it should be widely recognized—that, considered as a concrete realization of the abstract ideas of the relational model, SQL is very deeply flawed (that's why I put "relational" in quote marks in the previous sentence). And since for obvious practical reasons everyone in the database world has to know something about SQL, the emphasis in almost all relational (or would-be relational) education tends to be on SQL as such, instead of on the underlying theory. As a consequence, it's all too common for people to think that, just because they know SQL, they know relational theory. Sadly, however, the truth is that if you know only SQL as such, then you most certainly don't know that theory. And what you don't know can hurt you.

The principal aim of this book, then, is to teach relational theory, very carefully (indeed, as carefully as I can). A secondary aim is to describe SQL—or what might be regarded as the core features of SQL, at any rate—from the standpoint of that theory. Which brings me to another point ... Some readers will be aware that not all that long ago I published another book on such matters, with the title *SQL and Relational Theory: How to Write Accurate SQL Code* (2nd edition, O'Reilly, 2012). Unlike the present book, however, that earlier book was aimed at database practitioners specifically, meaning, typically, people with at least three or four years experience "working in the trenches" with a database system and using it regularly as part of their normal job (and therefore certainly having a working knowledge of SQL). What that book tried to do was show how to apply relational principles to the use of SQL, thereby making SQL behave almost as if it were a truly relational language (a discipline I referred to in that book as "using SQL relationally"). Now, there's unavoidably some overlap between that book and the present one; indeed, there are places in the present book where text has been copied and pasted

---

[1] The SQL standard has been through several versions, or editions, over the years. The version current at the time of writing is the 2011 version ("SQL:2011"). Here's the formal reference: International Organization for Standardization (ISO), *Database Language SQL*, Document ISO/IEC 9075:2011. Chapter 10 and Appendix E each have a little more to say about this reference, and Chapter 10 in particular briefly reviews the pertinent history.

from the earlier book, sometimes almost verbatim. Nonetheless, what you're looking at now is definitely a different book, in part because it's aimed at a different audience (see further explanation below). Of necessity, however, there are frequent references in what follows to that earlier book, and in the interest of brevity all such references are given in the form of the abbreviated title alone (viz., *SQL and Relational Theory*). What's more, I think it's only fair to say that if you're familiar with that earlier book, then you probably won't have much to gain from the present one. Of course, I don't want to discourage you from reading it!—but if you do, I doubt whether you'll find much that's really new to you.

Who Should Read This Book

My target audience is computer professionals. Thus, I assume you know something about computers and programming in general, and I assume you're reasonably familiar with at least one conventional programming language. But I don't assume you know anything about databases, relational or otherwise, nor about SQL in particular. Of course, you very likely do at least know that modern database systems are almost all supposed to be "relational" (whatever that might mean), but I won't rely even on that assumption. Please note, however, that if you do happen to know something about databases already, then you probably need to pay extra careful attention to what this book has to say!—you might find you have some *un*learning to do (and unlearning, as we all know, can be very difficult). The point is, existing database products, even those that are labeled "relational," are in fact not so—they depart from the theoretical relational ideal in far too many ways, as you'll soon discover. As I wrote in *SQL and Relational Theory*:

> I apologize for the possibly offensive tone here [, but] if your knowledge of the relational model derives only from your knowledge of SQL, then I'm afraid you won't know the relational model as well as you should, and you'll probably know "some things that ain't so." I can't say it too strongly: *SQL and the relational model aren't the same thing.*

Note: I'd like to mention that I have a live seminar available based on the material in this book. For further details, please go to the website *www.justsql.co.uk/chris_date/chris_date.htm.* A video version is available too—please go to *http://oreilly.com/go/date.*

Structure of the Book

The book is divided into three main parts, plus a collection of appendixes. Part I, "Foundations," is concerned with the relational model as such—in other words, with the theory underlying relational database technology (though it does also stress the practical applications of that theory throughout). Part II, "Transactions and Database Design," is devoted to a discussion of certain material that (a) you do need to know in order to understand what databases in general, and relational databases in particular, are all about, but (b) doesn't really have all that much to do with the relational model as such (except inasmuch as it does build on that model as a foundation). Part III, "SQL," then revisits the material of Part I and shows how the concepts discussed in that first part are realized in the SQL language as such. As for the appendixes, they're something of a mixed bag (as appendixes tend to be), and I don't think it's worth my while trying to describe them further here.

Note: Review questions and exercises are an integral part of most of the chapters, and I'd like to recommend that you try answering those questions and exercises for yourself before going on to read the ensuing discussion of the answers. In particular, you should be aware that those exercises frequently, and of course intentionally, go some way—sometimes a fairly long way—beyond the material as described in the immediately preceding text.

Acknowledgments

Once again I'd like to begin by thanking my wife Lindy for her support throughout the production of this book, as well as all of its predecessors. I'd also like to thank David Livingstone for originally suggesting the idea of this particular book—or one something like it, at any rate!—and Allen Noren for pressuring me to write it. (Allen's idea was that my other O'Reilly books needed a foundation on which to build, and a book like this could provide that foundation. And I believe he's correct. Certainly that's the book I've tried to write.) Finally, I'd like to thank the attendees at live classes, too numerous to mention individually, whose questions and comments helped me structure the book appropriately, and helped me also to decide what to include and what to exclude. As always, of course, any errors, of either fact or judgment, remain my own responsibility.

C. J. Date
Healdsburg, California
2013

Part I

FOUNDATIONS

Chapter 1

Basic Database Concepts

Our life is frittered away by detail ... Simplify, simplify.
—Henry David Thoreau: *Walden* (1854)

This introductory chapter is just meant to provide "the view from 30,000 feet," as it were. It's deliberately not deep, and if you do already know something about database management you probably won't find anything here you don't already know. But I think it's worth your while to give the material a "once over lightly" reading anyway, if only to get a sense of what background knowledge I'll be assuming and relying on in subsequent chapters. Also, the chapter introduces the running example, which you'll definitely need to be familiar with when we get to those later chapters.

WHAT'S A DATABASE?

A database can be thought of as a kind of electronic filing cabinet; it contains digitized information ("data"), which is kept in persistent storage of some kind, typically on magnetic disks. Users can insert new information into the database, and delete, change, or retrieve existing information in the database, by issuing *requests* or *commands* to the software that manages the database—which is to say, the database management system (DBMS for short). *Note:* Throughout this book, I take the term *user* to mean either an application programmer or an interactive user[1] or both, as the context demands.

 Now, in practice, those user requests to the DBMS can be formulated in a variety of different ways (e.g., by pointing and clicking with a mouse). For our purposes, however, it's more convenient to assume they're expressed in the form of simple text strings in some formal language. Given a human resources database, for example, we might write:

```
EMP WHERE JOB = 'Programmer'
```

And this expression represents (let's agree) a *retrieval request*—more usually known as a *query*—for employee information for employees whose job title is 'Programmer'.

---

[1] But still a computer professional, not a genuine "end user," who might reasonably be quite ignorant of most of the matters to be discussed in this book.

The Running Example

Fig. 1.1 below shows sample values for a typical database, having to do with *suppliers*, *parts*, and *shipments* (of parts by suppliers).

S

SNO	SNAME	STATUS	CITY
S1	Smith	20	London
S2	Jones	10	Paris
S3	Blake	30	Paris
S4	Clark	20	London
S5	Adams	30	Athens

P

PNO	PNAME	COLOR	WEIGHT	CITY
P1	Nut	Red	12.0	London
P2	Bolt	Green	17.0	Paris
P3	Screw	Blue	17.0	Oslo
P4	Screw	Red	14.0	London
P5	Cam	Blue	12.0	Paris
P6	Cog	Red	19.0	London

SP

SNO	PNO	QTY
S1	P1	300
S1	P2	200
S1	P3	400
S1	P4	200
S1	P5	100
S1	P6	100
S2	P1	300
S2	P2	400
S3	P2	200
S4	P2	200
S4	P4	300
S4	P5	400

Fig. 1.1: The suppliers-and-parts database—sample values

As you can see, this database contains three *files*, or *tables*. (Actually they're *relations*, as we'll see in Chapter 2, but for the purposes of this introductory chapter "files" or "tables" will do.) The tables are named S, P, and SP, respectively, and since they're tables they're made up of rows and columns (in conventional file terms, the rows correspond to records of the file in question and the columns to fields). They're meant to be understood as follows:

- Table S represents *suppliers under contract*. Each supplier has one supplier number (SNO), unique to that supplier; one name (SNAME), not necessarily unique (though the sample values shown in Fig. 1.1 do happen to be unique); one status value (STATUS); and one location (CITY). *Note:* In the rest of this book I'll abbreviate "suppliers under contract," most of the time, to just *suppliers*.

- Table P represents *kinds of parts*. Each kind of part has one part number (PNO), which is unique; one name (PNAME); one color (COLOR); one weight (WEIGHT); and one location where parts of that kind are stored (CITY). *Note:* In the rest of this book I'll abbreviate "kinds of parts," most of the time, to just *parts*.

- Table SP represents *shipments*—it shows which parts are shipped, or supplied, by which suppliers. Each shipment has one supplier number (SNO); one part number (PNO); and one quantity (QTY). Also, there's at most one shipment at any given time for a given supplier and given part, and so the combination of supplier number and part number is unique to any given shipment.

Examples throughout the rest of this book are based for the most part on the foregoing database. Now, you might well have seen this database before—I've used it in several other books and writings, including *SQL and Relational Theory* in particular,[2] as well as in numerous live presentations—and you might be forgiven for getting a little tired of it. But as I've written elsewhere, I believe using the same example in a variety of different publications can be a help, not a hindrance, in learning. Of course, it's true that real databases tend to be much more complicated than this "toy" example; but the trouble with using more realistic examples is that they tend to be *too* complicated (they make it difficult to see the forest for the trees, as it were). Let me say too that even if it is somewhat unrealistic, the suppliers-and-parts database has at least been very carefully tailored to illustrate all kinds of points that we need to be examining later on; thus, it's more than adequate for our purposes in this book. Please note, therefore, that in examples throughout the rest of this book, I'll be assuming the specific sample values shown in Fig. 1.1, barring explicit statements to the contrary.

WHAT'S A DBMS?

Now, when I say a figure like Fig. 1.1 "shows ... a typical database," what I mean is it shows that database *as perceived by the user* (what's sometimes called a *logical* database). That logical database is contrasted with the corresponding *physical* database, which is the database *as perceived by the DBMS* (i.e., it's the database as physically stored inside the computer system). Note carefully, therefore, that what I'm calling here the logical and physical databases aren't two totally different things; rather, they're two different *perceptions* of the *same* thing. Refer to Fig. 1.2. As that figure is meant to suggest, the DBMS—the software that manages the database—effectively serves as a kind of intermediary between the logical and physical levels of the system: User requests for access to the database are expressed in terms of the logical database, and they're implemented by the DBMS ("executed") in terms of the corresponding physical database.

---

[2] I remind you from the preface that throughout this book I use "*SQL and Relational Theory*" as an abbreviated form of reference to my book *SQL and Relational Theory: How to Write Accurate SQL Code* (2nd edition, O'Reilly, 2012).

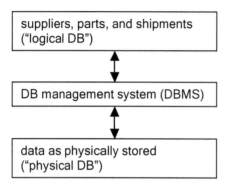

Fig. 1.2: Database system architecture

One general function provided by the DBMS is thus the shielding of users from details of the physical level of the system (very much as programming language systems also shield users from details of the physical level of the system). In other words, the DBMS provides users with a perception of the database that's more abstract, and thus more user friendly, than the way the database looks physically—i.e., the way it's physically stored inside the system.[3]

Now, a DBMS is a complex piece of software, and it consists of many components. But there's one component I'd like to mention right away, since it's so important to the subject of this book, and that's the *optimizer*. The optimizer is the DBMS component that's responsible for deciding exactly how to implement user requests. The point is this: Most requests (indeed, very likely all requests) are capable of being implemented in a variety—typically a very large variety—of different ways. Moreover, those different ways will typically have widely differing performance characteristics; in particular, they could have execution times that vary, quite literally, from fractions of a second to many days. Thus, it's very important that the optimizer choose a "good" way to implement any given request, where "good" essentially means *having good performance*.

One immediate and significant implication of the foregoing is this: Assuming the optimizer makes a reasonably good job of things, users shouldn't have to get involved in performance issues at all. As a matter of fact—to jump ahead of myself for a moment—let me state here for the record that it is and always was a major objective of the relational model that it should be the system, not the user, that has to worry about performance issues. Indeed, to the extent this objective is not met, the system can be said to have failed (or certainly to be less than fully successful, at any rate).

---

[3] By the way, that physical database, although it's less abstract than the logical database, is still an abstraction; it consists, typically, of things like stored files and indexes, and those stored files and indexes are represented in terms of various lower level constructs such as pages and disk spaces. And these latter constructs in turn are abstractions of still lower level constructs such as bits and bytes—which are, of course, themselves abstractions as well (and so on, as deep as you care to go).

Data Independence

The fact that the logical and physical databases are distinguished and (ideally, at least) kept rigidly apart is what allows us to achieve the important goal of *data independence*. Data independence—not a very good term, by the way, but we seem to be stuck with it—means we have the freedom to change the way the database is physically stored and accessed without having to make corresponding changes to the way the database is perceived by the user. Now, the reason we might want to change the way the database is physically stored and accessed is almost always *performance*; and the fact that we can make such changes without having to change the way the database looks to the user means that existing application programs, queries, and the like can all still work after the change. Very importantly, therefore, data independence means *protecting existing investment*—investment in user training, in existing applications, and in existing database designs (among other things).

Other DBMS Functions

To repeat, the DBMS acts as an intermediary between the logical and physical databases; in other words, it supports the *user interface* to the database. (For the rest of this book, I'll take the term *database*, unqualified, to mean a logical database specifically, unless the context demands otherwise—which in fact it almost never will.) Thus, the DBMS is responsible for (a) accepting user requests, be they queries or updates, that are expressed in terms of the logical database and (b) responding to those requests by interpreting and implementing them, or in other words executing them, in terms of the physical database. *Note:* The term *update*, in lower case,[4] is used to refer generically to requests that insert new data or delete or change existing data.

So the DBMS "protects users from the data" (i.e., it protects users from the details of how the data is physically represented inside the system). We might also say, somewhat glibly, that it protects the data from users!—by which I mean it provides certain *security, concurrency, integrity*, and *recovery* controls. To elaborate briefly:

- ■ *Security controls* are needed to ensure that user requests are legitimate, in the sense that the user in question is requesting an operation he or she is allowed to carry out on data he or she is allowed to access. In the case of the suppliers-and-parts database, for example, some users might not be allowed to see supplier status values; others might not be allowed to see suppliers at all; others might be allowed to see suppliers in London but not in other cities; others might be allowed to retrieve supplier information but not to update it; and so on. In a nutshell, users must be limited to performing only those operations they're allowed to perform. *Note:* Security is important, of course, but further details of security controls are mostly beyond the scope of this book (except for a brief mention in Chapter 7).

---

[4] That lower case is important! See the answer to Exercise 1.2 at the end of the chapter.

■ *Concurrency controls* have to do with the possibility that several users might be using the database at the same time. Suppose you were to ask the database whether there were any shipments for supplier S1 and, on receiving an answer in the affirmative, went on to ask what the average quantity was for those shipments; it would be very annoying (to say the least) to then be told there weren't any such shipments after all—presumably because some other user had just deleted them. Concurrency controls are intended to take care of such issues, and I'll have more to say about them in Part II of this book.

■ *Integrity controls* have to do with guaranteeing that the data in the database is correct (insofar as it's possible to provide any such guarantee). For example, an attempt to insert a shipment for supplier S6 into the shipments table must surely be rejected if there's no supplier S6 in the suppliers table. Likewise, an attempt to update the status for supplier S1 to 200 must also be rejected, if status values are supposed never to exceed 100. As these examples should be sufficient to illustrate, integrity controls are extremely important, and I'll have a lot more to say about them in Chapters 3 and 6 (also in Chapter 13).

■ *Recovery controls* have to do with the fact that the database is supposed never to "forget" anything it has been told to "remember." That is, data, once it has been inserted into the database, should never be deleted again, except as a result of some explicit user request—not even if some failure occurs, such as a system crash or a hard crash on the disk. I'll have a little more to say about such matters in Part II of this book.

There's one last thing I need to say regarding DBMSs in general. From everything I've said so far, it should be quite clear that there's a logical difference between a database, which is a repository for data, and a DBMS, which is the software that manages such a repository. Unfortunately, it has become common in the database field—I'm tempted to say, extremely common—to use the term *database* to mean a DBMS![5] I do *not* follow that usage in this book. The problem is, if you call the DBMS a database, what do you call the database?

WHAT'S A RELATIONAL DBMS?

So now we know what a DBMS is. But what's a *relational* DBMS? Well, first, of course, it's a DBMS, which means it provides all of the functionality mentioned in this chapter so far: data storage, query and update, recovery and concurrency, security and integrity, as well as other functions not discussed in this book. But second, it's also *relational*, which means the user interface is based on—better: *is a faithful implementation of*—the relational model. In other

---

[5] A typical example, found almost at random on the Internet: "MySQL [is] the world's most popular open source database." No, it isn't. It might be the world's most popular open source DBMS—I wouldn't know—but a database it's most certainly not.

words, the relational model can be thought of as a kind of recipe for what the user interface is supposed to look like in such a DBMS.

Before going any further, I'd like to stress the fact that that recipe (viz., the relational model) is very simple! The prescriptions of the relational model aren't a straitjacket—rather, they're a discipline, a discipline that makes life much easier for the user. (Easier for the system too, in certain respects; but the emphasis is on the user.) Now, it's true that the recipe might sometimes look a little complicated, but that's because the relational model is, above all, precise, and precision requires precise terminology, and precise terminology can sometimes be a little daunting. But the concepts the terminology refers to are actually quite simple (after all, the suppliers-and-parts database was pretty easy to understand, wasn't it?). In fact, it seems to me that the concepts in question are much simpler than their counterparts were in older, prerelational (and nonrelational) systems such as IMS and IDMS.[6]

To repeat, then, a relational DBMS is a DBMS that supports a user interface that's a faithful implementation of the relational model—meaning, as far as the user is concerned, that:

- The data looks relational.

- Relational operators (i.e., operators that operate on data in relational form) are available to serve as a basis for formulating retrieval and update requests. Here's a simple example:

```
S WHERE CITY = 'London'
```

This expression—which of course represents the query "Get suppliers in London"—is making use of the relational *restriction* operator; formally, it's asking for the set of suppliers represented in table S to be *restricted* to just the ones in London.

In this first part of the book, then, we'll take a closer look at exactly what it means for data to "look relational," and we'll examine various relational operators and see how they can be used in practice. Please note, however, that the treatment isn't meant to be exhaustive (a more complete treatment of these topics can be found in *SQL and Relational Theory*); but it *is* meant to be comprehensive, as far as it goes, and it's certainly meant to be accurate.

Unfortunately, there's a problem. In order to illustrate the concepts I'm going to be discussing, I obviously need to show coding examples; thus, I clearly need some formal language in which to express those examples. But the relational model doesn't prescribe any such language; that is, it doesn't prescribe a concrete syntax for how its concepts are to be realized in practice. Rather, it's defined at a high level of abstraction, and is in principle capable of concrete

---

[6] Much simpler too than their counterparts in the various proposals—which crop up all too frequently, I'm sorry to say—for replacing the relational model (see, e.g., XML, NoSQL, the Actor Model, and on and on). Incidentally, I've never seen such a proposal in which the person doing the proposing really understood the relational model. Surely, if you want to claim that Technology *A* is no good and needs to be replaced by Technology *B*, then it's incumbent on you to understand Technology *A* in the first place? And, more particularly, to demonstrate how Technology *B* solves some specific problem that Technology *A* doesn't?

realization in any number of different syntactic forms. Now, a standard concrete language does exist: viz., SQL (pronounced "ess cue ell," or sometimes "sequel"), which is supported, more or less, by all of the mainstream database products on the market today. As noted in the preface, however, SQL is very deeply flawed: It's complex, incomplete, hard to learn, and indeed actively misleading in numerous ways. So what I plan to do in this book is this:

- First, I'll explain the relational model without using SQL at all (that's Part I of the book). In place of SQL, I'll use a language called **Tutorial D**—note the boldface—that has been expressly designed for the purpose. *Note:* I believe **Tutorial D** is pretty much self-explanatory; however, a comprehensive description can be found if needed in the book *Databases, Types, and the Relational Model: The Third Manifesto*, by Hugh Darwen and myself (3rd edition, Addison-Wesley, 2007).[7]

- Second, I'll show how ideas from the relational model are realized in concrete form in SQL specifically (that's Part III of the book). Please be aware, therefore, that I'm definitely not attempting to cover the whole of the SQL language in this book, but only as much as I need—what I called in the preface the core features of the language.

(As fort Part II, a brief explanation of what that's about can be found in the preface.) *Note:* Perhaps I should warn you that, precisely because of the foregoing plan, what follows doesn't look much like most of the books and presentations currently available in the marketplace that purport to be "an introduction to relational databases."

One last point to close this section: You might or might not know (but I hope you do) that the relational model was originally the invention of E. F. Codd, when he was employed as a researcher at IBM (E for Edgar and F for Frank—but he always signed with his initials; to his friends, among whom I was proud to count myself, he was Ted). It was late in 1968 that Codd, a mathematician by training, first realized that the discipline of mathematics could be used to inject some solid principles and rigor into a field, database management, that prior to that time was all too deficient in any such qualities. His original description of the ideas of the relational model appeared in an IBM Research Report in 1969 (see Appendix E for further discussion).

DATABASE SYSTEMS vs. PROGRAMMING SYSTEMS

The point doesn't often seem to be recognized, but there are some analogies that can helpfully be drawn between database systems (relational or otherwise) and programming systems; in fact, it doesn't often seem to be recognized that a database system actually *is* a programming system (more precisely, a special case of such a system). Consider the code fragment shown in Fig. 1.3.

---

[7] **Tutorial D** has been revised and extended somewhat since that book was first published. A description of the revised version (which is essentially the version I'll be using in this book) can be found in another book by Hugh Darwen and myself, *Database Explorations: Essays on The Third Manifesto and Related Topics* (Trafford, 2010). See also ***www.thethirdmanifesto.com***.

The purpose of that code fragment—which is expressed in a hypothetical but self-explanatory language—is to compute and display the sum of the integers in a certain one-dimensional array called A.

```
VAR I , N, SUM INTEGER ;
VAR A ARRAY [1..N] OF INTEGER ;

SUM := 0 ;
I := 0 ;
DO WHILE I < N ;
    I := I + 1 ;
    SUM := SUM + A[I] ;
END DO ;
DISPLAY 'The sum is ' || SUM ;
```

Fig. 1.3: A code fragment

Note the following points:

- **Statements:** The code overall consists of nine statements. A *statement* in a programming language is a construct that causes some action to occur, such as defining or updating a variable or changing the flow of control. Observe that there's a logical difference between a statement and an *expression*, which is a construct that denotes a value (it can be thought of as a rule for computing, or determining, the value in question). In Fig. 1.3, for example, "I := I + 1 ;" is a statement—an assignment statement, as it happens (see further discussion below)—while "I + 1" is an expression. *Note:* Throughout this book, I adopt the common syntactic convention that statements terminate in a semicolon and expressions don't.

- **Types:** A *type* is a named set of values: namely, all legal values of some particular kind. Every value and every variable (see further discussion below) is of some type.[8] The code fragment in Fig. 1.3 involves three types: INTEGER (the set of all integers); ARRAY [1..N] OF INTEGER (the set of all one-dimensional arrays of integers with lower bound 1 and upper bound N); and CHAR (the set of all character strings). *Note:* As we'll see in a few moments—see the discussion of comparison operators below—it also implicitly involves type BOOLEAN, the set of all truth values. Of course, there are exactly two such values, denoted by the literals TRUE and FALSE.

- **Variables:** A *variable* is a container for a value (different values at different times, in general). The code fragment in Fig. 1.3 involves four variables: I, N, SUM, and A. The "current value" of a given variable—meaning the value the variable contains at some particular time—can be changed in one and only one way: namely, by executing an

---

[8] In fact, of exactly one type, unless type inheritance is a consideration, which in this book it isn't. *Note:* It follows that types are disjoint (at least as far as we're concerned)—no value is of two or more types.

assignment statement in which the variable in question serves as the target. In fact, to be a variable is to be assignable to, and to be assignable to is to be a variable.

■ **Assignment:** *Assignment* (denoted ":=" in Fig. 1.3) is an operator for updating a variable—that is, assigning a value, probably different from the previous value, to the variable in question. The code fragment in Fig. 1.3 contains four assignment statements.

■ **Literals:** A *literal* is a "self-defining symbol"—i.e., it's a symbol that denotes a value, and the value in question, and hence the type of that value also, are fixed and determined by the symbol in question (and are therefore known at compile time, incidentally). The code fragment in Fig. 1.3 involves three literals—0, 1, and 'The sum is ' (the first two of these are of type INTEGER and the third is of type CHAR).

■ **Values:** A *value* is an "individual constant"; it's what's denoted by an expression, and it's what can be assigned to a variable. Note in particular that literals and variable references are both expressions, since they certainly both denote values. Note too that every value effectively carries its type around with it.

■ **Read-only operators:** A *read-only operator* is an operator like "+" that "derives new values from old ones"; for example, the expression 2 + 3 derives the "new" value 5 from the "old" values 2 and 3. Note carefully that a read-only operator, when it's invoked, returns a result but doesn't update anything (in particular, it doesn't update its operands).[9] Note too that an expression, which I said earlier was a rule for computing a value, can equivalently be said to represent an invocation of some read-only operator; in fact, the terms *expression* and *read-only operator invocation* are effectively interchangeable. Note finally that read-only operators don't have to be denoted by a special symbol such as "+"; in fact, the vast majority of such operators are denoted by means of some more conventional identifier. For example, many programming languages support a read-only operator called RANDOM (or some such) for generating pseudorandom numbers.

■ **Comparison operators:** A *comparison operator* is an operator like "<" that, when it's invoked, returns a truth value (either TRUE or FALSE). In fact, of course, such operators are in fact read-only operators; they're just a special case, in which the type of the result they return is BOOLEAN.

---

[9] The obvious question arises: Is there any such thing as an operator that isn't read-only? The answer is yes, there are *update operators*, which are operators that, when invoked, don't return a result but do update some variable. As we'll see later, however, any given update operator invocation is functionally equivalent to some assignment operation. It follows that, logically speaking, assignment is the only update operator we need.

Finally, the reason for rehearsing all of this extremely familiar material is that (as I hope you were expecting) all of the foregoing concepts are directly relevant to databases, as we'll see in the chapters to come.

More on Types

I need to say a little more about the concept of types in particular. The code fragment in Fig. 1.3 didn't illustrate the point, but types in general can be either system defined (i.e., built in) or user defined. They can also be arbitrarily complex. For example, in a geometric application, we might have user defined types called POINT, LINE, RECTANGLE, CIRCLE, and so on. However, to the user who merely uses them (as opposed to the user who actually defines them), these user defined types will look exactly like system defined types anyway—indeed, that's the whole point (or a large part of the point, at any rate). So little or no generality is lost if, in my examples later in this book, I limit myself to system defined types such as INTEGER and CHAR (see below), and so I will, most if not quite all of the time.

Next, I've said that every value is of some type. It follows that every variable, every parameter to every operator, every read-only operator, and every expression—in particular, every literal and every variable reference—is of some type as well, because all of these constructs, when they're used, certainly do denote values. To be specific:

- In the case of variables, parameters, and read-only operators, the type in question is specified when the construct in question is defined. For example, see the variable definitions—i.e., the VAR statements—in Fig. 1.3.

- In the case of expressions, the type in question is simply the type of the result returned when the expression in question is evaluated. For example, the expression $2 + 3$ is of type INTEGER, because the result 5 of evaluating that expression is of type INTEGER.

Third and last, it's important to understand that associated with any given type T, there's a set of operators defined for operating on values and variables of type T (because types without operators are useless). For example, in the case of type INTEGER, which for simplicity I take to be system defined, the agency responsible for defining the type—in other words, the system, by my assumption—must define:

- Operators ":=", "=", "<", etc., for assigning and comparing integers

- Operators "+", "*", etc., for performing arithmetic on integers

- Perhaps a CAST operator, for converting integers to character strings

■ But *not* character string operators such as "| |" ("concatenate"), SUBSTR ("substring"), etc., because—let's agree, for the sake of the example at least—these operators make no sense for integers

It's also important to understand that the set of operators associated with any given type *T must* include both assignment (":=") and equality comparison ("="). What's more, the semantics of these operators must be such that the following requirements are satisfied:

■ **Assignment:** After assignment of value *v* to variable *V*, the comparison *V* = *v* must give TRUE. *Note:* This requirement is sometimes referred to as *The Assignment Principle*.

■ **Equality:** The comparison *v1* = *v2* must give TRUE if and only if *v1* and *v2* are the very same value (implying, incidentally, that they must certainly be of the same type). Note the following important corollary: If there exists some operator *Op* such that *Op(v1)* ≠ *Op(v2)*, then *v1* = *v2* must give FALSE.

Note: Of these two operators (":=" and "="), equality in particular is absolutely fundamental—for without it, we couldn't even tell, given some value *v* and some set of values *S*, whether *v* appears in *S* (i.e., whether *v* is an element of *S*).

Finally, let me say again that the reason for rehearsing all of this extremely familiar material is that once more (as I hope you were expecting) all of these concepts are directly relevant to databases, as we'll see in the chapters to come.

EXERCISES

Now it's your turn. Of course, it isn't possible to set any particularly searching exercises at this early point in the book, and the following are little more than review questions. Nevertheless, I'd like to recommend that you try to answer them yourself before going on to read my answers in the next section. *Note:* The first two exercises in particular are slightly unfair, because I haven't yet told you enough to answer them properly—but I think you should have a go at them anyway. They're not very difficult.

1.1   What do you think the following **Tutorial D** expressions represent?

a. `P WHERE WEIGHT < 12.5`

b. `P { PNO , COLOR , CITY }`

1.2   What do you think the following **Tutorial D** statements do?

a.   `DELETE S WHERE STATUS = 10 ;`

b.   `UPDATE S WHERE STATUS > 10 : { STATUS := STATUS + 5 } ;`

1.3   What's a database? What's a DBMS?

1.4   What do you understand by the following terms: (a) security controls; (b) integrity controls; (c) concurrency controls; (d) recovery controls?

1.5   What's SQL? What's **Tutorial D**?

1.6   Explain the following in your own words:

type
value
variable
literal
assignment
comparison
read-only operator
update operator

1.7   (*Try this exercise without looking back at the body of the chapter.*) What tables does the suppliers-and-parts database contain? What columns do they involve? *Note:* The point of this exercise is that it's worth making yourself as familiar as possible with the structure, at least in general terms, of the running example. It's not so important to remember the actual data values in detail—though it certainly wouldn't hurt if you did.

ANSWERS

1.1   a. Parts with weight less than 12.5. This example involves a relational restriction operation. b. Part number, color, and city for every part. This part of the exercise was definitely unfair, but you probably guessed the answer anyway—just as restriction picks out certain rows, so the operation of *projection*, illustrated by this example, picks out certain columns. See Chapter 4 for further explanation.

1.2   a. Delete all suppliers with status 10. b. Increase the status by 5 for all suppliers with status greater than 10. By the way, notice the use of the keyword UPDATE (in upper case) in this exercise. Perhaps a little confusingly, it has become standard practice in the database world to use the uppercase term UPDATE to refer to the specific operator that changes existing data (as opposed to DELETE, which deletes existing data, and INSERT, which inserts new data), and the lowercase term *update* to refer to the INSERT, DELETE, and UPDATE operators considered generically. In this book, therefore, when I want to refer to the UPDATE operator as such, I'll set it in upper case ("all caps") as just shown. As for the INSERT and DELETE operators, however, where no ambiguity arises, it can be a little tedious always to set them in all caps—especially when they're being used as qualifiers, as in, e.g., "INSERT statement" ("insert statement"?). I've therefore decided to use both forms in this book, letting context be my guide in any given situation (and I won't pretend I've been all that consistent in this regard, either).

1.3   A database is a repository for data stored electronically (an "electronic filing cabinet"). A DBMS is a software system that manages databases and access to those databases.

1.4   Security controls protect the database from unauthorized operations. Integrity controls protect the database from authorized but invalid operations. Concurrency controls protect user operations from interfering with one another. Recovery controls protect against data loss.

1.5   SQL is the standard language for interacting with "relational" databases; it's supported by just about every mainstream database product on the market today. **Tutorial D** is a language expressly designed for use in illustrating relational concepts; prototype implementations do exist—see the website *www.thethirdmanifesto.com*—but, at the time of writing, no commercial products.

1.6   A type is a named set of values. A value is an "individual constant"—e.g., the integer three—and it can't be changed. A variable is a holder for (some encoded representation of) some value, and it can be changed—i.e., its current value can be replaced by another value. A literal is a "self-defining symbol" denoting a value—e.g., the numeral 3. Assignment is the operator by which a variable is updated. A comparison is a read-only operator that (usually) takes two values as operands and returns a truth value. A read-only operator is an operator that takes zero or more values as operands and returns a value. An update operator is an operator that updates some variable; in other words, it's an assignment, logically speaking. *Note:* The operators INSERT, DELETE, and UPDATE mentioned in the answer to Exercise 1.2 are all relational update operators, and are thus by definition all effectively relational assignments. For further explanation of this point, see Chapter 2.

1.7   See Fig. 1.1.

Chapter 2

Relations and Relvars

There's nothing like a relation to do the business.
—with apologies to William Makepeace Thackeray:
Vanity Fair (1847-1848)

In this chapter, I want to explain exactly what it means for data to "look relational," as I put it in Chapter 1; in other words, I want to explain exactly what relations are (among other things). First, however, I need to remind you of something else I said in that chapter: namely, (a) that the relational model is, above all, precise; (b) that such precision requires precise or formal terminology; and (c) that such formal terminology can be a little daunting (indeed, it can act as a barrier to understanding). But the concepts the terminology refers to are really quite straightforward, once you've struggled through the formalism, and I hope you're ready now to make the necessary effort.

RELATIONS

Consider the suppliers-and-parts database once again (see Fig. 2.1, a repeat of Fig. 1.1 from Chapter 1). From a relational point of view, what I previously called the "files" or "tables" in that database are really *relations*. Now, a relation is a mathematical construct, and it has a very precise mathematical definition, which I'll give at the very end of the chapter—but for the moment it's sufficient to know that a relation can be thought of, and depicted, as a certain kind of table. Moreover, every relation consists of a *heading* and a *body*, where:

- The heading consists of a set of *attributes* (represented as columns in those tabular pictures).

- The body consists of a set of *tuples* (represented as rows in those tabular pictures). *Note:* The word *tuple* is usually pronounced to rhyme with "couple."

So let's take a closer look at exactly what attributes and tuples are.

S

SNO	SNAME	STATUS	CITY
S1	Smith	20	London
S2	Jones	10	Paris
S3	Blake	30	Paris
S4	Clark	20	London
S5	Adams	30	Athens

SP

SNO	PNO	QTY
S1	P1	300
S1	P2	200
S1	P3	400
S1	P4	200
S1	P5	100
S1	P6	100
S2	P1	300
S2	P2	400
S3	P2	200
S4	P2	200
S4	P4	300
S4	P5	400

P

PNO	PNAME	COLOR	WEIGHT	CITY
P1	Nut	Red	12.0	London
P2	Bolt	Green	17.0	Paris
P3	Screw	Blue	17.0	Oslo
P4	Screw	Red	14.0	London
P5	Cam	Blue	12.0	Paris
P6	Cog	Red	19.0	London

Fig. 2.1: The suppliers-and-parts database—sample values

Attributes

An attribute consists of a *name* and a corresponding *type* (more formally, we can say an attribute is an *attribute-name : type-name pair*). For example, the suppliers relation has an attribute ("the status attribute") in which the attribute name is STATUS and the corresponding type name is— let's agree for the sake of the example—INTEGER, meaning that legal values of that attribute are INTEGER values (or just integers for short), and INTEGER values only.

A couple of points arise immediately from this definition:

- What I'm here calling the *type* of an attribute is also known as a *domain*; i.e., *domain* and *type* mean exactly the same thing. (Earlier relational writings favored the term *domain*; more recent ones favor the term *type* instead. I'll stick to *type* in this book.)

- Tabular pictures of relations like those in Fig. 2.1 typically don't bother to mention the attribute types. For example, the STATUS attribute does have a type (namely, INTEGER), but I didn't show it in the figure. But please don't forget that, conceptually, it's there!

So the attributes of the suppliers relation in particular might perhaps be as indicated here—

```
SNO      :   SNO
SNAME    :   NAME
STATUS   :   INTEGER
CITY     :   CHAR
```

—where the first name in each pair is the attribute name and the second is the corresponding type name, and I'm assuming for the sake of the example that types SNO ("supplier numbers") and NAME ("names") are user defined and types INTEGER (the set of all legal integers) and CHAR (the set of all legal character strings) are system defined. But now let me remind you that, as I put it in Chapter 1, the whole point about user defined types is that they're supposed to look like system defined types anyway (at least to the user who uses them, as opposed to the user who actually defines them). So from this point forward I'm going to simplify the example and assume attributes SNO and SNAME are both of type CHAR (a system defined type), thus:

```
SNO      :   CHAR
SNAME    :   CHAR
STATUS   :   INTEGER
CITY     :   CHAR
```

In fact, I won't have much to say about user defined types at all in this book. This simplification allows me to ignore a lot of details that are certainly important for type definers but not for type users (and not all that important for relational databases as such, either).

The heading of the suppliers relation is thus the set

```
{ SNO CHAR , SNAME CHAR , STATUS INTEGER , CITY CHAR }
```

This is **Tutorial D** notation. As you can see, therefore, in headings in **Tutorial D** we use one or more spaces instead of a colon to separate attribute names from type names; we use commas (preceded and/or followed by zero or more spaces) to separate each attribute from the next; and we enclose the whole thing in braces—"{" and "}"—since the conventional representation of a set on paper consists of a commalist of elements enclosed in braces.

> *A remark on syntax:* The foregoing paragraph contains the first mention in this book of the useful term *commalist*, which I'll be using quite a lot in the pages ahead. It can be defined as follows: Let *xyz* be some syntactic construct (e.g., "attribute"). Then the term *xyz commalist* denotes a sequence of zero or more *xyz*'s in which each pair of adjacent *xyz*'s is separated by a comma, as well as, optionally, one or more spaces before or after the comma or both. *End of remark.*

The number of attributes in a given heading is called the *degree*, both of that heading as such and also of every relation with that heading. Thus, we can say of the suppliers-and-parts database that the degree of the suppliers relation is four, that of the parts relation is five, and that of the shipments relation is three. *Note:* If relation r is of degree n, we call that relation n-*ary*. If $n = 1$, the relation is unary; if $n = 2$, it's binary; if $n = 3$, it's ternary; and so on.

One last point: As we've seen, an attribute is defined, formally, to be an attribute-name : type-name pair. Informally, however, we often refer to attributes by their name alone, thereby talking about things like "the STATUS attribute" (of the suppliers relation). Likewise, we often refer informally to headings as if they were just sets of attribute names instead of sets of attribute-name : type-name pairs, thereby saying things like "the heading of the suppliers relation is the set {SNO, SNAME, STATUS, CITY}." These simplifications, or shorthands, save us a certain amount of circumlocution; moreover, they're legitimate (more or less) because there's another rule—I didn't mention this one before, but it's basically common sense—to the effect that, within a given heading, no two distinct attributes are allowed to have the same attribute name.

Tuples

Every tuple in the body of a given relation is required to *conform* to the heading of that relation, in the sense that it—the tuple in question—contains exactly one value, of the applicable type, for each attribute, and nothing else besides. For example, the body of the suppliers relation is the set of tuples for suppliers S1, S2, S3, S4, and S5, and each of those five tuples does contain exactly one value for each of the attributes SNO, SNAME, STATUS, and CITY, and nothing else besides; what's more, of course, those values are indeed values of the applicable types, namely, CHAR, CHAR, INTEGER, and CHAR, respectively. *Note:* It would be simpler—and actually more correct, in a way—to say just that each of those tuples *has* the pertinent heading, because in fact tuples have headings, just as relations do.

The number of tuples in a given body is called the *cardinality*, both of that body as such and also of every relation with that body.[1] Thus, we can say of the suppliers-and-parts database in Fig. 2.1 that the cardinality of the suppliers relation is five, that of the parts relation is six, and that of the shipments relation is twelve. *Note:* If the cardinality is zero, the relation is said to be empty. An empty relation is like a file that contains no records, loosely speaking.

Incidentally, it follows from what I've said so far that relations don't really contain tuples—they contain a body, and that body in turn contains the tuples—but in practice we do usually talk as if relations contained tuples directly, for simplicity.

Properties of Relations

So much for attributes and tuples; now we're ready to consider relations as such. The overriding point I want to make here is that (as I've said) relations are very precisely and formally defined, and as a consequence they enjoy a variety of formal properties, properties that are extremely important from both a theoretical and a practical point of view. *Note:* As I've written elsewhere (see, e.g., *SQL and Relational Theory*), it's an article of faith with me that *theory is practical!* The purpose of relational theory in particular isn't just theory for its own sake; rather, the purpose of that theory is to allow us to build systems that are 100 percent practical. That's why I believe strongly that, in the relational context in particular, departures from the underlying theory

---

[1] See footnote 10 in Chapter 3 regarding the meaning of "every relation" here.

are A Big Mistake. Indeed, so called (or would-be) "relational" systems are at their least attractive precisely at those points where they depart from that underlying theory.

Be that as it may, there are four properties of relations that I want to talk about here. I'll list them first, then elaborate on each in turn.

- Relations never contain duplicate tuples.

- The tuples of a relation are unordered, top to bottom.

- The attributes of a relation are unordered, left to right.

- Relations are always normalized (i.e., in "first normal form," abbreviated 1NF).

Relations never contain duplicate tuples: This property is a logical consequence of the fact that the body of a relation is defined to be a *set* (of tuples), because sets in mathematics don't contain duplicate elements.

The tuples of a relation are unordered, top to bottom: This property too is a logical consequence of the fact that the body of a relation is a set, because sets in mathematics have no ordering to their elements (thus, e.g., $\{a,b,c\}$ and $\{c,a,b\}$ both denote the same set). Of course, when we depict a relation as a table (e.g., on paper), we do have to show the rows in some top to bottom order, but that ordering doesn't correspond to anything relational, and you should ignore it. In the case of the suppliers relation as depicted in Fig. 2.1, for example, I could have shown the rows in any order—say supplier S3, then S1, then S5, then S4, then S2—and the picture would still represent the same relation. Note, therefore, that there's no such thing as "the first tuple" or "the fifth tuple" or "the 87th tuple" of a relation, and there's no such thing as "the next tuple"; in other words, there's no concept of positional addressing, and there's no concept of "nextness" among tuples. (Note, incidentally, that if we did have such concepts, we would need certain additional operators as well—e.g., "retrieve the nth tuple," "insert this new tuple *here*," "move this tuple from *here* to *there*," and so on. I'll have more to say about this particular issue when we get to Chapter 7.)

The attributes of a relation are unordered, left to right: In similar fashion, the attributes of a relation are also unordered, left to right, because a heading too is a mathematical set. Again, when we depict a relation as a table (e.g., on paper), we do have to show the columns in some left to right order, but that ordering doesn't correspond to anything relational, and again you should ignore it. In the case of the suppliers relation as depicted in Fig. 2.1, for example, I could have shown the columns in any left to right order—say STATUS, SNAME, CITY, SNO—and the picture would still represent the same relation as far as the relational model is concerned. Thus, there's no such thing as "the first attribute" or "the second attribute" (etc.), and there's no "next attribute" (i.e., there's no concept of "nextness" among attributes); attributes of a relation are always referenced by name, never by position.[2]

Relations are always normalized (i.e., in "first normal form" or 1NF):[3] Informally, all this statement means is that every tuple in the relation in question conforms to the pertinent heading (which of course we already know it does). So the obvious question is: What could it possibly mean for a relation to be *un*normalized? The answer is that it can't happen—"unnormalized relation" is simply a contradiction in terms. The point is, however, that *tables*, as opposed to relations, might indeed not be normalized. I'll have more to say about this possibility when we get to Part III of this book.

RELVARS

Take another look at Fig. 2.1. That figure shows three relations: namely, the relations that happen to exist in the database at some particular time. But if we were to look at the same database at some different time, we would probably see three different relations appearing in their place. In other words, the objects labeled S, P, and SP in that figure are really *variables*— relation variables, to be specific—and like all variables they have different values at different times, in general. And since they're relation variables specifically, their values at any given time are, of course, relation values (thus, what Fig. 2.1 really shows is three relation *values*).

Now, since S, P, and SP are indeed variables, they can of course be updated, or assigned to. (As I put it in Chapter 1, to be a variable is to be assignable to, and to be assignable to is to be a variable.) For example, suppose variable S currently has the value shown in Fig. 2.1, and suppose we execute the following relational assignment:

```
S := S WHERE CITY ≠ 'London' ;
```

As with all assignments, what happens here is that (a) the source expression on the right side is evaluated and then (b) the value resulting from that evaluation is assigned to the target variable on the left side. So relation variable S now looks like this:

---

[2] Actually, for reasons that need not concern us here, relations in mathematics, unlike their counterparts in the relational model, do have a left to right ordering to their attributes (see Appendix C).

[3] "First" normal form because, as you might know, it's possible to define a series of "higher" normal forms—second normal form, third normal form, and so on—that are relevant to the discipline of database design. I'll have a little more to say about such matters in Part II of this book.

SNO	SNAME	STATUS	CITY
S2	Jones	10	Paris
S3	Blake	30	Paris
S5	Adams	30	Athens

In other words, the tuples for suppliers S1 and S4 (both of which had CITY value London) have been deleted. In fact, the original assignment statement is logically equivalent to the following explicit DELETE statement:

```
DELETE S WHERE CITY = 'London' ;
```

Thus, this DELETE statement can be regarded as a more user friendly "shorthand" for the original assignment statement (shorthand in quotes because it's actually longer than what it's supposed to be short for!). Either way, however—i.e., regardless of whether the update is formulated as an explicit relational assignment or as an invocation of the user friendly shorthand—what's happened conceptually is that the old value of S (a relation value, of course) has been replaced in its entirety by a new value (another relation value). And while the old value (with five tuples) and the new one (with three) are clearly rather similar, in a sense, they're certainly different values.

Now, in practice, a relational DBMS will surely support explicit INSERT, DELETE, and UPDATE operators on relation variables, but conceptually, at least, these operators are all just shorthand for certain relational assignments. Logically speaking, in fact, relational assignment is the only update operator we need (a point I'll elaborate on in Chapter 4). For now, however, let me just show some more examples of the shorthands. Here first is another DELETE example:

```
DELETE SP WHERE QTY < 150 ;
```

I'll leave it as an exercise to show the effect of this DELETE, given the sample values shown in Fig. 2.1.

Next INSERT:

```
INSERT SP RELATION { TUPLE { SNO 'S5' , PNO 'P1' , QTY 250 } ,
                     TUPLE { SNO 'S5' , PNO 'P3' , QTY 450 } } ;
```

The effect of this INSERT is to insert a relation consisting of two tuples into the relation variable SP. If that variable has as its initial value the shipments relation shown in Fig. 2.1, then after the INSERT it will have as its value a relation of cardinality 14, consisting of the twelve existing tuples plus two new ones.

Finally UPDATE:

```
UPDATE SP WHERE SNO = 'S2' : { QTY := 2 * QTY } ;
```

If, again, relation variable SP has as its initial value the relation shown in Fig. 2.1, then after the UPDATE it will differ only in that the tuples for supplier S2 will have their QTY values doubled. Incidentally, note the *attribute assignment* QTY := 2 * QTY (enclosed in braces) in this UPDATE statement.

To say it again, then, in practice relational DBMSs will surely support explicit INSERT, DELETE, and UPDATE operators on relation variables, despite the fact that, conceptually at least, these operators are all just shorthand for certain relational assignments. Do please note, however, that the target for all of these operators (relational assignment included) is *not* a relation value but, rather, a relation variable. By contrast, operators such as restrict and project, both of which were mentioned in the previous chapter, do operate on relation values. (The point is, of course, that restrict and project, together with a variety of other operators to be discussed in Chapters 4 and 5, are read-only operators, whereas INSERT, DELETE, and UPDATE—and relational assignment—are update operators. Refer to Chapter 1 if you need to refresh your memory regarding the logical difference between these two kinds of operators.)

To sum up: There's a logical difference between relation values and relation variables. For that reason, I'll distinguish very carefully between the two from this point forward—I'll talk in terms of relation values when I mean relation values and relation variables when I mean relation variables. However, I'll also abbreviate *relation value,* most of the time, to just *relation* (exactly as we abbreviate *integer value* most of the time to just *integer*). And I'll abbreviate *relation variable* most of the time to **relvar**; for example, I'll say the suppliers-and-parts database contains three *relvars.*[4] *Note:* The term *relvar*—like the term *relation variable,* come to that—isn't widely used, but it should be.

One last point. Let *R* be a relvar. Then, just like a relation, *R* has a certain heading *H* (and a fortiori it has certain attributes and a certain degree as well). That heading *H* is specified when *R* is defined (see Chapter 3), and every relation *r* that can legally be assigned to *R* must then also have that same heading *H*. Moreover, if the relation that's assigned to *R* at some particular time *t* is *r*, then the body, tuples, and cardinality of *r* are considered to be the body, tuples, and cardinality, respectively, of *R* at that time *t*. Note, therefore, that the body, tuples, and cardinality of a relvar vary over time, while the heading, attributes, and degree don't.

EXERCISES

Which of the following statements are true?

2.1   Relations (and hence relvars) have no ordering to their tuples.

---

[4] More precisely, three "real" or base relvars, so called to distinguish them from so called "virtual" relvars or views (see Chapters 3 and 7 for further discussion).

2.2　Relations (and hence relvars) have no ordering to their attributes.

2.3　Relations (and hence relvars) never have any unnamed attributes.

2.4　Relations (and hence relvars) never have two or more attributes with the same name.

2.5　Relations (and hence relvars) never contain duplicate tuples.

2.6　Relations (and hence relvars) are always in 1NF.

2.7　The types over which relational attributes are defined can be arbitrarily complex.

2.8　Relations (and hence relvars) themselves have types.

As an additional exercise, try giving a definition, as precise as you can make it, of the term *relation* (as that term is used in the relational model).

ANSWERS

The short answer is: They're all true! But some of them do merit further discussion. To be specific, Exercises 2.1, 2.2, 2.4, 2.5, and 2.6 were answered in the body of the chapter. Exercise 2.3 was answered implicitly, too: Since an attribute is, by definition, an attribute-name : type-name pair, an unnamed attribute is a contradiction in terms. So that leaves Exercises 2.7 and 2.8.

Let me take Exercise 2.8 first: "Relations (and hence relvars) themselves have types." As I've already said, this statement is true; in fact, of course, a relation is a value and a relvar is a variable, and we know from Chapter 1 that every value is of some type and every variable is of some type, so the statement is *obviously* true. But I deliberately had nothing to say in the body of this chapter about relation and relvar types as such; I had my reasons for wanting to defer such a discussion to Chapter 3, and I'll refer you to that chapter for further explanation.

Turning now to Exercise 2.7: "The types over which relational attributes are defined can be arbitrarily complex." Again, I've already said this statement is true; so we can have relations, and relvars, with attributes that contain values that are as complex as we like—e.g., values that are polygons; or values that are arrays; or values that are XML documents; or values that are photographs; or values that are audio or video recordings; and on and on. However, there are a couple of limitations:

■　First, the relational model expressly prohibits relvars, and hence relations, in the database from having any attributes whose values are pointers—meaning no relation in the database is allowed to have an attribute whose values are pointers to tuples in some other such relation (or possibly in the same relation). *Note:* The foregoing statement is pretty loose, but it captures the essence of the situation. As for why the relational model imposes such a prohibition, there are many reasons. One such was stated by Codd in his book *The Relational Model for Database Management Version 2* (Addison-Wesley, 1990) in the following terms:

> It is safe to assume that all kinds of users understand the act of comparing values, but that relatively few understand the complexities of pointers ... [The] manipulation of pointers is more bug-prone than the act of comparing values, even if the user happens to understand the complexities of pointers.

In other words, pointers are complex, error prone, and logically unnecessary.[5] For example, to find the shipment tuples corresponding to a given supplier tuple, what we *don't* do is follow some kind of pointer; instead, what we do is compare the SNO value in that given supplier tuple with the SNO values in the available shipment tuples. *Note:* It's worth mentioning in passing that the prohibition of pointers in the relational model can be seen as an implicit—or maybe not so implicit—criticism of prerelational systems like IMS and IDMS, in which pointers were a sine qua non. It's worth mentioning too that the various schemes proposed from time to time as a replacement for the relational model (which were mentioned in footnote 6 in Chapter 1) also tend to be riddled with pointers.

■ The second limitation is a little harder to state, but what it boils down to is this: If relation *r* has heading *H*, then no attribute of *r* can be defined in terms of a relation type—or tuple type—that has that same heading *H*, at any level of nesting. (Yes, tuples have types too, of course, just as relations do.) The purpose of this prohibition is to rule out the possibility of infinite regress. Again, see Chapter 3 for further discussion of relation types in general.

As for a precise definition of the term *relation*: Well, it's convenient to begin by first giving a precise definition of the term *tuple*. Here is such a definition:

Definition: Let *T1, T2, ..., Tn* (*n* ≥ 0) be type names, not necessarily all distinct. Associate with each *Ti* a distinct *attribute name, Ai*; each of the *n* attribute-name : type-name combinations that results is an **attribute**. Associate with each attribute an *attribute value*, *vi*, of type *Ti*; each of the *n* attribute : value combinations that results is a *component*.

---

[5] Understand that we're talking here about what in the previous chapter I called "the logical database." The physical database by contrast almost certainly will contain pointers, and lots of them—but of course those pointers won't be visible to the user (they'll be "under the covers," to use the jargon).

Then the set of all *n* components thus defined, *t* say, is a *tuple value* (or just a **tuple** for short) over the attributes *A1, A2, ..., An*. The value *n* is the **degree** of *t*; a tuple of degree one is *unary*, a tuple of degree two is *binary*, a tuple of degree three is *ternary*, ..., and more generally a tuple of degree *n* is *n-ary*. The set of all *n* attributes is the **heading** of *t*.

And now I can define *relation*:

Definition: Let *H* be a tuple heading as just defined, and let *t1, t2, ..., tm* ($m \geq 0$) be distinct tuples, all with heading *H*. Then the combination, *r* say, of *H* and the set of tuples {*t1, t2, ..., tm*} is a *relation value* (or just a **relation** for short) over the attributes *A1, A2, ..., An*, where *A1, A2, ..., An* are all of the attributes in *H*. The **heading** of *r* is *H*; *r* has the same attributes (and hence the same attribute names and types) and the same degree as that heading does. The set of tuples {*t1, t2, ..., tm*} is the **body** of *r*. The value *m* is the **cardinality** of *r*.

Chapter 3

Keys, Foreign Keys, and

Related Matters

Keep breathing!—that's the key.

—Gimli the Dwarf,
in Peter Jackson's film *The Two Towers* (2002),
based on the book of the same name
by J. R. R. Tolkien (1954)

Every relvar has a key (sometimes more than one), and some relvars have foreign keys as well. This chapter explains these observations and explores some of their implications.

INTEGRITY CONSTRAINTS

Every database is subject to certain *integrity constraints* (constraints for short), which update operations must never be permitted to violate. Here are some examples of constraints that might apply to the suppliers-and-parts database:

- Supplier status values must be in the range 1 to 100 inclusive.

- Part weights must be greater than zero.

- London suppliers must have status 20.

- Red parts must be stored in London.

- Suppliers with status less than 20 aren't allowed to supply part P6.

And so on. Now, one particular kind of constraint that applies to *every* relvar is what's called a *key* constraint, which means, loosely, that some combination of the attributes of the relvar in question serves as a unique identifier—a *key*—for tuples in that relvar. For example, every tuple in relvar S at any given time *t* has a supplier number (i.e., SNO value) that's unique, meaning it's different from the SNO value in every other tuple appearing in that same relvar at that same time *t*. Thus, tuples in relvar S at any given time are uniquely identified by supplier number. Likewise, tuples in relvar P are uniquely identified by part number, and tuples in relvar SP are uniquely identified by the combination of supplier number and part number.

By the way, note that a key constraint is certainly an integrity constraint as such. For example, consider the suppliers relvar S. The fact that supplier numbers are supposed to be unique in that relvar implies that an attempt to insert a tuple with a duplicate SNO value (i.e., an SNO value that's the same as one that already exists in that relvar), or an attempt to change the SNO value in some tuple to one that already exists elsewhere in that relvar, must certainly fail.

I've said that every relvar has a key. In fact it should be obvious that such is the case. The reason is as follows: First, the value of a relvar at any given time is a relation; second, relations never contain duplicate tuples. As a consequence, the combination of all of the attributes (i.e., the entire heading) certainly has the property of uniqueness. Now, in practice it's usually the case that some proper subset of the entire heading also has the uniqueness property—but at least we're guaranteed that the entire heading does, and so there's always a key.

> *A remark on set theory:* The previous paragraph made use of the set theory term *proper subset*. Not everyone is familiar with such terminology, however, so let me digress for a moment to explain it. Let *A* and *B* be sets. Then "*A* is a subset of *B*" (or "*A* is included in *B*"), written $A \subseteq B$, means every element of *A* is also an element of *B*. By contrast, "*A* is a *proper* subset of *B*" (or "*A* is *properly* included in *B*"), written $A \subset B$, means *A* is a subset of *B* but there exists at least one element of *B* that isn't also an element of *A*. Note, therefore, that every set is a subset of itself, but no set is a proper subset of itself.
>
> All of the foregoing applies to supersets also, mutatis mutandis. Thus, "*B* is a superset of *A*" (or "*B* includes *A*"), written $B \supseteq A$, means the same as "*A* is a subset of *B*." Similarly, "*B* is a *proper* superset of *A*" (or "*B* properly includes *A*"), written $B \supset A$, means the same as "*A* is a proper subset of *B*." Note, therefore, that every set is a superset of itself, but no set is a proper superset of itself.
>
> Finally, a little more terminology. First, the *empty* set is the unique set with no elements at all; it's written { }, or sometimes $\emptyset$. Note that the empty set is a subset of

every set, and indeed a proper subset of every set except itself.[1] Second, note that a set *contains* its elements but *includes* its subsets.

For further discussion of such matters, please refer to Appendix C. *End of remark.*

KEYS

Here then is a precise definition of the relational term *key*:[2]

Definition: Let K be a subset of the heading of relvar R. Then K is a **key** for R if and only if it possesses both of the following properties:

1. **Uniqueness:** No possible relation that can ever legally be assigned to R has two distinct tuples with the same value for K.

2. **Irreducibility:** No proper subset of K has the uniqueness property.

If K consists of n attributes, then n is the **degree** of K.

Several points arise from this definition. First of all, note that keys are *sets* of attributes, not attributes per se (even when the set in question contains just one attribute), because they're defined to be a subset—not necessarily a proper subset—of the pertinent heading. Thus, the sole key for relvar S is {SNO} (note the braces), not SNO. Likewise, the sole key for relvar P is {PNO}, and the sole key for relvar SP is {SNO,PNO}. By the way, note that {SNAME} isn't a key for relvar S, even though the SNAME values shown in Figs. 1.1 and 2.1 do happen to be unique. The point is, there's no constraint in effect that says supplier names *have* to be unique.

Second, the uniqueness property is self-explanatory, but I need to say a little more about the irreducibility property. Consider relvar S and the set of attributes—call it SC—{SNO,CITY}, which is certainly a subset of the heading of S that has the uniqueness property (no relation that's a valid value for relvar S ever has two distinct tuples with the same SC value).

---

[1] It's important, too!—but this isn't the place to elaborate on this point. Let me just say that sets in general are ubiquitous in the relational world, and the question of what happens if some such set happens to be empty is far from a frivolous one. For further details, see (a) Appendixes B and C of the present book and (b) Hugh Darwen's paper "The Nullologist in Relationland," in *Relational Database Writings 1989–1991*, by Hugh and myself (Addison-Wesley, 1992). *Note:* The term *nullologist* is derived from *nullology*, which is defined, slightly tongue in cheek, to be "the study of nothing at all" (in other words, it's the study of the empty set). It has nothing to do with SQL-style nulls!—which are very strongly deprecated, as we'll see in Part III of this book.

[2] What I'm here referring to as simply a key, unqualified, is sometimes called a *candidate* key in the literature.

But it doesn't have the irreducibility property, because we could discard the CITY attribute and what's left, the *singleton set* {SNO}, would still have the uniqueness property. So we don't regard SC as a key, because it's "too big." By contrast, {SNO} is irreducible, and it's a key.

So why do we want keys to be irreducible? One important reason is that if we were to specify a "key" that wasn't irreducible, the DBMS wouldn't be able to enforce the proper uniqueness constraint. For example, suppose we told the DBMS (lying!) that {SNO,CITY} was a key for relvar S. Then the DBMS wouldn't—in fact, couldn't—enforce the constraint that supplier numbers are "globally" unique; instead, it would and could enforce only the weaker constraint that supplier numbers are "locally" unique, in the sense that they're unique within the pertinent city. So this is one reason—not the only one—why we require keys not to contain any attributes that aren't needed for unique identification purposes.

Third, please note that the key concept applies specifically to relvars, not relations. Why? Because to say something is a key is to say a certain integrity constraint is in effect, and integrity constraints apply to variables, not values. (By definition, integrity constraints constrain updates, and updates apply to variables, not values. See Chapter 6 for further discussion.)

Fourth and last, all of the relvars in the suppliers-and-parts database happen to have just one key. But it's certainly possible for a relvar to have two or more. Here are several more or less self-explanatory examples of such relvars (in outline only):

```
TAX_BRACKET { LOW ... , HIGH ... , RATE ... }
   KEY { LOW }
   KEY { HIGH }
   KEY { RATE }
```

The idea in this first example is that if your taxable income is in the range LOW to HIGH, you pay tax at the specified RATE. For example, if your taxable income is in the range $10,000 to $19,999, you pay 10% (say); if it's in the range $20,000 to $29,999, you pay 15%; and so on. Assuming an equitable tax system in which rates increase as taxable income increases (?), {LOW}, {HIGH}, and {RATE} are clearly all keys.

```
ROSTER { DAY ... , TIME ... , GATE ... , PILOT ... }
   KEY { DAY , TIME , GATE }
   KEY { DAY , TIME , PILOT }
```

This relvar represents a simplified version of an airline schedule: On a certain day at a certain time, a certain pilot takes a certain flight out from a certain gate. Since it's physically impossible for the same pilot to be at two different gates at the same time on the same day, it follows that {DAY,TIME,GATE} and {DAY,TIME,PILOT} are both keys. Note the overlapping nature of the keys in this example; note too that the overlap is possible because, and only because, the keys in question (like the sole key of the shipments relvar SP) are *composite*. *Note:* A key that's not composite, like {SNO} in relvar S and {PNO} in relvar P, is sometimes said to be *simple*.

```
PLUS { A ... , B ... , C ... }
   KEY { A , B }
   KEY { B , C }
   KEY { C , A }
```

In this last example, the idea is that the C value in each tuple is equal to the sum of the A and B values.[3] Clearly, {A,B}, {B,C}, and {C,A} are all keys (again the keys are composite, and again they overlap).

> *A remark on primary keys:* If relvar R has more than one key, as in the foregoing examples, then it's usual, but *not* required,[4] to single out one of those keys and call it "primary." And if relvar R has just one key, it's also usual, but not required, to call that key "primary." However, whether some key is labeled primary, and if so which one (if there's a choice), are essentially psychological issues, beyond the purview of the relational model as such. Keys as such are fundamental, but primary keys aren't. In pictures like Figs. 1.1 and 2.1, however, when a relvar has just one key, I'll mark it as primary by using the convention of "double underlining" the attributes that constitute the key in question. *End of remark.*

FOREIGN KEYS

So now we know that every relvar does have at least one key—i.e., is subject to at least one key constraint. But some relvars are additionally subject to certain *foreign key* constraints as well. For example, {SNO} is a foreign key in relvar SP, referencing the sole key, {SNO}, of relvar S. What this means is that if, at some given time *t*, relvar SP contains a tuple in which the SNO value is (let's say) S3, then relvar S must also contain a tuple at that same time *t* in which the SNO value is S3—for otherwise relvar SP would show some part as being supplied by a nonexistent supplier, and the database would thus not be "a faithful model of reality."

---

[3] Actually PLUS might be a relation *constant* rather than a relation variable. See *SQL and Relational Theory* for further discussion of the notion of relation constants.

[4] As a matter of fact it was required in the relational model as originally defined, but there was never any good logical reason for such a requirement.

Of course, {PNO} is also a foreign key in relvar SP, referencing the sole key, {PNO}, of relvar P. *Very* loosely, we might think of foreign key constraints as the "glue" that holds the database together, as it were. Be that as it may, here's a definition:

Definition: Let relvars *R2* and *R1* be such that:

1.   *K* is a key for *R1*.

2.   *FK* is a subset of the heading of *R2*.

3.   At any given time, every *FK* value in *R2* is required to be equal to the *K* value in some (necessarily unique) tuple in *R1*.

Then *FK* is a **foreign key** in *R2*, referencing *K* in *R1*. *Note:* If *FK* consists of *n* attributes, then *n* is the **degree** of *FK*.

Actually the foregoing definition is considerably simplified, but it's good enough for present purposes. However, let me just point out that it does tacitly assume that *K* and *FK* each consist of the very same attributes; for example, in the case of relvars S and SP, the sole key attribute in relvar S is called SNO and is of type CHAR, and so the corresponding foreign key attribute in relvar SP must also be called SNO and be of type CHAR. That is (to spell the point out), every attribute in each of *K* and *FK* must have the same name and be of the same type as the corresponding attribute in the other; formally, in fact, they must be the very same attribute. See Exercise 3.2 at the end of the chapter for further explanation.[5]

Note: Once again I need to spell out a few matters of terminology. First of all, foreign keys are the relational model's way of maintaining what's usually called *referential integrity*.[6] The idea is that a foreign key value, like the SNO value S3 in relvar SP, represents a *reference* to the corresponding tuple in relvar S—and what the referential integrity rule says, in essence, is simply this: If tuple *t2* references tuple *t1*, then tuple *t1* must exist. Thus, for example, an attempt to delete a supplier tuple must fail if it would otherwise leave any "dangling references"—i.e., references in relvar SP to the supplier tuple that now no longer exists.

---

[5] If a given attribute of *FK* and the attribute of *K* that's supposed to correspond to it are of the same type but have different names—a situation that, as explained in *SQL and Relational Theory*, ought to be rare in practice—then the RENAME operator, described in Chapter 4, can help. Examples to illustrate this point can be found in *SQL and Relational Theory*. See also the answer to Exercise 9.5 in Chapter 9.

[6] As a historical note, I remark that the term *referential integrity* was due to Codd, and he defined it in connection with the relational model specifically. But the concept, as opposed to the term, predates the relational model.

Relvars *R2* and *R1* in the definition are said to be the *referencing* relvar and the *referenced* (or *target*) relvar, respectively. By the same token, a particular tuple *t2* in *R2* and the corresponding tuple *t1* in *R1* are a referencing tuple and the corresponding referenced (or target) tuple, respectively. And if *FK* is the foreign key in *R2*, then the corresponding key *K* in *R1* is the referenced (or target) key.

RELVAR DEFINITIONS

Now (at last!) you should be in a position to understand the **Tutorial D** definitions of relvars S, P, and SP. Here's the definition of relvar S:

```
VAR S BASE
      RELATION
           { SNO     CHAR ,
             SNAME   CHAR ,
             STATUS  INTEGER ,
             CITY    CHAR }
      KEY { SNO } ;
```

Explanation:

■ The keyword VAR indicates that the statement overall defines a variable (a relation variable, of course, in the case at hand). The variable in question is called S. The keyword BASE indicates the kind of variable we're defining; it stands for "base relvar," which is the kind of relvar S is. (Loosely speaking, a base relvar is a relvar that "stands alone" and isn't defined in terms of any other relvars. Other kinds of relvars do exist, the most important of which is the so called *virtual* relvar or *view*, which I'll be discussing briefly in Chapter 7. Prior to that point, however, I'm just going to assume for simplicity that all relvars are base ones.)

■ The next five lines define the type of this variable (a relation type, of course—recall from the answer to Exercise 2.8 in Chapter 2 that relvars, like all variables, certainly do have a type). The keyword RELATION shows it's a relation type, and the next four lines together specify the corresponding heading. No significance attaches to the order in which the attributes are specified within that heading, because a heading is a *set* of attributes. (As explained in Chapter 2, the conventional representation of a set on paper is as a commalist of elements enclosed in braces. However, the sequence of elements in that commalist is irrelevant, of course; thus, for example, {*a,b,c,d*} and {*d,a,c,b*} both denote the same set.)

■ The last line defines {SNO} to be a key for this relvar. Note that the KEY specification is
part of the relvar definition, not part of the type specification (why, exactly?).

Let me say a little more about the notion of relation types. First (again as we saw in the
answer to Exercise 2.8 in Chapter 2), relations as well as relvars certainly do have a type. And as
the definition of relvar S demonstrates, relation types in **Tutorial D** have names of the form

```
RELATION heading
```

where *heading* takes the form

```
{ attribute commalist }
```

and *attribute* in turn takes the form

```
attribute-name type-name
```

(and the order in which the attributes are listed in the heading is irrelevant). In fact, it turns out
that there's an extremely good reason for requiring relation types to have names of this particular
form, as should become clear from the remarks concerning *closure* in Chapters 4 and 5, q.v.

Here now is the definition of relvar P:

```
VAR P BASE
     RELATION
          { PNO      CHAR ,
            PNAME    CHAR ,
            COLOR    CHAR ,
            WEIGHT   RATIONAL ,
            CITY     CHAR }
     KEY { PNO } ;
```

The only new thing here is the type, RATIONAL, of the WEIGHT attribute. RATIONAL
is the **Tutorial D** name for a type that in other languages is more usually called REAL. It's a
system defined type, and it consists of numbers that can be expressed as the ratio of two integers
(e.g., 3/8, 5/12, -4/3).

A note on rational numbers: Rational numbers (only) have the property that, in decimal
notation, the fractional part of such a number can be expressed as either (a) a possibly

empty finite sequence of nonzero digits followed by an infinite sequence of zeros, which can be ignored without loss (e.g., 3/8 = 0.375000..., 2/1 = 2.000...), or (b) a possibly empty finite sequence of digits followed by another finite sequence of digits, the first of which is nonzero, that infinitely repeats (e.g., 5/12 = 0.41666...). *End of note.*

Finally, here's the definition of relvar SP:

```
VAR SP BASE
      RELATION
           { SNO   CHAR ,
             PNO   CHAR ,
             QTY   INTEGER }
      KEY { SNO , PNO }
      FOREIGN KEY { SNO } REFERENCES S
      FOREIGN KEY { PNO } REFERENCES P ;
```

The only new things here are the FOREIGN KEY specifications, which I take to be self-explanatory.

LOADING THE DATABASE

By default, base relvars are empty when they're first created (i.e., when they're defined); that is, their initial value is the (unique) empty relation of the pertinent type.[7] In order to "populate" or *load* the database, we could of course use relational assignment statements. For example, the assignment statement

```
S := RELATION
        { TUPLE { SNO 'S1' , SNAME 'Smith' , STATUS 20 , CITY 'London' } ,
          TUPLE { SNO 'S2' , SNAME 'Jones' , STATUS 10 , CITY 'Paris'  } ,
          TUPLE { SNO 'S3' , SNAME 'Blake' , STATUS 30 , CITY 'Paris'  } ,
          TUPLE { SNO 'S4' , SNAME 'Clark' , STATUS 20 , CITY 'London' } ,
          TUPLE { SNO 'S5' , SNAME 'Adams' , STATUS 30 , CITY 'Athens' } } ;
```

would be sufficient to assign to relvar S the relation shown as the value of that relvar in Figs. 1.1 and 2.1. Alternatively, of course, we could use an explicit INSERT statement, thus:

---

[7] It's possible to specify a nonempty initial value, but the details are beyond the scope of this book.

```
INSERT S RELATION
      { TUPLE { SNO 'S1' , SNAME 'Smith' , STATUS 20 , CITY 'London' } ,
        TUPLE { SNO 'S2' , SNAME 'Jones' , STATUS 10 , CITY 'Paris'  } ,
        TUPLE { SNO 'S3' , SNAME 'Blake' , STATUS 30 , CITY 'Paris'  } ,
        TUPLE { SNO 'S4' , SNAME 'Clark' , STATUS 20 , CITY 'London' } ,
        TUPLE { SNO 'S5' , SNAME 'Adams' , STATUS 30 , CITY 'Athens' } } ;
```

(though this INSERT does rely, as the explicit assignment did not, on the target relvar S being initially empty). And relvars P and SP could be populated in the same kind of way, of course. *Note:* In both of the foregoing statements, the expression denoting the relation to be assigned to relvar S is an example of a *relation literal.*[8] As you can see, therefore, relation literals in **Tutorial D** take the form

```
RELATION body
```

where *body* takes the form

```
{ tuple literal commalist }
```

and *tuple literal* in turn takes the form

```
TUPLE { component commalist }
```

and *component* in turn takes the form

```
attribute-name literal
```

Of course, the order in which the tuple literals are listed in the body is irrelevant, and so is the order in which the components are listed in each tuple literal.

Back to loading the database. In practice, of course, for all but the tiniest databases it would be intolerably tedious to use explicit relational assignments and/or explicit INSERT statements to carry out the load process in the manner just illustrated. Real databases are therefore not usually loaded "by hand" in such a manner; rather, they're typically loaded by a specially privileged user called the *database administrator* (DBA), using some kind of utility program that's specifically intended for the purpose ("the load utility"). However, whatever that

---

[8] Two points: First, a relation literal is a special case of a more general construct called a relation *selector invocation*; second, the syntax I give here for such literals (or, more generally, for such selector invocations) is simplified, just slightly. The first of these points is explained in Chapter 7. As for the second, see Exercise 3.3 at the end of the chapter.

load utility actually does, it has to be logically equivalent to executing some set of relational assignments.

Note: In a real database, the relvars are probably defined, as well as being loaded (and the database itself is probably created in the first place), by the DBA. The DBA is responsible for a great many other matters of an administrative nature as well, but such matters are mostly beyond the scope of this book.

DATABASE SYSTEMS vs. PROGRAMMING SYSTEMS *bis*

Recall now the code fragment shown in Fig. 1.3 in Chapter 1, which I used to illustrate various familiar concepts from the world of programming: statements, types, variables, assignment, literals, and read-only operators (including comparison operators as a special case). Recall too that I claimed that all of those concepts were directly relevant to databases (to relational databases in particular, of course). So let's see how far we've come in this regard. In brief:

- **Relational statements:** We've seen the relational assignment statement, the more "user friendly" INSERT, DELETE, and UPDATE statements, and the VAR statement (which is used to define variables in general and relvars in particular).

- **Relation types:** We've seen that relations and relvars have such types, denoted in **Tutorial D** by the keyword RELATION followed by the applicable heading. We've also seen various attribute types—INTEGER, CHAR, RATIONAL—and I've said a little about user defined types as well.

- **Relation variables:** Relvars S, P, and SP are examples of such variables.

- **Relational assignment:** See the bullet item on relational statements above.

- **Relation literals:** The section "Loading the Database" gave an example of such a literal. We've also seen examples of scalar literals (e.g., 'S1', 'Smith', 20, 'London), and tuple literals (e.g., TUPLE { SNO 'S1', SNAME 'Smith', STATUS 20, CITY 'London'}).

- **Relation values:** The values of relvars S, P, and SP at any given time are relation values. So too is the value denoted by a relation literal, of course.

■ **Relational read-only operators:** These are still to be discussed in detail (in Chapters 4 and 5), though we've seen a couple of examples in passing—see, e.g., Exercise 1.1 in Chapter 1.

■ **Relational comparison operators:** These too will be discussed in Chapter 4.

EXERCISES

3.1   Consider the following relation type (extracted from the definition of relvar P in the body of the chapter):

```
RELATION { PNO CHAR , PNAME CHAR , COLOR CHAR ,
                            WEIGHT RATIONAL , CITY CHAR }
```

If left to right attribute order were significant after all, how many different "parts relvars" could be defined?

3.2   With respect to the definition I gave for the foreign key concept in the body of the chapter, I pointed out that it tacitly assumed that the foreign key *FK* and the target key *K* consisted of the very same attributes. But what exactly was it about that definition that led me to make this claim? I mean, how exactly did the definition rely on that assumption?

3.3   In the section "Loading the Database," I said a relation literal in **Tutorial D** took the form of the keyword RELATION followed by a commalist of tuple literals enclosed in braces. What I didn't say, though, was that every one of those tuple literals must have the same set of attributes, and further that that set of attributes implicitly defined the heading, and hence the type, of the relation that's denoted by that relational literal. But suppose the commalist of tuple literals is empty—i.e., suppose we're trying to write a literal that represents an empty relation. How then can the pertinent relation type be determined?

3.4   What do you think should happen on an attempt to delete a supplier, if there are currently some shipments for the supplier in question?

3.5   I've said the relational model prohibits pointers. But aren't foreign keys just pointers in a different guise?

ANSWERS

3.1   Well, there'd be five possible choices for the "first" attribute; then, for each of those five possibilities, there'd be four choices for the "second" attribute; then, for each of those four possibilities, there'd be three choices for the "third" attribute; and so on. In all, therefore, there'd be 5! ("factorial 5") = 5 * 4 * 3 * 2 * 1 = 120 different possible "parts relvars." (Maybe this exercise will give you some inkling as to why it's such an advantage of the relational model that relations have no left to right ordering to their attributes. Recall the quote from Thoreau at the head of Chapter 1!)

3.2   This one requires a certain amount of background explanation. First of all, I need to stress the point that a tuple is a *set*—a set of components, where each component consists of an attribute and a corresponding attribute value. Now, recall from Chapter 1 that two values *v1* and *v2* are equal if and only if they're the very same value (which implies among other things that they're certainly of the same type); for example, the integer 3 is equal to the integer 3 and not to any other integer (and not to anything else, either). It follows that two tuples *t1* and *t2* are equal if and only if they're the very same tuple. And *that* means that, first, *t1* and *t2* must both have exactly the same set of attributes, say *A1, A2, ..., An*; second, for all *i* (*i* = 1, 2, ..., *n*), the value of *Ai* in *t1* must be equal to the value of *Ai* in *t2*. For example, consider the tuple shown for supplier S1 in Figs. 1.1 and 2.1. That tuple is equal to itself, and it isn't equal to any other tuple (nor to anything else, either).

The next point is this: Since a tuple is a set, it has subsets. For example, here are two of the many[9] subsets of the tuple shown for supplier S1 in Figs. 1.1 and 2.1 (**Tutorial D** notation):

```
TUPLE { SNO 'S1' , CITY 'London' }

TUPLE { CITY 'London' }
```

And just as, in mathematics, a subset is in fact a set (see Appendix C), so in the relational model a "subtuple" is in fact a tuple.

Now back to foreign keys. As in the definition of the foreign key concept in the body of the chapter, let *FK* be a foreign key and let *K* be the corresponding target key. Now, *FK* and *K*

---

[9] How many, actually?

are both sets of attributes (since they're each a subset of the pertinent heading); thus, *FK* and *K* values are *tuples* (very likely "proper subtuples," but certainly tuples). For example, the key value in the tuple shown for supplier S1 in Figs. 1.1 and 2.1 is this "proper subtuple":

```
TUPLE { SNO 'S1' }
```

Now suppose we try to insert a tuple into the referencing relvar (relvar *R2*, in the definition). In order to ensure that the foreign key constraint isn't violated—i.e., in order to ensure that referential integrity is maintained—the system is going to have to perform equality comparisons between the *FK* value in that new tuple and the *K* values currently existing in the referenced relvar (relvar *R1*, in the definition). But those comparisons are between tuples! Thus, the only way they can possibly make sense—I mean, the only way those comparisons can even be legal in the first place, let alone evaluate to TRUE—is if *FK* and *K* are of the same type, which means (as originally claimed) they must both involve the same set of attributes.

> *Aside:* The foregoing discussion shows that every subset of a tuple is a tuple. What's more, it's worth pointing out in passing that, by the same token, (a) every subset of a heading is a heading, and (b) every subset of a body is a body. *End of aside.*

3.3   Before I answer this question, let me point out explicitly that although (as stated in the body of the chapter) there's only one empty set in mathematics, there are many distinct empty relations in the relational model; in fact, there's exactly one empty relation for each possible relation type. For example, the empty suppliers relation and the empty parts relation are certainly distinct, because although they have the same body, they have different headings—in fact, they're of different types.[10]

Now to the question. Clearly, if we want to write a literal that denotes the empty relation of some particular relation type, there's no way that relation type can be inferred from the tuples in the body, because there *are* no tuples in that body. For that reason, the full **Tutorial D** syntax for a relation literal isn't quite what I said it was earlier in the chapter:

```
RELATION body
```

---

[10] As an aside, I remark that two distinct relations can have the same body only if that body is empty. In other words, apart from this special case, two relations can have the same body only if they're the same relation.

Rather, it's:

```
RELATION [ heading ] body
```

The syntax of *heading* and *body* was explained earlier in the chapter; but the point is, while *heading* is, in general, optional (that's why it's shown in brackets), it must be specified if *body* is empty.

3.4   One possibility is that the attempt should simply fail on a referential integrity violation. A more sophisticated possibility (supported by both **Tutorial D** and SQL, as it happens) is to allow a "cascade delete rule" to be specified in connection with the foreign key from SP to S, such that a DELETE on relvar S "cascades" to cause an automatic DELETE on SP as well—to be specific, a DELETE for all tuples with the same supplier number as any tuple being deleted from S.

3.5   No, they're not. The paper "Inclusion Dependencies and Foreign Keys"—Chapter 13in the book *Database Explorations: Essays on The Third Manifesto and Related Topics*, by Hugh Darwen and myself (Trafford, 2010)—lists some 14 logical differences between the two concepts. Here I'll mention just one. The fact is, pointers *point*; that is, they have directionality, and they have a single, specific target. Foreign key values, by contrast, are regular data values, and they're thus, like all data values in a relational database, what might be called "multiway associative." For example, a shipment tuple containing the PNO value P4 (which does happen to be a foreign key value, of course) is simultaneously linked—speaking purely logically—not just to the part tuple for part P4 but to all other shipment tuples, and indeed to all tuples anywhere (in the database or otherwise), that happen to include that same PNO value P4.

Chapter 4

Relational Operators I

It's been a hard day's night
And I've been working like a dog
—John Lennon and Paul McCartney:
"A Hard Day's Night" (1964)

Having defined the relvars in the suppliers-and-parts database (see Chapter 3), and having "loaded" or initialized them (again, see Chapter 3), we can now start to use them for "real work." More specifically, we can now issue queries—i.e., retrieval requests—against those relvars, using operators of what's called the *relational algebra*, and in this chapter I want to start our investigation into those operators. *Caveat:* The chapter is, regrettably, quite long, and you might want to take it a piece at a time. To help you in this regard, I haven't left all of the exercises and answers to the very end of the chapter but have instead interspersed them at intervals among the regular explanatory text.

CODD'S ORIGINAL ALGEBRA

The relational algebra consists of a set of operators that (speaking very loosely) allow us to derive "new" relations from "old" ones. Each such operator takes one or more relations as input and produces another relation as output. For example, the difference operator (MINUS, in **Tutorial D**) takes two relations as input and "subtracts" one from the other, to derive another relation as output. And it's very important that the output is another relation (that's the so called *closure* property of the relational algebra). The reason it's so important is this: *It allows us to write nested relational expressions.* To spell the point out, since the output from every operation is the same kind of thing as the input, the output from one operation can become the input (or one of the inputs) to another. For example, we can take the difference *r1* MINUS *r2*, feed the result as input to a union with some relation *r3*, feed *that* result as input to an intersection with some relation *r4*, and so on.

There's an analogy here that might help, to do with ordinary arithmetic. In arithmetic, we can (for example) take the sum of two numbers *a* and *b* to obtain a result, *c*; and that output *c* is the same kind of thing as the input—they're all numbers—and so we can take that output and feed it as input to, say, a multiplication operation; and then we can feed the result of that multiplication as input to a subtraction (and so on). In other words, numbers form a closed system under the regular arithmetic operators, and it's that fact that allows us to write nested arithmetic expressions. Likewise, relations are closed under the operators of the relational algebra, and the significance is precisely analogous: As I've said, we can write nested relational expressions.

Now, any number of operators can be defined that fit the simple definition of "one or more relations in, exactly one relation out." Below I briefly describe what are usually thought of as the original operators (essentially the ones that Codd defined in his earliest papers);[1] I'll give more details of those operators in subsequent sections of the chapter, and then in Chapter 5 I'll describe a number of additional operators. Fig. 4.1 gives a pictorial representation of those original operators. *Note:* If you're unfamiliar with these operators and find the descriptions in this preliminary section a little hard to understand, don't worry about it. As I've already said, I'll be going into much more detail, with lots of examples, later in the chapter.

Restrict

Returns a relation containing all tuples from a specified relation that satisfy a specified condition. For example, we might restrict the suppliers relation to just those tuples where the STATUS value is less than 25.

Project

Returns a relation containing all (sub)tuples that remain in a specified relation after specified attributes have been removed. (As noted in the answer to Exercise 3.2 in Chapter 3, a subtuple is still a tuple, just as—and indeed precisely because—a subset is still a set.) For example, we might project the suppliers relation on just the SNO and CITY attributes (thereby removing the SNAME and STATUS attributes).

Product

Returns a relation containing all possible tuples that are a combination of two tuples, one from each of two specified relations. For example, let *r1* be the projection of the suppliers relation on SNO and let *r2* be the projection of the parts relation on PNO. Then—thanks to the closure property—we could form the product of *r1* and *r2*, and the result would consist of all possible SNO-PNO pairs such that the SNO value is a supplier number appearing in the suppliers relation and the PNO value is a part number appearing in the parts relation. *Note:* "Product" here really means *cartesian* product, and the operator is sometimes so called.

---

[1] Except that Codd additionally defined an operator he called *divide*. I omit that operator here because the problems that divide is supposed to address can be handled much better by means of *image relations*, a construct I'll be discussing in Chapter 5.

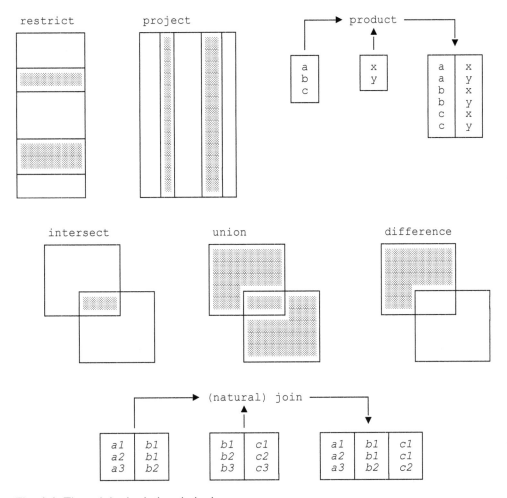

Fig. 4.1: The original relational algebra

Intersect

Returns a relation containing all tuples that appear in both of two specified relations.

Union

Returns a relation containing all tuples that appear in either or both of two specified relations.

Difference

> Returns a relation containing all tuples that appear in the first and not the second of two specified relations.

Join

> Returns a relation containing all possible tuples that are a combination of two tuples, one from each of two specified relations, such that the two tuples contributing to any given result tuple have common values for the common attributes of the two relations (and those common values appear just once, not twice, in that result tuple). *Note:* This kind of join was originally called the *natural* join, to distinguish it from various other kinds—especially the so called θ-join ("theta join"), to be discussed briefly in Chapter 11 in Part III of this book. Since natural join is far and away the most important kind, however, it's become standard practice to take the unqualified term *join* to mean the natural join specifically, and I'll follow that practice throughout this book.

> Finally, there are a number of additional points I need to make before I close this section:

■ The operators of the algebra are *generic:* They apply, in effect, to *all possible relations*. For example, we don't need one join operator to join (say) suppliers and shipments and another totally different join operator to join (say) departments and employees.

■ The operators are also *set level*, or (perhaps better) *relation level*: They take whole relations as operands, not individual tuples, and they return whole relations as their result.[2]

■ The operators are also *read-only:* They "read" their operands and they return a result, but they don't update anything. In other words, they operate on relations, not relvars.

■ Of course, the previous point doesn't mean that relational expressions can't refer to relvars. For example, if *R1* and *R2* are relvar names, then *R1* MINUS *R2* is certainly a valid relational expression in **Tutorial D** (just so long as the relvars denoted by those names are of the same type, that is—see later). In that expression, however, *R1* and *R2* don't denote those relvars as such; rather, they denote the relations that happen to be the current values of those relvars at the time the expression is evaluated. In other words, we can certainly use a relvar name to denote an operand to a relational algebra operator—and such a *relvar reference* thus constitutes one simple kind of relational expression—but in principle we

---

[2] INSERT, DELETE, and UPDATE (and relational assignment) are set level operators too, of course. In fact, the relational model includes no operators at all that work on relations (or relvars) one tuple at a time—despite the fact that it's sometimes convenient to explain certain operations in such terms, informally (see, for example, the explanation of image relations in Chapter 5 or the explanation of quantified expressions in Appendix D).

could equally well denote the very same operand by means of an appropriate relation literal instead.

An analogy might help clarify this point. Suppose N is a variable of type INTEGER, and at time *t* it has the value 3. Then N + 2 is certainly a valid arithmetic expression, but at time *t* it means exactly the same as the expression 3 + 2 does, no more and no less.

■ Finally, given that the operators of the algebra are indeed all read-only, it follows that INSERT, DELETE, and UPDATE (and relational assignment), though they're certainly *relational* operators, aren't relational *algebra* operators as such—though, regrettably, you'll often come across statements to the contrary in the literature. (In fact, of course, INSERT, DELETE, UPDATE, and relational assignment are all, specifically, *update* operators, whereas the algebraic operators are, as I've said, all read-only.)

RESTRICT

Now we can begin to examine the operators of the algebra in more detail. I'll start with restrict. Consider this query: "Get part information for parts whose weight is less than 12.5 pounds." (I'm assuming here, just to be definite, that part weights are recorded in relvar P in pounds avoirdupois.) Here then is a **Tutorial D** formulation of this query:

```
P WHERE WEIGHT < 12.5
```

And here's the result, given our usual sample values:[3]

PNO	PNAME	COLOR	WEIGHT	CITY
P1	Nut	Red	12.0	London
P5	Cam	Blue	12.0	Paris

As you can see, the result is certainly a relation; what's more, the heading of that result is the same as that of the input (i.e., the parts relation, which is to say the current value of relvar P), and the body of that result consists of just those tuples of the input for which the specified *restriction condition*—viz., WEIGHT < 12.5—evaluates to TRUE.

Here then for the record is a precise definition of the restriction operator:

Definition: Let *r* be a relation and let *bx* be a **restriction condition** on *r* (i.e., a boolean expression in which every attribute reference identifies some attribute of *r* and there aren't

---

[3] I won't keep saying this, since (to repeat from Chapter 1) I'm going to assume the specific sample values shown in Fig. 1.1 in examples throughout this book, barring explicit statements to the contrary.

any relvar references). Then the expression *r* WHERE *bx* denotes the **restriction** of *r* according to *bx*, and it returns a relation with heading the same as that of *r* and body consisting of all tuples of *r* for which *bx* evaluates to TRUE.

Points arising from this definition:

■ The definition mentions the term *restriction condition*, defining it to be a boolean expression in which every attribute reference identifies some attribute of the pertinent relation and there aren't any relvar references. (Note that the boolean expression in the example is indeed a restriction condition by this definition.) As you might have realized, the point about a boolean expression that takes this very simple form is that it can be evaluated for a given tuple of the pertinent relation "in isolation," as it were—there's no need to examine any other tuples in that relation, and there's no need to examine any other relations, either. For example, the restriction condition WEIGHT < 12.5 can be determined to be true or false (as applicable) for a given tuple in the parts relation "in isolation" in exactly the foregoing sense.

■ To repeat, the boolean expression in the WHERE clause is supposed to be a restriction condition. As a matter of user convenience, however, real languages, including both **Tutorial D** and SQL in particular, usually allow WHERE clauses to contain boolean expressions that are more general than this. Examples are given in later chapters. *Note:* It's legitimate to relax the strict requirement in this way because, if *exp* is an expression of the form *r* WHERE *bx* in which *bx* is *not* a restriction condition as such, then *exp* can always be shown to be equivalent to some more complicated expression in which any restrictions involved do in fact abide by the requirement after all.

■ It follows from the definition that the type of the result from a restriction operation is always the same as that of the input (since they both have the same heading).

■ Restriction is sometimes known as *selection*, but this latter term is deprecated, slightly, because of the potential confusion with (a) the SELECT operation of SQL (see Part III of this book) and (b) selector operators in the relational model (see Chapter 7).

PROJECT

Now on to project. Consider the query "For each part, get part number, color, and city." Here's a **Tutorial D** formulation:

```
P { PNO , COLOR , CITY }
```

And here's the result:

PNO	COLOR	CITY
P1	Red	London
P2	Green	Paris
P3	Blue	Oslo
P4	Red	London
P5	Blue	Paris
P6	Red	London

As you can see, the result is a relation once again; its heading consists of the attributes specified in the projection, and its body consists of the corresponding (sub)tuples of the input.

Here's another example, to illustrate another point. The query is "What part color and city combinations currently exist?" **Tutorial D** formulation:

```
P { COLOR , CITY }
```

Here's the result:

COLOR	CITY
Red	London
Green	Paris
Blue	Oslo
Blue	Paris

The point about this example is that the cardinality of the result is four, not six; even though there are six tuples in the input (the parts relation), three of those six contain the same color and city combination. Now, we want the result to be a relation—i.e., we want to preserve the closure property—and relations by definition never contain duplicate tuples; thus, those three tuples with the same color and city combination together contribute just one tuple to the overall result. In other words, "duplicates are eliminated," to use the common phrase.

> *Aside:* Observe that the result in this example is "all key," meaning the sole key is the entire heading (note the double underlining in the picture). However, see Exercise 5.1 in the next chapter for further discussion of this point. *End of aside.*

By the way, I'd like to point out that it's intuitively reasonable, as well as being logically correct, to do duplicate elimination in the foregoing example. Consider the original query once again: "What part color and city combinations currently exist?" Well, the combination "red and London" certainly exists; in fact, of course, it appears three times. But the query didn't ask how many times that combination appeared, it merely asked whether it existed. And the right answer to a question of the form "Does *x* exist?" is either yes or no, not a count.[4]

Note: In principle duplicate elimination was done in the previous projection example too, but in that case it had no effect. And the reason it had no effect was that, in that example, the set of attributes on which the projection was being done included a key (actually the only key) of the underlying relvar. To jump ahead of myself for a moment, let me add that conceptually, at least, duplicate elimination is *always* done as part of the process of producing the result of some algebraic operator. In practice, however, the only operators (out of the ones discussed in this chapter) for which duplicate elimination might actually be required—i.e., might actually have some effect on the result—are projection, which is the topic of the present section, and union, to be discussed later in the chapter.

Here then is a definition of the projection operator:

Definition: Let relation *r* have attributes called *A1*, *A2*, ..., *An* (and possibly others). Then the expression *r{A1,A2,...,An}* denotes the **projection** of *r* on *{A1, A2, ..., An}*, and it returns a relation with heading *{A1,A2,...,An}* and body consisting of all tuples *t* such that there exists a tuple in *r* that has the same value for attributes *A1*, *A2*, ..., *An* as *t* does.

Points arising from this definition:

- Of course, the order in which the attributes are specified in a projection operation is irrelevant. That's why the commalist of attribute names is enclosed in braces.[5] Thus, for example, these two expressions are logically equivalent and therefore effectively interchangeable:

```
P { COLOR , CITY }

P { CITY , COLOR }
```

- As a matter of user convenience, **Tutorial D** also allows projection operations to be expressed in terms of the attributes to be removed instead of the ones to be retained. For example, the two projection examples discussed so far in this section could alternatively have been formulated in **Tutorial D** as follows:

```
P { ALL BUT PNAME , WEIGHT }

P { ALL BUT PNO , PNAME , WEIGHT }
```

---

[4] We could have asked for the count if we had wanted to, of course, but that would have been a different query. I'll show how to do that kind of query in Chapter 5.

[5] At least in formal syntax. In informal prose, it's usual to skip the braces, thereby writing, e.g., "the projection of S on SNO" (instead of "the projection of S on {SNO}").

Note: **Tutorial D** allows this ALL BUT style throughout the language (wherever it makes sense, in fact). In the VAR statement that defined relvar SP, for example, we could have specified KEY {ALL BUT QTY} instead of KEY {SNO,PNO}.

- The type of the result from a projection operation is RELATION *H*, where the heading *H* consists of the attributes on which the projection was done. *Note:* In fact, of course, the type of the result of any relational operation is always RELATION *H*, where *H* is the applicable heading. Thus, I won't bother to point this fact out explicitly any more.

Closure Revisited

Consider the query "Get part number, color, and city for parts whose weight is less than 12.5 pounds." The obvious **Tutorial D** formulation is:

```
( P WHERE WEIGHT < 12.5 ) { PNO , COLOR , CITY }
```

Here's the result:

PNO	COLOR	CITY
P1	Red	London
P5	Blue	Paris

Note the use of parentheses, which forces the subexpression P WHERE WEIGHT < 12.5— which represents a restriction, of course—to be evaluated first. The result of that restriction is then projected on attributes PNO, COLOR, and CITY. So here we're explicitly making use of closure again: The result of the restriction is a relation, and so it's legitimate to perform a projection on it.

It follows from this example that when we say (as I did in the definition) that projection is denoted by an expression of the form *r{A1,A2,...,An}*, it's important to understand that the symbol *r* in that expression itself represents a relational expression of, in general, arbitrary complexity. And, of course, the same goes for the symbol *r* in the restriction expression *r* WHERE *bx*, and more generally for any mention of a relation as such in any of the relational operator definitions.

EXERCISES I

4.1   We have a formal reason for prohibiting duplicate tuples in relations (what is it?), but can you think of a pragmatic reason?

4.2   Why do you think relational algebra is *called* "relational algebra"?

4.3   What do the following **Tutorial D** expressions denote?

  a. `SP { SNO , PNO , QTY }`

  b. `P WHERE CITY = CITY`

  c. `P WHERE FALSE`

ANSWERS I

4.1   The formal reason is simply that the body of a relation is defined to be a set, and sets in mathematics don't permit duplicate elements. As for pragmatic reasons: Actually there are many, but we haven't covered enough groundwork to explain most of them here. But there's at least one that should make good intuitive sense, as follows.[6] Suppose "relvar" R permits duplicates. Then we can't tell the difference between "genuine" (i.e., explicitly intended) duplicates in R and "accidental" ones (i.e., ones caused by some kind of user error). Nor can we easily delete those "accidental" ones, even if we can recognize them.

There's another point too that applies specifically to the results of relational operations: If we don't eliminate duplicates from those results, then those results won't be relations, and we won't be able to perform further relational operations to them. In other words, we'll have violated closure, and we won't be able to write proper nested expressions.

4.2   Now *this* is a complicated question, and I don't think it has a simple, succinct answer.[7] Speaking a little loosely, however, an *algebra* can be defined as a formal system that consists of (a) a set of objects of some kind, together with (b) a set of read-only operators that apply to those objects, such that (c) those objects and operators together satisfy certain laws and properties, such as the closure property (see Appendix C). The word algebra itself derives from Arabic *al-jebr*, meaning a resetting (of something broken) or a combination. And relational algebra in particular does conform, somewhat, to the foregoing loose definition.

4.3   a. The projection of the relation that's the current value of relvar SP on all of its attributes. The result is of course necessarily identical to that current value; indeed, a

---

[6] Other reasons are discussed in some of the references listed in Appendix E, q.v.

[7] In fact I wrote an entire paper on the question—"Why Is It Called Relational Algebra?"—which appeared in my book *Logic and Databases: The Roots of Relational Theory* (Trafford, 2007).

projection of a relation on all of its attributes is sometimes referred to as an *identity projection* for that very reason.

　　b. This expression—it's a restriction expression, of course—returns the relation that's the current value of relvar P, because the boolean expression in the WHERE clause evaluates to TRUE for every tuple in that current value. In fact, the restriction expression overall is logically equivalent to the restriction expression P WHERE TRUE. *Note:* Any restriction expression that's logically equivalent to one of the form *r* WHERE TRUE is said to denote an *identity restriction*.

　　c. This expression (a restriction expression again) returns the empty parts relation. Any restriction expression that's logically equivalent to one of the form *r* WHERE FALSE is said to denote an *empty restriction*.

UNION, INTERSECTION, AND DIFFERENCE

Now I turn to union, intersection, and difference. These three operators all follow the same general pattern. I'll start with union.

Union

Consider the query "Get cities in which at least one supplier or at least one part is located." Here's a **Tutorial D** formulation (note the appeal to closure yet again):

```
S { CITY } UNION P { CITY }
```

And here's the result:

```
CITY
━━━━━
Athens
London
Oslo
Paris
```

　　As you can see, the result is a relation once again; its heading is the same as that of each of the two input relations, and its body consists of tuples that appear in one or both of those two relations (with duplicates eliminated, as mentioned earlier). Note, therefore, that the two input relations must have the same heading—equivalently, they must be of the same type—for otherwise the union operation is undefined. But if it *is* defined, then the result too is of the same type as both of the inputs.

Here's another example, to illustrate another (very simple) point. Suppose for the sake of the example that parts have an extra attribute called STATUS, of type INTEGER, and consider the query "Get status and city pairs such that at least one supplier or part has that combination." In **Tutorial D**:

```
S { STATUS , CITY } UNION P { CITY , STATUS }
```

The point of this example, of course, is simply that (as always) the left to right order in which attributes are specified within a heading is irrelevant.

Here then is a definition of the union operator:

Definition: Let relations *r1* and *r2* be of the same type *T*. Then the expression *r1* UNION *r2* denotes the **union** of *r1* and *r2*, and it returns the relation of type *T* with body the set of all tuples *t* such that *t* appears in either or both of *r1* and *r2*.

Intersection

Intersection is very similar to union, mutatis mutandis; in particular, the two input relations must again be of the same type, and the result is of the same type also. Here's an example (the query is "Get cities in which at least one supplier and at least one part are both located"). **Tutorial D** formulation:

```
S { CITY } INTERSECT P { CITY }
```

Result:

Here's the definition:

Definition: Let relations *r1* and *r2* be of the same type *T*. Then the expression *r1* INTERSECT *r2* denotes the **intersection** of *r1* and *r2*, and it returns the relation of type *T* with body the set of all tuples *t* such that *t* appears in both *r1* and *r2*.

Difference

Difference—MINUS in **Tutorial D**—is also somewhat similar to union; in particular, the two input relations must again be of the same type, and the result is of the same type also. Here's an example (the query is "Get cities in which at least one supplier is located and no part is"). In **Tutorial D**:

```
S { CITY } MINUS P { CITY }
```

Result:

There is, however, one point on which difference is *not* similar to union and intersection: *Operand order matters.* With union, *r1* UNION *r2* and *r2* UNION *r1* both mean the same thing; likewise, with intersection, *r1* INTERSECT *r2* and *r2* INTERSECT *r1* both mean the same thing. But with difference, *r1* MINUS *r2* and *r2* MINUS *r1* most definitely don't mean the same thing, even if they return the same result (which can happen only if *r1* and *r2* are equal, in which case both results are empty). Thus, for example, the expression

```
P { CITY } MINUS S { CITY }
```

evaluates to:

Here's the definition:

Definition: Let relations *r1* and *r2* be of the same type *T*. Then the expression *r1* MINUS *r2* denotes the **difference** between *r1* and *r2* (in that order), and it returns the relation of type *T* with body the set of all tuples *t* such that *t* appears in *r1* and not in *r2*.

Some Formal Properties

The union operator in particular possesses a number of attractive formal properties that can help the user's task of query formulation.[8] To be specific, the operator is commutative, associative, and idempotent. *Commutative* means *r1* UNION *r2* and *r2* UNION *r1* are equivalent (this property follows immediately from the fact that the definition of the operator is symmetric in *r1* and *r2*); as already noted, therefore, the order in which the operands are specified makes no difference. *Associative* means *r1* UNION (*r2* UNION *r3*) and (*r1* UNION *r2*) UNION *r3* are equivalent, so the parentheses aren't needed and both of these expressions can be simplified to just *r1* UNION *r2* UNION *r3*. *Idempotent* means *r* UNION *r* reduces to simply *r*.

The foregoing paragraph applies 100 percent, mutatis mutandis, to intersection also; that is, intersection too is commutative, associative, and idempotent. However, it doesn't apply at all to difference, for which none of those three properties holds.

RENAME

Consider the following query: "Get names such that at least one supplier or at least one part has the name in question." (This query is very contrived and probably doesn't make much intuitive sense, but it suffices to illustrate the point I want to make here.) Now, the following formulation *doesn't* work:

```
S { SNAME } UNION P { PNAME }
```

The reason it doesn't work is that UNION requires its operands to be of the same type, meaning that corresponding attributes have to be of the same type *and have the same name*. (Formally, in fact, they have to be the very same attribute.) In order to meet this requirement in the case at hand, therefore, we must *rename* at least one of SNAME and PNAME before we do the union (these attributes are at least of the same type, but they obviously have different names). Here then is a possible formulation of the query that does work, in which, purely for reasons of symmetry, I've renamed both of the pertinent attributes:

```
( ( S RENAME { SNAME AS NAME } ) { NAME } )
  UNION
( ( P RENAME { PNAME AS NAME } ) { NAME } )
```

Before explaining in detail how this formulation works (if you haven't figured it out for yourself already), let me discuss the RENAME operator as such.[9] Here's the definition:

---

[8] They can also help the optimizer, but it's not my aim in this book to get into too much detail about the optimizer.

[9] You might have noticed that RENAME wasn't shown in Fig. 4.1. Indeed, it wasn't one of Codd's original operators. But that was because Codd never did properly spell out the details of how operators like UNION were supposed to work.

Definition: Let relation *r* have an attribute called *A* and no attribute called *B*. Then the expression *r* RENAME {*A* AS *B*} returns a relation with heading identical to that of *r* except that attribute *A* in that heading is renamed *B*, and body identical to that of *r* except that all references to *A* in that body—more precisely, in tuples in that body—are replaced by references to *B*.

And here's an example:

```
S RENAME { CITY AS SCITY }
```

The result looks like this (it's identical to our usual suppliers relation, except that the city attribute is called SCITY):

SNO	SNAME	STATUS	SCITY
S1	Smith	20	London
S2	Jones	10	Paris
S3	Blake	30	Paris
S4	Clark	20	London
S5	Adams	30	Athens

Important: Relvar S has *not* been changed in the database here! The expression S RENAME {CITY AS SCITY} is only an expression (just as, e.g., *r1* MINUS *r2* or N + 2 are only expressions), and like any expression it simply denotes a value. What's more, of course, since it *is* an expression and not a statement, it can be nested inside other expressions.

RENAME is needed primarily as a preliminary to a JOIN or UNION invocation.[10] The details of JOIN are still to be discussed, of course, but here again is the UNION example that introduced this section:

```
( ( S RENAME { SNAME AS NAME } ) { NAME } )
  UNION
( ( P RENAME { PNAME AS NAME } ) { NAME } )
```

Explanation:

■ The subexpression S RENAME {SNAME AS NAME} returns a relation essentially identical to the current value of relvar S, except that the SNAME attribute is renamed NAME. Let's call that result *r1*. Relation *r1* is then projected on NAME, to give as a result relation *r2*, say.

---

[10] It's also needed in connection with certain foreign key specifications (see *SQL and Relational Theory*, also the answer to Exercise 9.5 in Chapter 9).

- The subexpression P RENAME {PNAME AS NAME} returns a relation essentially identical to the current value of relvar P, except that the PNAME attribute is renamed NAME. Let's call that result *r3*. Relation *r3* is then projected on NAME, to give as a result relation *r4*, say.

- Finally, the expression *r2* UNION *r4* is evaluated, to produce a relation of degree one, with sole attribute NAME (of type CHAR) and body consisting of all tuples of the form

```
TUPLE { NAME name }
```

such that *name* appears as a value of the SNAME attribute in the current value of relvar S or a value of the PNAME attribute in the current value of relvar P or both.

EXERCISES II

4.4   Why exactly is duplicate elimination not an issue for intersection and difference?

4.5   The relational union, intersection, and difference operators are each based on the set theory operator of the same name. Give definitions, as precise as you can make them, of those set theory operators.

4.6   What do the following **Tutorial D** expressions denote? *Note:* You can assume, here and throughout this book, that in **Tutorial D** projection has the highest precedence of all relational operators.

a.   P { PNO } MINUS (SP WHERE SNO = 'S2') { PNO }

b.   (S { CITY } INTERSECT P { CITY }) UNION P { CITY }

c.   S { SNO } MINUS (S { SNO } MINUS SP { SNO })

d.   SP MINUS SP

e.   S INTERSECT S

f.   (S WHERE CITY = 'Paris') UNION (S WHERE STATUS = 20)

4.7   Write **Tutorial D** expressions for the following queries:

a. Get all shipments.

b. Get part numbers for parts supplied by supplier S2.

c. Get suppliers with status in the range 15 to 25 inclusive.

d. Get supplier numbers for suppliers with status lower than that of supplier S2.

e. Get part numbers for parts supplied by all suppliers in Paris.

4.8   Try writing **Tutorial D** expressions for some queries of your own—preferably on a database of your own but, failing that, on the suppliers-and-parts database.

ANSWERS II

4.4   Well, there are certainly no duplicates in the inputs, because the inputs are relations. Next, observe that *r1* INTERSECT *r2* can be loosely defined to mean "return the maximal subset *r* of *r1* such that every tuple appearing in *r* also appears in *r2*"—from which it's obvious that there aren't any duplicates to be eliminated. Likewise, *r1* MINUS *r2* can be loosely defined to mean "return the maximal subset *r* of *r1* such that no tuple appearing in *r* also appears in *r2*," from which, again, it's obvious that there aren't any duplicates to be eliminated.

4.5   Let *A* and *B* be sets. Then the set theory union of *A* and *B* is the set of all elements appearing in at least one of *A* and *B*; the set theory intersection of *A* and *B* is the set of all elements appearing in both *A* and *B*; and the set theory difference between *A* and *B*, in that order, is the set of all elements appearing in *A* and not in *B*. See Appendix C for further discussion.

4.6   *Note:* My characterizations below of what the various expressions denote are deliberately quite informal.

  a. Part numbers for parts not supplied by supplier S2.

  b. All part cities. The expression overall reduces to just P{CITY}. *Note:* This exercise illustrates one of the so called *absorption laws*, which for the record I spell out here:

```
( r1 INTERSECT r2 ) UNION r2  ≡  r2

( r1 UNION r2 ) INTERSECT r2  ≡  r2
```

(The symbol "≡" denotes logical equivalence.)

    c. Supplier numbers for suppliers who supply at least one part.

    d. The empty set of shipments.

    e. All suppliers.

    f. Suppliers with city Paris or status 20 or both.

4.7   The following answers aren't the only ones possible, in general.

    a. `SP`

    b. `( SP WHERE SNO = 'S2' ) { PNO }`

    c. `S WHERE STATUS ≥ 15 AND STATUS ≤ 25`. As this answer illustrates, the boolean expression in a WHERE clause is of course allowed to use logical connectives such as AND, OR, and NOT.

    d. `( S WHERE STATUS < STATUS FROM`
`( TUPLE FROM`
`( S WHERE SNO = 'S2' ) ) ) { SNO }`

    This expression needs a certain amount of explanation!—though the explanation that follows is deliberately somewhat informal. First, note that we have here an illustration (the first we've seen) of the point that, in **Tutorial D** at least, the boolean expression in a WHERE clause can, in general, be more complicated than just a simple restriction condition. Second, the innermost subexpression S WHERE SNO = 'S2' evaluates to a relation containing just one tuple. But that relation is still a relation, and what we need is not that relation as such, but rather the status value that's contained in the single tuple that's contained in that single-tuple relation. So first we need to extract the pertinent tuple from that relation, using TUPLE FROM (which is an operator that extracts the unique tuple from a one-tuple relation); then we need to extract the pertinent status value from that tuple, using STATUS FROM (in general, the operator "*attribute name* FROM *t*" extracts the value of the specified attribute from the tuple denoted by the tuple expression *t*). The status value so obtained—call it *x*—is the status value for supplier S2, and the expression overall thus reduces to the restriction expression S WHERE STATUS < *x*.

Note: An alternative answer to this exercise is given in footnote 14 in the section "Update Operator Expansions" later in the chapter.

```
e. WITH ( t1 := S WHERE CITY = 'Paris' ,
          t2 := t1 { SNO } ,
          t3 := SP RENAME { PNO AS x } ) :
    ( P WHERE ( t3 WHERE x = PNO ) { SNO } ⊇ t2 ) { PNO }
```

Again a certain amount of (deliberately informal) explanation is needed. First, WITH isn't an operator as such, it's just a syntactic trick that lets us introduce names for subexpressions and thereby enables us to see the forest as well as the trees, as it were. Thus, *t1* is suppliers in Paris; *t2* is supplier numbers for suppliers in Paris; and *t3* is the whole shipments relation, except that the PNO attribute is renamed *x*. Then the last line asks for an expression of the form P WHERE *bx* to be evaluated—in other words, it picks out a certain subset of the parts relation—and then it projects that subset on PNO, thereby returning part numbers as desired. As for that boolean expression *bx*, observe first that it involves a comparison between two relations (let's call them *r1* and *r2*).[11] Note that those two relations are both of degree one; what's more, their single attribute is the same, viz., SNO, in both cases (thus, the relations are both of the same type). Relation *r2* is just *t2*; in other words, it's supplier numbers for suppliers in Paris. As for relation *r1*: Well, I shouldn't really refer to it as "relation *r1*" (as if it were a single thing) at all, because actually it depends on which tuple of the parts relation we happen to be talking about. In fact, if we consider the parts tuple for part *p*, then *r1* is effectively the supplier numbers for the suppliers who supply part *p*. So, for each part *p*, *bx* is effectively asking whether the supplier numbers for suppliers who supply that part *p* are a superset of the supplier numbers for suppliers in Paris. Thus, *bx* evaluates to TRUE precisely for those parts that are supplied by all suppliers in Paris, as required.

Of course, we don't have to use WITH if we don't want to. The following **Tutorial D** expression is logically equivalent to the one shown above:

```
( P WHERE ( ( SP RENAME { PNO AS x } ) WHERE x = PNO ) { SNO } ⊇
                       ( ( S WHERE CITY = 'Paris' ) { SNO } ) ) { PNO }
```

Note: SQL supports a WITH construct too, but it's not as useful as its **Tutorial D** counterpart because (as we'll see in Part III of this book) the syntactic structure of SQL doesn't lend itself so readily to the idea of breaking large expressions down into smaller ones.

4.8   *No answer provided.*

---

[11] Relational comparisons are discussed in more detail later in the chapter.

JOIN

The next operator of Codd's original set I want to discuss is join, which, despite the fact that I've left it almost until last, is certainly one of the most important. I'll begin with an example. The query is "For each shipment, get the part number and quantity and corresponding supplier details." The **Tutorial D** formulation is very simple:

```
SP JOIN S
```

Here's the result:

SNO	SNAME	STATUS	CITY	PNO	QTY
S1	Smith	20	London	P1	300
S1	Smith	20	London	P2	200
S1	Smith	20	London	P3	400
S1	Smith	20	London	P4	200
S1	Smith	20	London	P5	100
S1	Smith	20	London	P6	100
S2	Jones	10	Paris	P1	300
S2	Jones	10	Paris	P2	400
S3	Blake	30	Paris	P2	200
S4	Clark	20	London	P2	200
S4	Clark	20	London	P4	300
S4	Clark	20	London	P5	400

Explanation: As the definition below makes clear, joins in **Tutorial D** are performed on the basis of *common attributes*. In the case at hand, the join is done on the basis of supplier numbers, SNO being the sole attribute the two operand relations have in common. Thus, every SP tuple *t1* that has SNO value *s*, say, joins to every S tuple *t2* with that same SNO value *s*, and the result is as shown above. (Actually, of course, there'll be exactly one such *t2* for any given *t1*, because the sole common attribute SNO constitutes a foreign key in SP and the corresponding target key in S. Also, note that there's no *t1* at all with SNO value S5, and so there's no tuple for supplier S5 in the overall result.) Note too that the common attribute SNO appears once, not twice, in the result.

Before I get to the definition of join as such, it's helpful to introduce the concept of *joinability*. I'll say relations *r1* and *r2* are *joinable* if and only if attributes with the same name are of the same type, meaning that in fact they're the very same attribute.[12] So here now is the join definition (note how it appeals to the fact that headings and tuples are both sets and can therefore be operated upon by set theory operators such as union):

---

[12] Despite the name, the notion of joinability applies not only to join but to certain other operations as well, as we'll see in Chapter 5. Also, observe that another way to define it is as follows: Relations *r1* and *r2* are joinable if and only if the set theory union of their headings is a legal heading.

Definition: Let relations *r1* and *r2* be joinable. Then the expression *r1* JOIN *r2* denotes the **join** of *r1* and *r2*, and it returns a relation with heading the set theory union of the headings of *r1* and *r2* and body the set of all tuples *t* such that *t* is the set theory union of a tuple from *r1* and a tuple from *r2*.

Perhaps I should remind you that I'm using the abbreviated name *join* to refer to the natural join specifically. Here's another example:

```
P JOIN S
```

The join here is done, by definition, on the basis of part and supplier cities, CITY being the sole attribute that P and S have in common. Here's the result:

SNO	SNAME	STATUS	CITY	PNO	PNAME	COLOR	WEIGHT
S1	Smith	20	London	P1	Nut	Red	12.0
S1	Smith	20	London	P4	Screw	Red	14.0
S1	Smith	20	London	P6	Cog	Red	19.0
S2	Jones	10	Paris	P2	Bolt	Green	17.0
S2	Jones	10	Paris	P5	Cam	Blue	12.0
S3	Blake	30	Paris	P2	Bolt	Green	17.0
S3	Blake	30	Paris	P5	Cam	Blue	12.0
S4	Clark	20	London	P1	Nut	Red	12.0
S4	Clark	20	London	P4	Screw	Red	14.0
S4	Clark	20	London	P6	Cog	Red	19.0

Like union and intersection, join is commutative, associative, and idempotent.

Cartesian Product

In general, cartesian product—product for short—returns a relation containing all possible tuples that are effectively a concatenation of two tuples, one from each of two specified relations. Now, suppose we wanted to form the product of the current values of relvars S and P. Relvars S and P both have a CITY attribute, and so it looks on the face of it as if the result would have *two* CITY attributes. But then the result wouldn't be a relation!—recall from Chapter 2 that no relational heading is allowed to have two distinct attributes with the same name. For that reason, we require that the input relations to a product not have any attribute names in common (a requirement that can always be met, of course, thanks to the availability of the relational RENAME operator).

In order not to have to bother with RENAME, however, let's consider a simpler example. The query is "Get all current supplier and part number pairs." Here's a **Tutorial D** formulation:

```
S { SNO } TIMES P { PNO }
```

I won't bother to show the result in its entirety (it has 30 tuples in it), but here it is in outline:

```
┌─────────────┐
│ SNO │ PNO   │
├─────┼───────┤
│ S1  │ P1    │
│ S1  │ P2    │
│ ..  │ ..    │
│ S5  │ P6    │
└─────────────┘
```

And here's the definition of the product operator:

> **Definition:** Let relations *r1* and *r2* have no attribute names in common. Then the expression *r1* TIMES *r2* denotes the **product** of *r1* and *r2*, and it returns a relation with heading the set theory union of the headings of *r1* and *r2* and body the set of all tuples *t* such that *t* is the set theory union of a tuple from *r1* and a tuple from *r2*.

As you can see, this definition is identical to the definition I gave for join, except that instead of requiring *r1* and *r2* to be joinable we're now requiring them to have no common attribute names. But wait a minute ... *Joinable* just means attributes with the same name must be of the same type. But if there aren't any attributes with the same name, then this requirement is satisfied trivially! (If there aren't any attributes with the same name, then there certainly aren't any attributes with the same name that aren't of the same type.) Thus, *r1* and *r2* having no attribute names in common is just a special case of *r1* and *r2* being joinable, and TIMES is therefore just a special case of JOIN.

Here's another example, for interest. The query is "Get SNO-PNO pairs such that supplier SNO doesn't supply part PNO." **Tutorial D** formulation:

```
( S { SNO } TIMES P { PNO } ) MINUS SP { SNO , PNO }
```

We could replace TIMES here by JOIN without making any logical difference. In fact, TIMES is supported in **Tutorial D** mainly for psychological reasons.

Intersection Revisited

It turns out that intersection too is just a special case of join, as you might perhaps have already realized. To be specific, *r1* JOIN *r2* is logically equivalent to *r1* INTERSECT *r2* if and only if *r1* and *r2* are of the same type. Recall the following example: "Get cities in which at least one supplier and at least one part are both located." Here's the formulation I gave earlier:

```
S { CITY } INTERSECT P { CITY }
```

Well, we could replace INTERSECT here by JOIN without making any logical difference. In fact, INTERSECT too is supported in **Tutorial D** mainly for psychological reasons.

Primitive Operators

So INTERSECT and TIMES can be defined in terms of JOIN; in other words, not all of the operators I've discussed so far are primitive, where, loosely speaking, an operator is *primitive* if it can't be defined in terms of other operators. One possible primitive set is the set {restrict, project, join, union, difference}; another can be obtained by replacing join in this set by product. *Note:* You might be surprised to see no mention here of rename. In fact, however, rename isn't primitive, though I haven't covered enough groundwork yet to show why not (see the discussion of EXTEND in Chapter 5). As you can see, however, there's a difference between being primitive and being useful! I certainly wouldn't want to be without our useful rename operator, even if it isn't primitive—nor INTERSECT and TIMES, come to that.[13]

RELATIONAL COMPARISONS

Of course, relation types are no exception to the rule that the "=" comparison operator must be defined for every type; that is, given two relations *r1* and *r2* of the same relation type *T*, we must certainly be able to test whether they're equal. Here's a **Tutorial D** example:

```
S { CITY } = P { CITY }
```

The left comparand here is the projection of suppliers on CITY, the right comparand is the projection of parts on CITY, and the comparison returns TRUE if these two projections are equal, FALSE otherwise. (Given our usual sample values, it returns FALSE, of course.)
    The comparison operators "≠", "⊆" (is included in), "⊂" (is properly included in), "⊇" (includes), and "⊃" (properly includes) should obviously be supported as well. *Note:* Of these operators, the "⊆" operator in particular is usually referred to, a trifle arbitrarily, as "the" relational inclusion operator. Here's another example, this one making use of "⊃":

```
S { SNO } ⊃ SP { SNO }
```

The meaning of this expression, considerably paraphrased, is: "Some suppliers supply no parts at all" (which again necessarily evaluates to either TRUE or FALSE).

---

[13] As a matter of fact, it's possible to define a version of the relational algebra that has only two primitives! In the book *Databases, Types, and the Relational Model: The Third Manifesto* (3rd edition, Addison-Wesley, 2007), by Hugh Darwen and myself, we define such an algebra, which we call **A**.

Aside: There's a tiny technical issue here. Recall that the operators of the relational algebra are supposed to form a closed system, in the sense that the result of every such operator is supposed to be a relation. But the result of the relational comparison operators is, of course, not a relation but a truth value; thus, it's not entirely clear that these latter operators should really be regarded as part of the algebra as such (writers differ on this point). Still, we don't need to worry about this question; the important thing as far as we're concerned is that the operators are certainly available for use when we need them. *End of aside.*

Note: One very common requirement is to be able to perform an "=" comparison between some given relation *r* and an empty relation of the applicable type—in other words, a test to see whether *r* is empty. So it's convenient to define a shorthand:

```
IS_EMPTY ( r )
```

This expression is defined to return TRUE if *r* is empty and FALSE otherwise. I'll be relying on it heavily in chapters to come (especially Chapter 6). The inverse operator is useful too:

```
IS_NOT_EMPTY ( r )
```

This expression is logically equivalent to NOT (IS_EMPTY(*r*)).

UPDATE OPERATOR EXPANSIONS

As noted earlier in this chapter, INSERT, DELETE, and UPDATE, being update operators, aren't operators of the relational algebra as such. However, they can certainly be explained—in fact, they're *defined*—in terms of operators of the algebra. For example, the **Tutorial D** INSERT statement

```
INSERT R rx ;
```

(where *R* is a relvar name and *rx* is a relational expression denoting a relation *r* of the same type as *R*) is defined to be shorthand for the following explicit relational assignment:

```
R := R UNION rx ;
```

Thus, for example, the statement

```
INSERT SP RELATION { TUPLE { SNO 'S5' , PNO 'P6' , QTY 700 } } ;
```

inserts a relation containing just a single tuple into the shipments relvar SP—or, speaking rather loosely, albeit more intuitively, we can say it "inserts a tuple" into SP (recall that, strictly speaking, there aren't any tuple level operators, as such, in the relational model at all). *Note:* In case you're wondering here about TUPLE FROM, which is tuple level in a sense (recall from the answer to Exercise 4.7d that its purpose is to extract the single tuple from a single-tuple relation), that's an example of an operator that's clearly needed in the external environment surrounding the database but isn't part of the relational model as such.[14]

Observe now that the foregoing definition of INSERT in terms of union implies that an attempt to insert "a tuple that already exists"—i.e., an INSERT in which the relations denoted by *R* and *rx* aren't disjoint—will succeed. (It won't insert any duplicate tuples, of course—it just won't have any effect, as far as those existing tuples are concerned.) For that reason, **Tutorial D** additionally supports an operator called D_INSERT ("disjoint INSERT"), with syntax as follows:

```
D_INSERT R rx ;
```

This statement is defined to be shorthand for:

```
R := R D_UNION rx ;
```

D_UNION here stands for *disjoint union*. Disjoint union is just like regular union, except that its operand relations are required to have no tuples in common (otherwise an exception is raised). It follows that an attempt to use D_INSERT to insert a tuple that already exists will fail.

Turning now to DELETE, the **Tutorial D** DELETE statement

```
DELETE R rx ;
```

(where again *R* is a relvar name and *rx* is a relational expression denoting a relation *r* of the same type as *R*) is defined to be shorthand for the following explicit assignment:

```
R := R MINUS rx ;
```

For example, the DELETE statement

```
DELETE SP RELATION { TUPLE { SNO 'S1' , PNO 'P1' , QTY 300 } } ;
```

deletes a relation containing just a single tuple from the shipments relvar SP—or, more loosely, it "deletes a tuple" from SP. *Note:* What I've shown here is the most general form of DELETE. Earlier examples in this book took the form "DELETE *R* WHERE *bx*"; technically speaking,

---

[14] In case you're still skeptical, here's an answer to Exercise 4.7d that avoids the use of TUPLE FROM: ((S{SNO,STATUS} TIMES ((S WHERE SNO = 'S2'){STATUS} RENAME {STATUS AS *x*})) WHERE STATUS < *x*){SNO}.

however, that form is shorthand for a DELETE of the form "DELETE *R rx*" in which *rx* in turn takes the form "*R* WHERE *bx*".

Of course, the foregoing definition implies that an attempt to delete "a tuple that doesn't exist" (i.e., a DELETE in which the relation denoted by *rx* isn't wholly included in the relation denoted by *R*) will succeed. For that reason, **Tutorial D** additionally supports an operator called I_DELETE ("included DELETE"), with syntax as follows:

```
I_DELETE R rx ;
```

This statement is defined to be shorthand for:

```
R := R I_MINUS rx ;
```

I_MINUS here stands for *included minus;* the expression *r1* I_MINUS *r2* is defined to be the same as *r1* MINUS *r2*, except that every tuple appearing in *r2* must also appear in *r1*—in other words, *r2* must be included in *r1* (otherwise an exception is raised). It follows that an attempt to use I_DELETE to delete a tuple that doesn't exist will fail.

Finally, the **Tutorial D** UPDATE statement also corresponds to a certain explicit assignment. However, the details are a little more complicated in this case than they are for INSERT and DELETE, and for that reason I'll defer them to Chapter 5 (see Exercise 5.2).

EXERCISES III

4.9   As noted earlier in the chapter, closure is important in the relational model for the same kind of reason it's important in ordinary arithmetic. In arithmetic, however, there's one situation where closure breaks down, in a sense: namely, division by zero. Is there any analogous situation in the relational algebra?

4.10 What do the following **Tutorial D** expressions denote?

a. (S { SNO , CITY } JOIN P { PNO , CITY }) { PNO , SNO }

b. S JOIN SP JOIN P

c. ((S RENAME { CITY AS SC }) { SC }) JOIN
    ((P RENAME { CITY AS PC }) { PC })

d. SP { SNO } I_MINUS S { SNO }

e. (S WHERE STATUS = 20) { CITY } D_UNION
    (P WHERE COLOR = 'Blue') { CITY }

4.11 Write **Tutorial D** expressions for the following queries:

a. Get part numbers for parts supplied by a supplier in London.

b. Get part numbers for parts not supplied by any supplier in London.

c. Get all pairs of part numbers such that some supplier supplies both of the indicated parts.

4.12 Try writing **Tutorial D** expressions for some queries of your own—preferably on a database of your own but, failing that, on the suppliers-and-parts database.

ANSWERS III

4.9   No! But I can't explain why not here—we haven't covered enough of the background. (However, I can at least say that the reason has to do with the special relations TABLE_DUM and TABLE_DEE, which are discussed in Appendix B.) See *SQL and Relational Theory* for further explanation.

4.10 a. Part and supplier number pairs for parts and suppliers that are in the same city. By the way, notice that the two inner projections in the overall expression are logically unnecessary (though of course they're not wrong). Do you think the optimizer might ignore them? Would we want it to?

b. SNO – SNAME – STATUS – CITY – PNO – QTY – PNAME – COLOR – WEIGHT tuples such that supplier SNO both supplies, and is in the same city as, part PNO. (Note that the result of S JOIN SP has *two* attributes, PNO and CITY, in common with relvar P.)

c. SC – PC pairs such that some supplier is in city SC and some part is in city PC (the join in this example is really cartesian product).

d. Exception, unless every supplier supplies some part, in which case I_MINUS reduces to MINUS (and the result is then the empty set of supplier numbers).

e. Exception, unless no city is the city for both some supplier with status 20 and some blue part, in which case D_UNION reduces to UNION.

4.11 The following answers aren't the only ones possible, in general.

a. (SP JOIN (S WHERE CITY = 'London')) { PNO }

b. `P { PNO } MINUS ( SP JOIN ( S WHERE CITY = 'London' ) ) { PNO }`

c. `WITH ( t := SP { ALL BUT QTY } ) :`
`( ( t RENAME { PNO AS PX } ) JOIN ( t RENAME { PNO AS PY } ) )`
`{ PX , PY }`

Note: Given our usual sample data values, supplier S1, for example, supplies both part P1 and part P2, and so the pair (P1,P2) appears in the result here. But for exactly the same reason, so does the pair (P2,P1)! Come to that, so does the pair (P1,P1), necessarily. We could eliminate these redundancies, if we wanted to, by restricting the result to just those pairs where PX < PY.

4.12 *No answer provided.*

Chapter 5

R e l a t i o n a l   O p e r a t o r s   I I

Men of judgment ... so enclose
Infinite riches in a little room
—Christopher Marlowe: *The Jew of Malta* (c. 1592)

As noted in Chapter 4, any number of operators can be defined that fit the simple definition of "one or more relations in, exactly one relation out." That previous chapter described Codd's original operators (join, project, etc.); in this chapter, by contrast, I want to describe some of the many additional operators that have been defined since the relational model was first invented. Specifically, I want to discuss (a) MATCHING and NOT MATCHING; (b) EXTEND; (c) image relations; and (d) aggregation, summarization, and related matters.

MATCHING AND NOT MATCHING

It turns out in practice that most relational expressions—not all—that seem to need the join operator for their formulation really need a related but logically distinct operator called *semijoin* (MATCHING, in **Tutorial D**). Here's an example (the query is "Get supplier details for suppliers who supply at least one part"):

```
S MATCHING SP
```

Here's the result:

SNO	SNAME	STATUS	CITY
S1	Smith	20	London
S2	Jones	10	Paris
S3	Blake	30	Paris
S4	Clark	20	London

This result contains just the tuples for suppliers that "match" at least one shipment.

Here now is the semijoin definition (note how it appeals to the concept of joinability, which was defined in Chapter 4):

> **Definition:** Let relations *r1* and *r2* be joinable, and let *r1* have attributes called *A1*, *A2*, ..., *An* (only). Then the expression *r1* MATCHING *r2* denotes the **semijoin** of *r1* with *r2* (in that order), and it returns a relation equal to the relation returned by the projection on *{A1,A2, ...,An}* of the join of *r1* and *r2*.

In other words, the expression *r1* MATCHING *r2* returns a relation equal to the relation returned by the expression *r1* JOIN *r2*, projected back on the attributes of *r1*. Thus, for example, the expression S MATCHING SP is shorthand for the expression

```
( S JOIN SP ) { SNO , SNAME , STATUS , CITY }
```

Note that *r1* MATCHING *r2* and *r2* MATCHING *r1* aren't equivalent, in general.

In similar fashion, it turns out in practice that most relational expressions (not all) that seem to need the difference operator for their formulation really need a related but logically distinct operator called *semidifference* (NOT MATCHING, in **Tutorial D**). Here's an example (the query is "Get full supplier details for suppliers who supply no parts at all"):

```
S NOT MATCHING SP
```

Here's the result:

SNO	SNAME	STATUS	CITY
S5	Adams	30	Athens

This result contains just the tuples for suppliers that don't match any shipments at all.

Here now is the definition:

> **Definition:** Let relations *r1* and *r2* be joinable. Then the expression *r1* NOT MATCHING *r2* denotes the **semidifference** between *r1* and *r2* (in that order), and it returns a relation equal to the relation returned by the expression *r1* MINUS (*r1* MATCHING *r2*).

For example, the expression S NOT MATCHING SP is shorthand for the expression

```
S MINUS ( S MATCHING SP )
```

By the way, do you see what happens with NOT MATCHING if relations *r1* and *r2* aren't merely joinable but are actually of the same type? For example, consider the following expression:

```
S { CITY } NOT MATCHING P { CITY }
```

By definition, this expression is shorthand for the following:

```
S { CITY } MINUS ( S { CITY } MATCHING P { CITY } )
```

And as I'm sure you can see, this latter expression reduces to just:

```
S { CITY } MINUS P { CITY }
```

In other words, the regular difference operator—MINUS in **Tutorial D**—is actually a special case of NOT MATCHING. In a sense, therefore, NOT MATCHING is more fundamental than MINUS is. Note, however, that an analogous remark does *not* apply to MATCHING and JOIN: Neither of these operators is a special case of the other.

EXTEND

Consider this query: "For each part, get full part information, together with the part weight in grams." (Recall that part weights are given in relvar P in pounds.) A moment's thought should be sufficient to convince you that if the only operators we have are the ones described in Chapter 4 (and, of course, if the only relations we have are the ones shown in Fig. 1.1), then there's no way we can formulate this query. And that in essence is why we need EXTEND. Here's a formulation of the foregoing query that uses that operator:

```
EXTEND P : { GMWT := WEIGHT * 454 }
```

(Note that there are 454 grams to a pound.) Here's the result:

PNO	PNAME	COLOR	WEIGHT	CITY	GMWT
P1	Nut	Red	12.0	London	5448.0
P2	Bolt	Green	17.0	Paris	7718.0
P3	Screw	Blue	17.0	Oslo	7718.0
P4	Screw	Red	14.0	London	6356.0
P5	Cam	Blue	12.0	Paris	5448.0
P6	Cog	Red	19.0	London	8626.0

Important: Relvar P has *not* been changed in the database! The expression EXTEND P : {GMWT := WEIGHT * 454} is only an expression, and like any expression it simply denotes a value. What's more, of course, since it *is* an expression, not a statement, it can be nested inside other expressions.

As a matter of fact, EXTEND comes in two forms, or versions. We'll get to the second in a little while, but here's a definition of the first:

Definition: Let relation *r* not have an attribute called *A*. Then the expression EXTEND *r* : {*A* := *exp*} returns a relation with heading the heading of *r* extended with attribute *A* and body the set of all tuples *t* such that *t* is a tuple of *r* extended with a value for *A* that's computed by evaluating the expression *exp* on that tuple of *r*.

Now, I said a moment ago that EXTEND expressions can be nested inside other expressions. Here's an example to illustrate this point (the query is "Get part number and gram weight for parts with gram weight greater than 7000 grams"):

```
( ( EXTEND P : { GMWT := WEIGHT * 454 } )
                WHERE GMWT > 7000.0 )
                        { PNO , GMWT }
```

What we have here, as you can see, is a projection of a restriction of an extension. Here's the result:

PNO	GMWT
P2	7718.0
P3	7718.0
P6	8626.0

In practice, EXTEND is a really important operator. For that reason, I'll show a few more examples, with corresponding results (though little by way of further commentary):

1. `EXTEND S : { TAG := 'Supplier' }`

SNO	SNAME	STATUS	CITY	TAG
S1	Smith	20	London	Supplier
S2	Jones	10	Paris	Supplier
S3	Blake	30	Paris	Supplier
S4	Clark	20	London	Supplier
S5	Adams	30	Athens	Supplier

2. `EXTEND ( P JOIN SP ) : { SHIPWT := WEIGHT * QTY }`

PNO	...	WEIGHT	...	SNO	QTY	SHIPWT
P1	...	12.0	...	S1	300	3600.0
..	...	....	...	..	...	......

etc.

3. `( EXTEND S : { SCITY := CITY } ) { ALL BUT CITY }`

SNO	SNAME	STATUS	SCITY
S1	Smith	20	London
S2	Jones	10	Paris
S3	Blake	30	Paris
S4	Clark	20	London
S5	Adams	30	Athens

Note: This last example (i.e., Example 3) illustrates the point that, as mentioned in Chapter 4, RENAME isn't a primitive operator, because the expression shown—a projection of an extension—is logically equivalent to the following renaming:

```
S RENAME { CITY AS SCITY }
```

I turn now to the second form of EXTEND, which is aimed primarily at what are sometimes called "what if" queries. In other words, it can be used to explore the effect of making certain changes to the database without actually having to make (and subsequently unmake, possibly) the changes in question. Here's an example ("What if part weights were given in grams instead of pounds?"):

```
EXTEND P : { WEIGHT := WEIGHT * 454 }
```

The point about this example is simply that the target attribute in the attribute assignment in braces here isn't a "new" attribute as it was in all of the EXTEND examples prior to this point; instead, it's an attribute that already exists in the specified relation (that relation being the current value of relvar P, in the case at hand). The expression overall is defined to be equivalent to the following:

```
( ( EXTEND P : { GMWT := WEIGHT * 454 } ) { ALL BUT WEIGHT } )
                                        RENAME { GMWT AS WEIGHT }
```

Here for the record is a definition of this second form of EXTEND:

Definition: Let relation *r* have an attribute called *A*. Then the expression EXTEND *r* : {*A* := *exp*} returns a relation with heading the same as that of *r* and body the set of all tuples *t* such that *t* is derived from a tuple of *r* by replacing the value of *A* by a value that's computed by evaluating the expression *exp* on that tuple of *r*.

IMAGE RELATIONS

An *image relation* is, loosely, the "image" within some relation of some tuple (usually but not necessarily a tuple within some other relation). For example, given our usual suppliers-and-parts database, the following is the image within the shipments relation—i.e., the current value of relvar SP—of the supplier tuple for supplier S4:

PNO	QTY
P2	200
P4	300
P5	400

Clearly, this particular image relation can be obtained by means of the following **Tutorial D** expression:

```
( SP WHERE SNO = 'S4' ) { ALL BUT SNO }
```

But image relations in general are such a useful and widely applicable concept that it's desirable to define a shorthand for them, and so we do. The shorthand in question is illustrated in the following example:

```
S WHERE ( !!SP ) { PNO } = P { PNO }
```

In this expression, the subexpression !!SP—pronounced "bang bang SP" or "double bang SP"—is an *image relation reference*, and it denotes the image relation corresponding to "the current tuple" of S. Let me explain:

- To begin with, the expression overall (i.e., S WHERE ...) is asking for a certain subset of the relation that's the current value of relvar S (i.e., a subset of "the suppliers relation").

- The subset in question consists of all tuples from the suppliers relation for which the boolean expression in the WHERE clause evaluates to TRUE. I remark in passing that the boolean expression in question isn't a simple restriction condition—it involves references to attributes that aren't attributes of relvar S, and it also involves relvar references. In fact, as you can see, it's a relational equality comparison.

- The right comparand in that equality comparison is the projection on PNO of the current value of relvar P, and thus contains the six part numbers P1, P2, ..., P6 (or tuples containing these six part numbers, rather). The left comparand is also a projection on PNO of *something*, so at least the comparands are, as required, relations of the same type.

- We can imagine the equality comparison being carried out for each of the tuples of the suppliers relation one at a time in some arbitrary sequence. Consider one such tuple, say the tuple for supplier S*x* (let's call that tuple *t*). For tuple *t*, then, the expression !!SP denotes the corresponding image relation within the relation that's the current value of relvar SP (i.e., "the shipments relation"). In other words, it denotes the set of PNO-QTY pairs within SP for parts supplied by that supplier S*x*; for example, if S*x* is S4, it denotes the relation shown near the beginning of the present section.

■ For that tuple *t*, then, the expression (!!SP){PNO}—i.e., the projection of that image relation on PNO—denotes the set of part numbers for parts supplied by supplier S*x*.

■ The expression overall (i.e., S WHERE ...) thus denotes suppliers from S for whom the corresponding set of part numbers is equal to the set of all part numbers in the projection of P on PNO. Hence, the expression overall represents the query "Get suppliers who supply all parts" (speaking a little loosely). Here's the result:

SNO	SNAME	STATUS	CITY
S1	Smith	20	London

Let me point out before going any further that "Get suppliers who supply all parts" isn't at all a simple query. In SQL, for example, it would take several lines of fairly complex code, as we'll see in Part III of this book. Being able to formulate it as a "one liner," which is what the image relation construct has enabled us to do, is thus a significant usability benefit.

By way of a second example, recall Exercise 4.7e from Chapter 4: "Get part numbers for parts supplied by all suppliers in Paris." In that chapter I gave the following formulation as an answer to this exercise:

```
( P WHERE
    ( ( SP RENAME { PNO AS x } )
            WHERE x = PNO ) { SNO } ⊇
                ( ( S WHERE CITY = 'Paris' ) { SNO } ) ) { PNO }
```

But it can be done more succinctly with image relations:

```
( P WHERE ( !!SP ) { SNO } ⊇ ( S WHERE CITY = 'Paris' ) { SNO } ) { PNO }
```

For a third example, suppose we're given a revised version of the suppliers-and-parts database—one that's simultaneously both extended and simplified, compared to our usual running example—that looks like this (in outline):

```
S    { SNO }        /* suppliers              */
SP   { SNO , PNO }  /* supplier supplies part */
PJ   { PNO , JNO }  /* part is used in project */
J    { JNO }        /* projects               */
```

Relvar J here represents *projects* (JNO stands for project number), and relvar PJ indicates which parts are used in which projects. Now consider the query "Get all *sno-jno* pairs such that *sno* is an SNO value currently appearing in relvar S, *jno* is a JNO value currently appearing in relvar J, and supplier *sno* supplies all parts used in project *jno*." This is a pretty complicated query!—but a formulation using image relations is almost trivial:

```
( S TIMES J ) WHERE !!PJ ⊆ !!SP
```

We'll see further examples involving image relations in the next section, but for now just let me close this section with a definition. (I give this definition mainly for the record; don't worry if you find it a little hard to understand on a first reading.)

> **Definition:** Let relations *r1* and *r2* be joinable; let their common attributes be called *A1*, *A2*, ..., *An*; let *t1* be a tuple of *r1*; let *t2* be a tuple of *r2* that has the same values for *A1*, *A2*, ..., *An* as tuple *t1* does; let relation *r3* be that restriction of *r2* that contains all and only such tuples *t2*; and let relation *r4* be the projection *r3* {ALL BUT *A1*, *A2*, ..., *An*}. Then *r4* is the **image relation** (with respect to *r2*) corresponding to *t1*.

AGGREGATION AND SUMMARIZATION

An *aggregate operator* in the relational model is not, in general, a relational operator, because its result is usually not a relation. Rather, an aggregate operator is an operator that derives a single value from the "aggregate"—i.e., the set or *bag*[1]—of values of some attribute of some relation (or, in the case of COUNT, which is slightly special, from the "aggregate" that's the entire relation). Here are a few simple examples:

```
X.:= COUNT ( S ) ;              /* X = 5 */

Y := COUNT ( S { STATUS } ) ;   /* Y = 3 */

Z := SUM ( SP { QTY } ) ;       /* Z = 1000 */
```

As the comments indicate, the first of these statements assigns the value 5 (the cardinality of the suppliers relation) to the variable X; the second assigns the value 3 (the cardinality of the projection of the suppliers relation on STATUS) to the variable Y; and the third assigns the value

---

[1] A *bag*, also known as a *multiset*, is like a set but permits duplicate elements.

1000 (the sum of the values in the projection of the shipments relation on QTY) to the variable Z. In general, a **Tutorial D** aggregate operator invocation looks like this:

```
agg ( rel exp [, exp ] )
```

Available operators include COUNT, SUM, AVG, MAX, MIN, AND, OR, and XOR (the last three of which apply to aggregates of boolean values specifically). Within *exp*, an attribute reference can appear wherever a literal would be allowed. As indicated by the brackets, the expression *exp* is optional; it must be omitted for COUNT, but can be omitted otherwise only if the relational expression *rel exp* denotes a relation of degree one, in which case an *exp* consisting of a reference to the sole attribute of that relation is assumed. Here are some more examples:

1. `SUM ( SP , QTY )`

   This expression denotes the sum of all quantities in relvar SP (it can be read as "Sum the current value of relvar SP *over* quantities"). The result is 3100.

2. `SUM ( SP { QTY } )`

   This expression is shorthand for SUM(SP{QTY},QTY), and it denotes the sum of all *distinct* quantities in SP, which is 1000 (contrast the previous example).

3. `AVG ( SP , 3 * QTY )`

   This expression effectively asks what the average shipment quantity would be if quantities were all triple their current value (the answer is 775).

So much for the basic idea. Now, aggregate operators have two main uses:

- They can be used in a *summarization*, by which I mean, a trifle loosely, aggregating something for each tuple in some projection of some relation.

- They can be used in a WHERE clause, thereby supporting what I'll refer to—rather sloppily, and purely for present purposes, please note—as *generalized restriction*.

Incidentally, it's worth mentioning up front that, in both cases, image relations are almost always involved as well.

Summarization

Consider the following query: "For each supplier, get the supplier number and a count of the number of parts that supplier supplies." Here's a **Tutorial D** formulation:

```
EXTEND S { SNO } : { PCT := COUNT ( !!SP ) }
```

And here's the result (note the tuple for supplier S5 in particular):

SNO	PCT
S1	6
S2	2
S3	1
S4	3
S5	0

Observe that the foregoing result does indeed constitute a summarization (check the loose definition I gave earlier for this concept): It consists of an aggregation—actually a counting—of the shipments corresponding to each tuple in the projection of the suppliers relation on SNO.

By way of a second example, consider the query "For each supplier, get the supplier number and the corresponding total shipment quantity." **Tutorial D** formulation:

```
EXTEND S { SNO } : { TOTQ := SUM ( !!SP , QTY ) }
```

And here's the result (again note the tuple for supplier S5 in particular):

SNO	TOTQ
S1	1300
S2	700
S3	200
S4	900
S5	0

For a third and final example, consider the query "For each Athens supplier, get full supplier details and the corresponding total, maximum, and minimum shipment quantity."

Here's a tentative **Tutorial D** formulation (but it needs some refinement, as I'll explain in a moment):

```
EXTEND ( S WHERE CITY = 'Athens' ) : { TOTQ := SUM ( !!SP , QTY ) ,
                                        MAXQ := MAX ( !!SP , QTY ) ,
                                        MINQ := MIN ( !!SP , QTY ) }
```

This example illustrates the use of "multiple EXTEND." *Note:* I observe in passing that various other **Tutorial D** operators also exist in such "multiple" versions, including in particular RENAME and UPDATE, as well as other operators not discussed in this book.

A more important issue raised by the example is this: What happens if the argument to an aggregate operator, *agg* say, happens to be empty? Well, we've already seen what happens if *agg* is COUNT or SUM—the result is simply zero. As for the other operators: If *agg* is AND, the result is TRUE; if it's OR or XOR, the result is FALSE; and if it's AVG, MAX, or MIN, an exception is raised—in the case of AVG, because asking for the average of an empty set is effectively asking for zero to be divided by zero; in the case of MAX and MIN, because the result for those operators should clearly be some value in the input, and if the input is empty no such value exists. *Note:* The reason why COUNT and SUM return zero, AND returns TRUE, and OR and XOR return FALSE is that in each of these cases the indicated result is the pertinent *identity value.* Refer to *SQL and Relational Theory* for further explanation.

So what should we do about AVG, MAX, and MIN, if there's a possibility that the argument might be empty? Well, the following modified version of the foregoing example shows a trick that does at least work:

```
EXTEND ( S WHERE CITY = 'Athens' ) :
   { TOTQ := SUM ( !!SP , QTY ) ,
     MAXQ :=
     CASE WHEN IS_EMPTY ( !!SP ) THEN 0 ELSE MAX ( !!SP , QTY ) END CASE ,
     MINQ :=
     CASE WHEN IS_EMPTY ( !!SP ) THEN 0 ELSE MIN ( !!SP , QTY ) END CASE }
```

Result:

SNO	SNAME	STATUS	CITY	TOTQ	MAXQ	MINQ
S5	Adams	30	Athens	0	0	0

Whether it might be possible, and/or desirable, to find some more elegant solution to the problem illustrated by the foregoing example is open to debate.

A remark on MAX and MIN: Actually there's an argument that says the MAX and MIN of an empty argument shouldn't be undefined after all. For definiteness, consider MAX specifically (the following discussion applies equally well to MIN, mutatis mutandis). First let's define a dyadic operator LARGER that returns the larger of its two arguments. Then (a) a MAX invocation is essentially just shorthand for repeated invocation of LARGER, and (b) LARGER clearly has an identity value, viz., "negative infinity" (meaning the minimum value of the pertinent type); so we might reasonably define the MAX of an empty argument to be that identity value. Maybe the best approach in practice would be to provide both versions of MAX—they are, after all, different operators—and let the user decide. We might even provide a third version, one that takes an additional argument *x*, where *x* is the value to be returned if the aggregate argument is empty. But further discussion of such matters is beyond the scope of this book. *End of remark.*

Explicit SUMMARIZE

As we've seen, summarizations can be expressed in **Tutorial D** using EXTEND and image relations. However, **Tutorial D** currently supports an explicit SUMMARIZE operator as well. Let me show you what the summarization examples discussed so far in this section might look like if we used that operator. The first query was "For each supplier, get the supplier number and a count of the number of parts that supplier supplies":

```
SUMMARIZE SP PER ( S { SNO } ) : { PCT := COUNT ( ) }
```

The second query was "For each supplier, get the supplier number and the corresponding total shipment quantity":

```
SUMMARIZE SP PER ( S { SNO } ) : { TOTQ := SUM ( QTY ) }
```

And the third was "For each Athens supplier, get full supplier details and the corresponding total, maximum, and minimum shipment quantity":

```
SUMMARIZE SP PER ( ( S WHERE CITY = 'Athens' ) { SNO } ) :
                                 { TOTQ := SUM ( QTY ) ,
                                   MAXQ := MAX ( QTY ) ,
                                   MINQ := MIN ( QTY ) }
```

In my opinion, however, SUMMARIZE should be dropped from the language. For one thing, SUMMARIZE expressions tend to be clumsier and harder to understand than their EXTEND counterparts, as you can probably see. For another, they tend to exacerbate the empty argument problem (as I'm sure you noticed, I didn't even attempt to show an "empty argument" formulation of the third example). And—most damning of all, in my opinion—they rely on a rather suspect linguistic construct, viz., the *summary* (examples are COUNT(), SUM(QTY), and MAX(QTY)). *Note:* I call this construct "suspect" because it turns out to be extremely difficult to come up with a precise definition of the pertinent semantics (a criticism that does *not* apply to image relation references, please note). This book isn't the place to go into details; let me just point out that a summary is certainly not the same thing as an aggregate operator invocation. For example, the following is definitely not legal:

```
Z := SUM ( QTY ) ;            /*  Warning!  Illegal!  */
```

Because of such considerations, I'll have nothing more to say in this book regarding the explicit SUMMARIZE operator as such.

"Generalized Restriction"

As I suggested earlier, the term *generalized restriction* certainly isn't an "official" term (in some ways it isn't even a very good term), but I find it convenient as a label for what I want to talk about in this section: viz., expressions of the form *r* WHERE *bx*, where the boolean expression *bx* involves an aggregate operator invocation and, almost always, an image relation reference as well. Here's a self-explanatory example (the query is "Get suppliers with fewer than three shipments"):

```
S WHERE COUNT ( !!SP ) < 3
```

(The result contains just the supplier tuples for suppliers S2, S3, and S5.)
    Another example ("Get suppliers for whom the total shipment quantity is less than 1000"):

```
S WHERE SUM ( !!SP , QTY ) < 1000
```

And a couple more:

```
( EXTEND S { SNO } : { TOTQ := SUM ( !!SP , QTY ) } ) WHERE TOTQ > 250
```

("Get supplier number and total shipment quantity for suppliers where the total quantity is greater than 250.")

```
UPDATE S WHERE SUM ( !!SP , QTY ) < 1000 : { STATUS := 0.5 * STATUS } ;
```

("Update suppliers with total shipment quantity less than 1000, halving their status.")

EXERCISES

5.1   In Chapter 3 I said I'd be indicating primary key attributes, in tabular pictures of relations, by double underlining. But I also explained very carefully in that chapter that keys, primary or otherwise, apply to relvars, not relations. Yet I've shown numerous tabular pictures in the present chapter, as well as in Chapter 4, that represent relations as such (I mean, relations that aren't just a sample value for some relvar), and I've certainly been using the double underlining convention in those pictures. So what can we say about that convention now?

5.2   Consider the following **Tutorial D** UPDATE statement:

```
UPDATE S WHERE CITY = 'Paris' : { STATUS := 30 } ;
```

Can you give an explicit relational assignment that's precisely equivalent to this UPDATE? *Hint:* Remember the "what if" version of EXTEND.

5.3   The following **Tutorial D** expression was discussed in the body of the chapter, in the section "Image Relations":

```
S WHERE ( !!SP ) { PNO } = P { PNO }
```

Can you find a relational expression that's logically equivalent to the image relation reference in the WHERE clause here ("!!SP") but doesn't use an image relation reference as such?

5.4   What do the following **Tutorial D** expressions denote?

  a. P MATCHING S

b. S NOT MATCHING (SP WHERE PNO = 'P2')

c. EXTEND P : { SCT := COUNT (!!SP) }

d. P WHERE SUM (!!SP , QTY) < 500

5.5   Write **Tutorial D** expressions for the following queries:

a. Get supplier numbers for suppliers whose city is first in the alphabetic list of such cities. (You can assume at least one supplier exists.)

b. Get city names for cities in which at least two suppliers are located.

5.6   Show that any given "generalized restriction" can be expressed in terms of EXTEND and regular restriction.

ANSWERS

5.1   There are two cases to consider: (a) The relation depicted is a sample value for some relvar *R*; (b) the relation depicted is a sample value for some relational expression *rx*, where *rx* is something other than a simple relvar reference (recall that a relvar reference is basically just the pertinent relvar name). In the first case, double underlining simply indicates that a primary key *PK* has been—or could have been—declared for *R* and the pertinent attribute is part of *PK*. In the second case, you can think of *rx* as the defining expression for some temporary relvar *R* (think of WITH specifications, for example); then double underlining indicates that a primary key *PK* could in principle be declared for *R* and the pertinent attribute is part of *PK*.

5.2   One possible answer is as follows:

```
S := ( S WHERE CITY ≠ 'Paris' )
       UNION
     ( EXTEND S WHERE CITY = 'Paris' : { STATUS := 30 } ) ;
```

A slightly better answer is:

```
S := ( S WHERE CITY ≠ 'Paris' OR STATUS = 30 )
        UNION
      ( EXTEND S WHERE CITY = 'Paris' AND STATUS ≠ 30 ) :
                                { STATUS := 30 } ) ;
```

Subsidiary exercise: In what sense is this latter formulation "slightly better"?

5.3   It's convenient first to show a replacement for the entire original expression:

```
S WHERE
    ( SP MATCHING RELATION { TUPLE { SNO SNO } } ) { PNO } = P { PNO }
```

Explanation: Consider some tuple of S, say that for supplier Sx. For that tuple, then, the expression TUPLE {SNO SNO} denotes a tuple containing just the SNO value Sx (the first SNO in that TUPLE expression is an attribute name, the second denotes the value of the attribute of that name in the tuple for supplier Sx within relvar S). So the expression

```
RELATION { TUPLE { SNO SNO } }
```

(which in fact is a relation selector invocation—see Chapter 7) denotes the relation that contains just that tuple. Hence, the expression

```
SP MATCHING RELATION { TUPLE { SNO SNO } }
```

denotes a certain subset of SP: namely, that subset that contains just those shipment tuples that have the same SNO value as the supplier tuple for supplier Sx does. It follows that, in the context under consideration, the expression shown ("SP MATCHING ...") is logically equivalent to the image relation reference "‼SP".

5.4   a. Parts in the same city as some supplier. b. Suppliers who don't supply part P2. c. PNO – PNAME – WEIGHT – COLOR – CITY – SCT tuples such that part PNO is supplied by n suppliers, where n is the value of SCT. d. Parts with total shipment quantity less than 500.

5.5   a. (S WHERE CITY = MIN (S { CITY })) { SNO }

      b. S { CITY } WHERE COUNT (‼S) > 1

5.6   a. A single example should suffice to give the general idea. Consider the following expression (repeated from the body of the chapter):

```
S WHERE COUNT ( ‼SP ) < 3
```

This expression is clearly equivalent to the following:

```
( ( EXTEND S : { X := COUNT ( ‼SP ) } ) WHERE X < 3 ) { ALL BUT X }
```

Chapter 6

Constraints and Predicates

With integrity and consistency—your credits are piling up.
—message in a Chinese fortune cookie (November 15th, 2004)

Constraints and predicates are distinct but related concepts in the database world. They're also both extremely important! Constraints have to do with making sure the data in the database is correct, and predicates have to do with what that data means. Let's take a closer look.

DATABASE CONSTRAINTS

I first mentioned database constraints in Chapter 3, though in that chapter I called them integrity constraints. A database constraint, or just a *constraint* for short, is, loosely, a boolean expression that must evaluate to TRUE (because if it evaluates to FALSE, there must be something wrong with the database). Thus, any attempt to update the database in such a way as to cause some constraint to evaluate to FALSE must fail—and, in the relational model, fail *immediately*, meaning the exception must be raised as soon as the update is attempted.[1] *Note:* This requirement (that constraint violations be detected immediately) is sometimes referred to as **The Golden Rule**. Observe that it's an immediate consequence of this rule that no user ever sees the database in an inconsistent state—where an inconsistent state is, by definition, a state of the database that violates at least one known constraint. Observe further that an inconsistent state is certainly an *incorrect* state, in the sense that it can't possibly correspond to a true state of affairs in the real world. I'll return to this point near the end of the chapter.

Now, I discussed key and foreign key constraints in Chapter 3. Such constraints are extremely important, but they're also rather simple. Constraints of arbitrary complexity are possible, however, and do indeed occur in practice (sometimes they're called *business rules*). I'll give a few examples of such constraints, expressed in natural language first; then I'll show how those examples can be formulated in **Tutorial D**. *Note:* The list that follows is similar but not identical to the one I gave in Chapter 3.

---

[1] This requirement is surely obvious. I mention it here only because (as we'll see in Part III of this book) commercial DBMSs, perhaps a little surprisingly, don't always conform to it—i.e., sometimes they actually allow an update to produce a state of the database that they *know* is incorrect. What's more, they even allow users to see such an incorrect state!

1. Supplier status values must be in the range 1 to 100 inclusive.

2. Suppliers in London must have status 20.

3. Supplier numbers must be unique.

4. Suppliers with status less than 20 mustn't supply part P6.

5. Every supplier number in SP must also appear in S.

Now let's consider some possible **Tutorial D** formulations for these constraints (or business rules). Here again is the first one:

1. Supplier status values must be in the range 1 to 100 inclusive.

```
CONSTRAINT CX1 IS_EMPTY ( S WHERE STATUS < 1 OR STATUS > 100 ) ;
```

Constraints in general are expressed in **Tutorial D** by means of a CONSTRAINT statement. As the example indicates, such a statement consists of (a) the keyword CONSTRAINT, followed by (b) a constraint name (for use in error messages and the like that refer to the constraint in question), followed by (c) the boolean expression that must evaluate to TRUE. In the example, that boolean expression says, in effect, that if we restrict the suppliers relation—i.e., the relation that's the value of relvar S at the time the constraint is checked—to just those tuples where the status value is either less than zero or greater than 100, then the result of that restriction must be empty.

By the way, what happens if relvar S happens to be empty when the constraint is checked? (*Answer:* The constraint is satisfied trivially.)

Actually there's another way to formulate the foregoing constraint, a way that's arguably a little more satisfactory from an intuitive point of view (a little more user friendly, perhaps). Here it is:

```
CONSTRAINT CX1 AND ( S , STATUS ≥ 1 AND STATUS ≤ 100 ) ;
```

Explanation:

■ AND here is an aggregate operator (I mentioned that operator in Chapter 5 but gave no examples there). It works on aggregates of boolean values. In the example, the aggregate contains one boolean value for each tuple in the suppliers relation, that value being computed by evaluating the boolean expression STATUS ≥ 1 AND STATUS ≤ 100 against the tuple in question.

■ The suppliers relation contains tuples for suppliers S1, S2, S3, S4, and S5; the corresponding status values are 20, 10, 30, 20, and 30, respectively; thus, the corresponding boolean values are TRUE, TRUE, TRUE, TRUE, and TRUE, respectively.

■ Now, AND returns TRUE if and only if all of the values in the pertinent aggregate are TRUE, which can be the case in the example only if every supplier has a status value in the desired range (as indeed they all do, of course).

So this alternative formulation does indeed do the job.[2] And the reason I say it might be a little more user friendly than the previous version is that it lets us state the requirement in a positive fashion—i.e., it lets us say directly what we mean: namely, that status values must lie in a certain range. By contrast, the previous version effectively meant we had to state the requirement in a negative fashion, by saying, in effect, that those status values mustn't lie outside that certain range.

2. Suppliers in London must have status 20.

```
CONSTRAINT CX2 IS_EMPTY ( S WHERE CITY = 'London' AND STATUS ≠ 20 ) ;
```

Alternative formulation:

```
CONSTRAINT CX2 AND ( S , CITY ≠ 'London' OR STATUS = 20 ) ;
```

In this case there seems little to choose between the two formulations.

3. Supplier numbers must be unique.

```
CONSTRAINT CX3 COUNT ( S ) = COUNT ( S { SNO } ) ;
```

It might not be immediately obvious that this formulation achieves what we want, but in fact it does. Let the current value of relvar S be *s* (a relation, of course). Then (a) the expression COUNT (S) denotes the cardinality of *s*; (b) the expression COUNT (S{SNO}) denotes the cardinality of the projection of *s* on SNO; and (c) the constraint overall requires those two cardinalities to be equal. (If it's still not obvious that requiring these two counts to be equal is equivalent to requiring supplier numbers to be unique, try interpreting the constraint in terms of our usual sample value for relvar S.)

In practice, of course, we would almost certainly specify the desired constraint in this example—viz., that supplier numbers must be unique—not by means of a separate, explicit CONSTRAINT statement as shown, but rather by means of an appropriate KEY specification on

---

[2] But, again, what happens if relvar S happens to be empty when the constraint is checked?

the definition of the pertinent relvar (viz., relvar S, in the example). But it's interesting to note that such a specification is really nothing more than shorthand for something that can be expressed, albeit more longwindedly, using that explicit CONSTRAINT syntax.

4. Suppliers with status less than 20 mustn't supply part P6.

```
CONSTRAINT CX4
     IS_EMPTY ( ( S JOIN SP ) WHERE STATUS < 20 AND PNO = 'P6' ) ;
```

Observe that this constraint involves (better: *interrelates*) two distinct relvars, S and SP. In general, a constraint might involve, or interrelate, any number of distinct relvars. *Terminology:* A constraint that involves just a single relvar is known, informally, as a relvar constraint (sometimes a single-relvar constraint, for emphasis); a constraint that involves two or more distinct relvars is known, informally, as a multirelvar constraint. (Thus, constraints CX1–CX3 were all single-relvar constraints, while constraint CX4 is a multirelvar constraint.)

5. Every supplier number in SP must also appear in S.

```
CONSTRAINT CX5 SP { SNO } ⊆ S { SNO } ;
```

This example also involves a multirelvar constraint. More to the point, of course, we would almost certainly specify the constraint in question not by means of a separate, explicit CONSTRAINT statement as shown, but rather by means of an appropriate FOREIGN KEY specification on the definition of the pertinent relvar (viz., relvar SP, in the example). But as with Example 3 above, it's interesting to note that such a specification is really nothing more than shorthand for something that can be expressed, albeit more longwindedly, using that explicit CONSTRAINT syntax.

This brings me to the end of my list of sample constraints. Now, there's a great deal more that could be said about the topic of constraints in general; however, it wouldn't be in keeping with the introductory nature of this book to go into any more detail here, and so I won't. A much more comprehensive discussion of the topic can be found if you're interested in *SQL and Relational Theory*. Also, a detailed examination of certain specific kinds of constraints, usually known as *dependencies*—especially the so called *functional* and *join* dependencies—can be found in another book of mine, *Database Design and Relational Theory: Normal Forms and All That Jazz* (O'Reilly, 2012).[3]

A remark on multiple assignment: Actually there's one further point that I should at least mention here, though again it's not appropriate to get into too much detail on it in a book of this nature. Suppose the suppliers-and-parts database is subject to a constraint to the

---

[3] Functional dependencies, though not join dependencies, are also briefly discussed in Chapter 9 of the present book.

effect that supplier S1 and part P1 must never be in different cities (see Exercise 6.3e at the end of the chapter). Then if supplier S1 and part P1 are currently both in London, both of the following UPDATEs will fail:

```
UPDATE S WHERE SNO = 'S1' : { CITY = 'Paris' } ;

UPDATE P WHERE PNO = 'P1' : { CITY = 'Paris' } ;
```

In order to move both S1 and P1 to Paris, therefore, we need to be able to update relvars S and P "simultaneously," as it were (i.e., as a single combined operation). To that end, **Tutorial D** provides a *multiple* form of assignment, which allows any number of distinct variables all to be updated as part of the same statement, as here:

```
UPDATE S WHERE SNO = 'S1' : { CITY := 'Paris' } ,
UPDATE P WHERE PNO = 'P1' : { CITY := 'Paris' } ;
```

(Note the comma separator, which means the two UPDATEs are part of the same overall statement.) Of course, UPDATE is really assignment, so the foregoing "double UPDATE" is really shorthand for a double assignment that looks like this:

```
S := ... , P := ... ;
```

This double assignment assigns one value to relvar S and another to relvar P, both as part of the same overall operation, and no integrity checking is performed until the end of the statement (i.e., until the semicolon is reached, as it were).

Observe now that the constraint we're talking about here—"Supplier S1 and part P1 must never be in different cities"—is in fact a multirelvar constraint. And as I'm sure you can see, remarks similar to those above apply to many such constraints, if not all. For example, they certainly apply to constraint CX4, q.v. For further discussion of this issue, please refer to *SQL and Relational Theory. End of remark.*

RELVAR PREDICATES

Now I want to shift gears, so to speak, and turn to the other big topic of this chapter, viz., predicates. The essence of that topic is this: There's another way to think about relvars. I mean, most people think of relvars as if they were just files in the traditional computing sense—rather abstract files, perhaps (*disciplined* might be a better word than abstract), but files nonetheless. But there's a different way to look at them, a way that can lead to a much deeper understanding of what's really going on. It goes like this.

Consider the suppliers relvar S. Like all relvars, that relvar is supposed to represent some portion of the real world. In fact, I can be more precise: The heading of that relvar represents a certain *predicate*, meaning it's a kind of generic statement about some portion of the real world (it's generic because it's *parameterized*, as I'll explain in a moment). The predicate in question looks like this:

> *Supplier SNO is under contract, is named SNAME, has status STATUS, and is located in city CITY.*

This predicate is the *intended interpretation*—in other words, the meaning, also called the *intension* (note the spelling)—for relvar S.

In general, you can think of a predicate as *a truth valued function*. Like all functions, it has a set of parameters; it returns a result when it's invoked; and (because it's truth valued) that result is either TRUE or FALSE. In the case of the predicate just shown, for example, the parameters are SNO, SNAME, STATUS, and CITY (corresponding of course to the attributes of the relvar), and they stand for values of the applicable types (CHAR, CHAR, INTEGER, and CHAR, respectively). When we invoke the function—when we *instantiate the predicate,* as the logicians say—we substitute arguments for the parameters. Suppose we substitute the arguments S1, Smith, 20, and London, respectively. Then we obtain the following statement:

> *Supplier S1 is under contract, is named Smith, has status 20, and is located in city London.*

This statement is in fact a *proposition,* which in logic is something that's unequivocally either true or false. Here are a couple of examples:

1.   Barbara Kingsolver wrote *The Poisonwood Bible.*

2.   Jane Austen wrote *The Poisonwood Bible.*

The first of these is true and the second false. Don't fall into the common trap of thinking that propositions must always be true! However, the ones I'm talking about at the moment *are* supposed to be true ones specifically, as I now explain:

■ First of all, it should be obvious that *every* relvar has an associated predicate, called the *relvar predicate* for the relvar in question. (The predicate shown earlier in this section is thus the relvar predicate for relvar S.)

■ Let relvar *R* have predicate *P*. Then every tuple *t* appearing in *R* at some given time can be regarded as representing a certain proposition *p*, derived by invoking (or *instantiating*) *P* at that time with the attribute values from *t* as arguments.

- And (*very important!*) we assume by convention that each such proposition *p* that's obtained in this manner evaluates to TRUE.

Given our usual sample value for relvar S, for example, we assume the following propositions all evaluate to TRUE at this time:

Supplier S1 is under contract, is named Smith, has status 20, and is located in city London.

Supplier S2 is under contract, is named Jones, has status 10, and is located in city Paris.

Supplier S3 is under contract, is named Blake, has status 30, and is located in city Paris.

And so on. What's more, we go further: If at some given time *t* a certain tuple plausibly could appear in a certain relvar but doesn't, then we assume the corresponding proposition is false at that time *t*. For example, the tuple

```
TUPLE { SNO 'S6' , SNAME 'Lopez' , STATUS 30 , CITY 'Madrid' }
```

is certainly a plausible supplier tuple—but it doesn't appear in relvar S at this time, and so we're entitled to assume *it's not the case that* the following proposition is true at this time:

Supplier S6 is under contract, is named Lopez, has status 30, and is located in city Madrid.

To sum up: A given relvar *R* contains, at any given time, *all* and *only* the tuples that represent true propositions (true instantiations of the relvar predicate for *R*) at the time in question—or, at least, that's what we always assume in practice. In other words, in practice we adopt what's called *The Closed World Assumption*. Here's a definition:

Definition: Let relvar *R* have predicate *P*. Then ***The Closed World Assumption*** (CWA) says (a) if tuple *t* appears in *R* at time *T*, then the instantiation *p* of *P* corresponding to *t* is assumed to be true at time *T*; conversely, (b) if tuple *t* has the same heading as *R* but doesn't appear in *R* at time *T*, then the instantiation *p* of *P* corresponding to *t* is assumed to be false at time *T*. In other words, tuple *t* appears in relvar *R* at a given time if and only if it satisfies the predicate for *R* at that time.

More terminology: Again, let *P* be the relvar predicate, or intension, for relvar *R*, and let the value of *R* at some given time be relation *r*. Then *r*—or the body of *r*, to be more precise—constitutes the *extension* of *P* at that time.[4] Note, therefore, that the extension for a given relvar varies over time, but the intension does not.

---

[4] Nothing to do with the EXTEND operator of relational algebra discussed in Chapter 5.

Relations vs. Types

So a database at any given time can be thought of as a collection of true propositions—for example, the proposition *Supplier S1 is under contract, is named Smith, has status 20, and is located in city London*—such that the arguments appearing in such a proposition (i.e., S1, Smith, 20, and London, in the example) are, precisely, the attribute values from the corresponding tuple, where each such attribute value is a value of the associated type. It follows that:

Types are sets of things we can talk about;
relations are (true) statements we make about those things.

In other words, types give us our vocabulary (i.e., the things we can talk about), and relations give us the ability to say things about the things we can talk about. For example, suppose we limit our attention to suppliers only, for simplicity. Then:

- The things we can talk about are character strings and integers, and nothing else. (In a real database, of course, our vocabulary will usually be much more extensive than this, especially if any user defined types are involved.)

- The things we can say are things of the form "The supplier with the supplier number denoted by the specified character string is under contract; has the name denoted by another specified character string; has the status denoted by the specified integer; and is located in the city denoted by yet another specified character string"—and nothing else.

The foregoing state of affairs has at least three important corollaries. To be specific, in order to "represent some portion of the real world" (as I put it earlier):

1. *Types and relations are both necessary:* Without types, we would have nothing to talk about; without relations, we wouldn't be able to say anything.

2. *Types and relations are sufficient, as well as necessary:* We don't need anything else, logically speaking.[5] (Well, we do need relvars, in order to reflect the fact that the real world changes over time, but we don't need them to represent the situation at any *given* time.)

3. *Types and relations aren't the same thing.* Beware of anyone who tries to pretend they are! In fact, pretending that a type is just a special kind of relation is precisely what certain

---

[5] When I say types and relations are necessary and sufficient, I am of course talking only about what I called in Chapter 1 the logical database. Obviously other constructs (pointers, for example) are needed for the physical database—but that's because the design goals are different at that level. The physical database is beyond the purview of the relational model, deliberately.

nonrelational products do try to do (though it goes without saying that they don't usually talk in such terms)—and I hope it's clear that any product that's founded on such a logical error is doomed to eventual failure.

Here's a slightly more formal perspective on what I've been saying. As we've seen, a database can be thought of as a collection of true propositions. In fact, a database, together with the operators that apply to the propositions represented in that database (or to sets of such propositions, rather), is *a logical system.* And by "logical system" here, I mean a formal system—like euclidean geometry, for example—that has *axioms* ("given truths") and *rules of inference* by which we can prove *theorems* ("derived truths") from those axioms. Indeed, it was Codd's very great insight, when he invented the relational model back in 1969, that a database (despite the name) isn't really just a collection of data; rather, it's a collection of *facts,* or in other words true propositions. Those propositions—the given ones, that is to say, which are the ones represented by the tuples in the base relvars[6]—are the axioms of the logical system under discussion. And the inference rules are essentially the rules by which new propositions can be derived from the given ones; in other words, they're the rules that tell us how to apply the operators of the relational algebra. Thus, when the system evaluates some relational expression (in particular, when it responds to some query), it's really deriving new truths from given ones; in effect, it's proving theorems!

Once you understand the foregoing, you can see that the whole apparatus of formal logic becomes available for use in attacking "the database problem." In other words, questions such as

- What should the database look like to the user?

- What should integrity constraints look like?

- What should the query language look like?

- How can we best implement queries?

- More generally, how can we best evaluate database expressions?

- How should results be presented to the user?

- How should we design the database in the first place?

(and others like them) all become, in effect, questions in logic that are susceptible to logical treatment and can be given logical answers.

---

[6] Recall from Chapter 3 that a base relvar is a relvar that "stands alone" and isn't defined in terms of any other relvars. Relvars S, P, and SP in the running example are all base relvars.

Now, it goes without saying that the relational model supports the foregoing perception very directly—which is why, in my opinion, that model is rock solid, and "right," and will endure. It's also why, again in my opinion, other so called "models of data" are simply not in the same ballpark. Indeed, I seriously question whether those other models deserve to be called data models, as such, at all—at least not in the sense that the relational model does deserve to be so called. Certainly most of them are ad hoc to a degree, instead of being firmly founded, as the relational model is, on *set theory* and *predicate logic.*[7]

PREDICATES vs. CONSTRAINTS

So how are these two concepts, predicates and constraints, related to each other? Well, consider once again the predicate for relvar S:

> *Supplier SNO is under contract, is named SNAME, has status STATUS, and is located in city CITY.*

Now, this predicate is the intended interpretation (loosely, the meaning) for relvar S. In an ideal world, then, it would serve as *the criterion for acceptability of updates* on relvar S—that is, it would dictate whether or not any given update operation on that relvar can be accepted. But of course this goal is unachievable:

- For one thing, the system can't know what it means for a "supplier" to be "under contract" or to be "located" somewhere; to repeat, these are matters of interpretation. For example, if the supplier number S1 and the city name London happen to appear together in the same tuple, then the user can interpret that fact to mean that supplier S1 is located in London—or that supplier S1 *used to be* located in London, or that supplier S1 *has an office* in London, or that supplier S1 *maintains a warehouse* in London, or any of an infinite number of other possible interpretations (corresponding, of course, to an infinite number of possible relvar predicates)—but there's no way the system can do anything analogous.

- For another, even if the system could know what it means for a supplier to be under contract or to be located somewhere, it still couldn't know a priori whether what the user tells it is true! If the user asserts to the system, by means of some update operation, that there's a supplier S6 named Lopez with status 30 and city Madrid, then there's no way for the system to know whether that assertion is true. All the system can do is check that the user's assertion doesn't cause any integrity constraints to be violated. Assuming it doesn't, the system will accept the user's assertion *and will treat it as true from that point forward*

---

[7] This is the first time I've mentioned set theory and predicate logic in this book, though the relevance of set theory, at least, is surely obvious (see Appendix C for further discussion). As for predicate logic, see Appendix D.

(until such time as the user tells the system, by executing another update, that it isn't true any longer).

Thus, the pragmatic criterion for acceptability of updates, as opposed to the ideal one, is not the predicate but the corresponding set of constraints, which might thus be regarded as the system's approximation to the corresponding predicate. Equivalently:

The system can't enforce truth, only consistency.

Sadly, truth and consistency aren't the same thing. To be specific, if the database contains only true propositions, then it's consistent, but the converse isn't necessarily so; similarly, if it's inconsistent, then it contains at least one false proposition, but the converse isn't necessarily so. Or to put it another way, *correct* implies *consistent* (but not the other way around), and *inconsistent* implies *incorrect* (but not the other way around)—where:

■ To say the database is correct is to say it faithfully reflects the true state of affairs in the real world.

■ By contrast, to say the database is consistent is merely to say it doesn't violate any known integrity constraints.

EXERCISES

6.1   Give (plausible) predicates for relvars P and SP.

6.2   Consider constraints CX1–CX5 from the body of the chapter (restated here in natural language form):

CX1:   Supplier status values must be in the range 1 to 100 inclusive.

CX2:   Suppliers in London must have status 20.

CX3:   Supplier numbers must be unique.

CX4:   Suppliers with status less than 20 mustn't supply part P6.

CX5:   Every supplier number in SP must also appear in S.

Which operations have the potential to violate these constraints? *Note:* You don't need to give your answer in very precise form—e.g., "INSERT on S" is sufficient as the answer, or part of the answer, in the case of constraint CX1.

6.3 Write CONTRAINT statements for the suppliers-and-parts database for the following "business rules":

a. All red parts must weigh less than 50 pounds.

b. No two suppliers can be located in the same city.

c. At most one supplier can be located in Athens at any one time.

d. There must be at least one London supplier.

e. Supplier S1 and part P1 must never be in different cities.

6.4 Consider the projection of the current value of relvar S on all attributes but CITY. That projection contains all tuples of the form (*sno,sn,st*) such that a tuple of the form (*sno,sn,st,sc*) currently appears in relvar S for some CITY value *sc* (I'm using a highly simplified and, I hope, self-explanatory notation for tuples here). In other words, we can say the projection in question has a corresponding predicate that looks like this:

> *Supplier SNO is under contract, is named SNAME, has status STATUS, and is located somewhere*—i.e., in some city, but we don't know which.

Note that this predicate has just three parameters, corresponding of course to the three attributes of the projection.
    Analogous remarks apply to all possible relational expressions. In other words, it isn't just relvars as such that have predicates; rather, *every relational expression* has a predicate.[8] What's more, the predicate for a given relational expression can always be determined from the predicates for the relvars involved in that expression, together with the semantics of the relational operators involved in that expression. As an exercise, then, try giving predicates for the following expressions:

a. `( S JOIN P ) { PNO , SNO }`

b. `P MATCHING S`

---

[8] Indeed, users, possibly without realizing as much, rely on this fact whenever they write a formal query (in **Tutorial D** or some other relational language) and whenever they interpret the result of such a query.

c.　`S NOT MATCHING ( SP WHERE PNO = 'P2' )`

d.　`EXTEND P : { SCT := COUNT ( !!SP ) }`

e.　`P WHERE SUM ( !!SP , QTY ) < 500`

6.5　Near the beginning of this chapter, I claimed (in footnote 1) that **The Golden Rule** is "surely obvious." But *is* it obvious? What do you thing might go wrong if it's violated?

ANSWERS

6.1　Relvar P: *Part PNO is named PNAME, has color COLOR and weight WEIGHT, and is stored in city CITY.*[9] Relvar SP: *Supplier SNO supplies part PNO in quantity QTY.*

6.2　CX1:　INSERT on S, UPDATE on STATUS in S (or equivalent assignments)

　　　CX2:　INSERT on S, UPDATE on STATUS or CITY in S (or equivalent assignments)

　　　CX3:　INSERT on S, UPDATE on SNO in S (or equivalent assignments)

　　　CX4:　INSERT on SP, UPDATE on SNO or PNO in SP, INSERT on S, UPDATE on STATUS in S (or equivalent assignments)

　　　CX5:　INSERT on SP, UPDATE on SNO in SP, DELETE on S, UPDATE on SNO in S (or equivalent assignments)

6.3　a.　`CONSTRAINT CXA AND ( P , COLOR = 'Red' AND WEIGHT < 50.0 ) ;`

　　　b.　`CONSTRAINT CXB COUNT ( S { SNO } ) = COUNT ( S { CITY } ) ;`

　　　c.　`CONSTRAINT CXC COUNT ( S WHERE CITY = 'Athens' ) < 2 ;`

　　　d.　`CONSTRAINT CXD IS_NOT_EMPTY ( S WHERE CITY = 'London' ) ;`

---

[9] Perhaps a little more accurately, *Part PNO **is used in the enterprise**—whatever that enterprise might be—and is named PNAME* (and so on).

```
e. CONSTRAINT CXE COUNT ( ( S WHERE SNO = 'S1' ) { CITY }
                         UNION
                         ( P WHERE PNO = 'P1' ) { CITY } ) < 2 ;
```

6.4   a. *Supplier SNO and part PNO are in the same city.* b. *Part PNO is named PNAME, has color COLOR and weight WEIGHT, is stored in city CITY, and is supplied by at least one supplier.* c. *Supplier SNO is under contract, is named SNAME, has status STATUS, is located in city CITY, and does not supply part P2.* d. *Part PNO is named PNAME, has color COLOR and weight WEIGHT, is stored in city CITY, and is supplied by SCT suppliers.* e. *Part PNO is named PNAME, has color COLOR and weight WEIGHT, is stored in city CITY, and is supplied in a total quantity less than 500. Note:* This exercise is really nothing but a slightly more formal counterpart to certain of the exercises from earlier chapters (e.g., Exercise 4.6 in Chapter 4).

6.5   The truth is, we can never trust the answers we get from an inconsistent database. Here's a proof of this fact (the discussion that follows is based on one in *SQL and Relational Theory*). As we know, a database can be thought of as a collection of propositions. Suppose that collection is inconsistent; that is, suppose it states, explicitly or implicitly, that some proposition *p* and its negation NOT *p* are both true. Now let *q* be any arbitrary proposition. Then:

■   From the truth of *p,* we can infer the truth of *p* OR *q.*

■   From the truth of *p* OR *q* and the truth of NOT *p,* we can infer the truth of *q.*

But *q* was arbitrary! It follows that any proposition whatsoever (even ones that are obviously false, like 1 = 0) can be shown to be "true" in an inconsistent system.

Chapter 7

The Relational Model

The Relational Model: Information in Formation!
—Anon.: *Where Bugs Go*

This is the final chapter in this first part of the book. In previous chapters, I've described the most important features—at least, the features that are most important from a relational point of view—of a relational DBMS. Now it's time to review those features and bring them all together, so to speak, by defining the relational model as such and attempting to explain what that definition means. One small point for the record: The term *relational model* itself is taken from the title of Codd's famous paper "A Relational Model of Data for Large Shared Data Banks" (*CACM 13*, No. 6, June 1970), which I'll have a little more to say about in Appendix A.

THE RELATIONAL MODEL DEFINED

I don't know whether you noticed, but I deliberately gave no definition prior to this point of what exactly the relational model is[1]—even though I tacitly appealed to such a definition on numerous occasions, saying things like:

- The relational model has no tuple level operators

- The relational model prohibits pointers

- The relational model requires immediate integrity checking

and many other things of a similar nature. The closest I came to an actual definition was probably in Chapter 1, when I described the relational model as "a recipe for what the user interface is supposed to look like"—which is true, but is hardly much use as a precise definition. Now, I could alternatively have said the relational model is *an abstract externals specification for a DBMS*—but that's really just restating the "recipe" definition in slightly more high-flown language. Observe in particular that neither of these definitions (or would-be definitions) is anything like precise enough for us to say whether a given DBMS is relational or not.

---

[1] Interestingly, Codd's 1970 paper, despite its title, didn't actually give a definition either.

Actually, I regard it as a strength of the model that it can be explained—defined, even—very simply and briefly indeed at an intuitive level. In support of this contention, consider the following, which is a lightly edited version of the text I wrote for the web page describing Codd's background and his contribution and justifying his receipt of the 1981 ACM Turing Award (*http://amturing.acm.org/award_winners/codd_1000892.cfm*):

The Relational Model of Data

The relational model of data is, in essence, a formal and rigorous definition of what the data in a database should look like to the user; i.e., it's a somewhat abstract specification of the user interface to a database system. In other words, a database system is relational if and only if the user interface it supports is a faithful implementation of the relational model—meaning that, as far as the user of such a system is concerned, (a) the data looks relational, and (b) relational operators such as *join* are available for operating on data in that relational form.

Data Looks Relational

Relations can be depicted on paper as simple tables of rows and columns. Loosely, therefore, we can say the user sees the data in the form of such tables.

Relational Operators Are Available

Relational operators are operators that derive further relations from given relations. Since relations can loosely be thought of as tables, we can think of those operators (also loosely) as "cut and paste" operators for tables. For example, given a table of employee information, the *restrict* operator will let us "cut out" just the rows for employees with a certain salary. And if we're also given a table of department information, the *join* operator will then let us "paste on" to those employee rows department information for the employees in question.

Implementation

Since the user interface in a relational system is so radically different from (and of course so much simpler than) the way data is physically stored and manipulated inside the system, there are some significant implementation challenges to be faced. Researchers began to investigate this problem early in the 1970s, soon after the publication of Codd's original papers, and numerous prototypes were built throughout the 1970s. The first commercial products began to appear toward the end of that decade. And while it's unfortunately still true, even today, that none of those products is entirely faithful to Codd's original vision, they quickly came to dominate the marketplace. The relational model—thanks to its solid foundation in set theory and formal logic—is here to stay. It will stand the test of time.

But although it can be "defined" so simply, the model also has great depths. After all, I've just taken a hundred pages or so to describe some of those depths, and my treatment has certainly not been exhaustive. The truth is, even after all these years—I first heard about the relational model myself back in 1970, when I read that 1970 paper of Codd's—I'm still discovering new ramifications and new implications of the model myself. In a word, I'm still learning.

In this chapter, therefore, I'd like to give what I regard as a much more precise definition of the relational model. The trouble is, the definition I'll give is indeed precise: so much so, in fact, that I think it would have been quite hard to understand if I'd given it in Chapter 1. (Of course, that's why I didn't do anything of the kind. As Bertrand Russell once memorably said: *Writing can be either readable or precise, but not at the same time.*) So the definition I'm going to give will be followed, of necessity, by several pages of further explanation.

Without further ado, then, here's my proposed definition:

Definition: The **relational model** consists of five components:[2]

1.   An open ended collection of **types**, including type BOOLEAN in particular

2.   A **relation type generator** and an intended interpretation for relations of types generated thereby

3.   Facilities for defining **relation variables** of such generated relation types

4.   A **relational assignment** operator for assigning relation values to such relation variables

5.   A relationally complete, but otherwise open ended, collection of **generic relational operators** for deriving relation values from other relation values

The following sections elaborate on each of these components in turn. First, however, a word of caution. As John Muir once said, whenever we try to pick out anything by itself, we find it hitched to everything else in the universe (often quoted in the form "Everything is connected to everything else"). John Muir was talking about the natural world, of course, but he might just as well have been talking about the relational model. The fact is, the various features of the relational model are highly interconnected—remove just one of them, and the whole edifice crumbles. Translated into concrete terms, this metaphor means that if we build a "relational" DBMS that fails to support some aspect of the model, the resulting system (which shouldn't really be called relational, anyway) will be bound to display behavior on occasion that's certainly undesirable, and possibly unforeseeable. I can't stress the point too strongly: Every feature of the model is there *for solid practical reasons*; if we choose to ignore any of those features, then we do so at our own peril.

---

[2] By the way, do please note that definite article—*the* relational model. Yes, there's just one! Critics sometimes suggest that relational advocates (among whom I most certainly count myself) keep changing the definition and "moving the goalposts," as it were. I responded to this criticism in detail in the paper "There's Only One Relational Model" in my book *Date on Database: Writings 2000–2006* (Apress, 2006).

TYPES

To repeat, the first of the five components (in my definition of the model) is *an open ended collection of types, including type BOOLEAN in particular*. Note that the relational model certainly does need types, if only because relations are defined over them—that is, every attribute of every relation, and hence of every relvar, is of some type, by definition.

Incidentally, please note that the relational model doesn't say what types have to exist (with the sole exception already noted of type BOOLEAN). It's an unfortunate but common misconception that the relational model can handle only a few rather simple types: numbers, strings, perhaps dates and times, and not much else. But in fact relations, and relvars, can have attributes *of any type whatsoever* (other than as noted below). To put it another way, the question as to what types are supported is orthogonal to the question of support for the relational model as such.

Now, when I say *types* here, what I mean—primarily, although (please note) *not* exclusively—are what are often referred to more specifically as *scalar* types. (Indeed, in other writings I've often used the term *scalar types* in this context instead of just *types*, unqualified.) So what does it mean for a type to be scalar? Loosely, a type is said to be scalar if it has no user visible components; otherwise it's said to be nonscalar. And values, variables, attributes, operators, parameters, and expressions of some type *T* are said to be scalar or nonscalar according as type *T* itself is scalar or nonscalar. For example:

- Type INTEGER is scalar (it has no user visible components); hence, values, variables, and so on of type INTEGER are all scalar as well.

- Relation types are nonscalar (the pertinent user visible components being the corresponding attributes, of course) and hence relation values, relation variables, and so on are all nonscalar as well. *Note:* Tuple types, values, variables, etc. are nonscalar too (recall from the answer to Exercise 2.7 in Chapter 2 that tuples, like relations, certainly do have a type).

That said, I must now emphasize that the foregoing notions, while they can be helpful from an intuitive point of view, are actually quite informal, and indeed quite imprecise. Part of the reason for this state of affairs is that there are some types where it really isn't clear whether they're scalar or nonscalar. (For example, is a character string scalar, or do the individual characters in the string constitute "user visible components"?) For such reasons, the relational model nowhere relies in any formal way on the distinction between scalar and nonscalar types.[3] For present purposes, in fact, you can take the term *scalar* to refer (a trifle loosely) to any type that's neither a tuple nor a relation type, and the term *nonscalar* to refer (again a trifle loosely) to any type that *is* either a tuple or a relation type. And for the remainder of the present section,

---

[3] That's why I never mentioned that distinction in earlier chapters. Indeed, I mentioned the term *scalar* itself only very briefly, and in passing, twice—once when I discussed scalar literals in Chapter 3, and again when I referred to scalar operators in Chapter 4 (and even that was only in a footnote). And I never mentioned the term *nonscalar* at all.

you can take the term *type*, unqualified, to mean a scalar type specifically, barring explicit statements to the contrary.

Now, scalar types can be either system or user defined; thus, a means must be available for users to define their own scalar types. A means must therefore be available for users to define their own operators, too (scalar or otherwise), because types without operators are useless. As for system defined types, the set of such types is required to include type BOOLEAN—the most fundamental type of all, containing precisely two values (viz., the truth values TRUE and FALSE)—but a real system will surely support others as well (INTEGER, CHAR, and so on). Support for type BOOLEAN implies support for the usual *connectives* (i.e., the logical operators NOT, AND, OR, etc.) as well as other operators, system or user defined, that return boolean values. In particular, the equality comparison operator "="—which is a boolean operator by definition—must be available in connection with every type, nonscalar as well as scalar, for without it we couldn't even say what the values are that constitute the type in question. What's more, the model prescribes the semantics of that operator, too (see Chapter 1): The comparison $v1 = v2$ gives TRUE if $v1$ and $v2$ are the very same value (implying, incidentally, that they must certainly be of the same type) and FALSE otherwise.

Now, I've already suggested that it's not quite 100 percent true that relations and relvars can have attributes of any type whatsoever. In fact (as we saw in the answer to Exercise 2.7 in Chapter 2), there are essentially two exceptions. First, relvars, and hence relations, in the database aren't allowed to have attributes of any pointer type. Second, if relation r has heading H, then no attribute of r can be defined, directly or indirectly, in terms of a tuple or relation type that has that same heading H.

Finally—I mention this point mainly for completeness, and it's not important to understand it on a first reading—note that associated with every type T, scalar or nonscalar, there must exist at least one *selector* operator. A selector is a read-only operator with the properties that (a) every invocation of that operator returns a value of type T, and (b) every value of type T is returned by some invocation of that operator (more specifically, by some corresponding *literal*—note that a literal is a special case of a selector invocation). In particular, therefore, given some arbitrary type T, it must always be possible to write a literal to denote an arbitrary value of that type T. See *SQL and Relational Theory* for further explanation.

THE RELATION TYPE GENERATOR

The second component of the model is *a relation type generator and an intended interpretation for relations of types generated thereby.* Now, this is the first mention in this book of the term *type generator*, so let me digress for a moment to explain it. Essentially, a type generator is just a special kind of operator; it's special because (a) it returns a type instead of a value, and (b) it's invoked at compile time instead of run time. For example, the code fragment shown in Fig. 1.3 in Chapter 1 contains the following VAR statement:

```
VAR A ARRAY [1..N] OF INTEGER ;
```

This statement defines a variable called A whose permitted values are one-dimensional arrays of elements (referred to as A[1], A[2], ..., A[N]), such that each of those N elements is an integer. Here, then, the expression ARRAY [1..N] OF INTEGER can be regarded as an invocation of the ARRAY type generator, and it returns a specific array type. That specific array type is a *generated* type (a nonscalar generated type, as it happens, though scalar generated types are possible too). Please note, therefore, that there's a logical difference between a type generator and a type as such; more specifically, note that a type generator is *not* a type.

Getting back now to the relational model, the type generator we're mostly interested in here is, of course, the RELATION type generator. That type generator allows users to specify individual relation types as desired. Here are some examples (using **Tutorial D** syntax):

```
RELATION { SNO CHAR , SNAME CHAR , STATUS INTEGER , CITY CHAR }

RELATION { PNO CHAR , PNAME CHAR , COLOR CHAR ,
                                   WEIGHT RATIONAL , CITY CHAR }

RELATION { SNO CHAR , PNO CHAR , QTY INTEGER }
```

These types are, of course, the types of relvars S, P, and SP, respectively, in our running example. In other words, one important use of the RELATION type generator—in fact, easily the most important use in practice—is within some relvar definition (a VAR statement, in **Tutorial D**), to specify the type of the relvar being defined.

> *A remark on relation valued attributes:* This point is mostly beyond the scope of this book, but I just want to mention it in passing. As we know, (a) attributes have types and (b) relation types are types—so it shouldn't come as a surprise to learn that relations can have attributes that are of some relation type (i.e., *relation valued attributes*, which is to say attributes whose values are relations in turn).[4] Thus, another use of the RELATION type generator is in specifying the type of such an attribute, within a heading definition. See *SQL and Relational Theory* for further discussion of this possibility. *End of remark.*

As for that business of intended interpretations, the intended interpretation for a given relation of a given type, in a given context, is as a set of propositions. Each such proposition (a) constitutes an instantiation of some predicate that corresponds to the relation heading, (b) is represented by a tuple in the relation body, and (c) is assumed to be true. If the context in question is some relvar—that is, if we're talking about the relation that happens to be the current value of some relvar—then the predicate in question is the relvar predicate for that relvar.

---

[4] In fact, I touched on this possibility, somewhat obliquely, when I said in the previous section that if relation *r* has heading *H*, then no attribute of *r* can be defined, directly or indirectly, in terms of a (tuple or) relation type that has that same heading *H*.

Moreover, both relvars and relations are interpreted in accordance with *The Closed World Assumption* or CWA (see Chapter 6).[5]

Finally, let *RT* be some relation type. Associated with *RT*, then, there's a selector operator (a *relation* selector specifically, of course), with the properties that (a) every invocation of that operator returns a relation of type *RT*, and (b) every relation of type *RT* is returned by some invocation of that operator (more specifically, by some relation literal—see Chapter 3). Here are a couple of examples:

```
RELATION { TUPLE { SNO 'S1' , PNO 'P1' , QTY 300 } ,
           TUPLE { SNO 'S5' , PNO 'P6' , QTY 350 } }

RELATION { TUPLE { SNO SX , PNO PX , QTY QX } }
```

Each of these expressions evaluates to a relation of type RELATION {SNO CHAR, PNO CHAR, QTY INTEGER}, which could therefore (among other things) be assigned to relvar SP. The first denotes a relation of two tuples and is in fact a relation literal. The second denotes a relation of just one tuple and *isn't* a literal; in fact, a selector invocation (of any kind) is a literal if and only if all of its argument expressions are literals in turn.

Finally, since the equality comparison operator "=" is available in connection with every type, it's available in connection with relation types in particular. So too is the relational inclusion operator "⊆"; if relations *r1* and *r2* are of the same type, then *r1* is included in *r2* if and only if the body of *r1* is a subset of that of *r2*.

RELATION VARIABLES

The third component of the model—*facilities for defining relation variables of such generated relation types*—follows on logically from the previous one. That is, a major use for the RELATION type generator is (as stated in the previous section) in specifying the type of a relation variable, or relvar, when that relvar is defined. And relation variables are the only kind of variable permitted in a relational database; all other kinds, scalar variables or tuple variables or any other kind, are explicitly prohibited. (In programs that access such a database, by contrast, they're not prohibited—in fact, they're probably required.)

The statement that the database contains nothing but relvars is one possible formulation of what Codd originally called *The Information Principle*. However, I don't think it's a formulation he ever used himself. Instead, he usually stated the principle like this:

The entire information content of the database at any given time is represented in one and only one way: namely, as explicit values in attribute positions in tuples in relations.

---

[5] The CWA as defined in Chapter 6 referred to relvars, not relations, but I hope it's obvious that it extends naturally to relations (e.g., query results) as well.

This principle is a major source of the simplicity I claimed in Chapter 1 for relational systems in general. Indeed, I heard Codd refer to it on more than one occasion as *the* fundamental principle underlying the relational model. Any violation of it thus has to be seen as serious.[6] But why is the principle so important? The answer is bound up with the observations I made in Chapter 6 to the effect that (along with types) relations are both necessary and sufficient to represent any data whatsoever at the logical level. In other words, the relational model gives us everything we need in this respect, and it doesn't give us anything we don't need.

I'd like to pursue this issue a moment longer. First of all, it's axiomatic that if we have n different ways of representing data, then we need n different sets of operators (I touched on this point in Chapter 2). For example, if we had arrays as well as relations, we'd need a full complement of array operators as well as a full complement of relational ones. We'd also have to choose which data we wanted to represent as relations and which as arrays, probably without any good guidelines to help us in making such choices. So if n is greater than one, we have more operators to implement, document, teach, learn, remember, and use (and choose among). But those extra operators increase complexity, not power! There's nothing useful that can be done if n is greater than one that can't be done if n equals one (and in the relational model, of course, n does equal one). What's more, not only does the relational model give us just one way to represent data, but that one way is *extremely simple*.

> *A remark on database variables:* As Hugh Darwen and I demonstrate in our book *Databases, Types, and the Relational Model: The Third Manifesto* (3rd edition, Addison-Wesley, 2007), the database isn't really just "a container for relation variables," even though we usually talk about it as if it were. Rather, it's a variable in its own right! After all, it can certainly be updated—and that means it's a variable by definition. Logically speaking, in other words, the database in its entirety is one (typically rather large) variable in itself, which we might call a *dbvar*. To put the matter another way, database relvars are really an illusion (albeit an illusion that's extremely useful in practice and—as Einstein once remarked, albeit in a different context—one that's "stubbornly persistent"); the only true variable is the database itself, in its entirety. This notion is explored in depth in another book of mine, *View Updating and Relational Theory: Solving the View Update Problem* (O'Reilly, 2013).
>
> By the way: I don't know if you've noticed, but I haven't given anything even close to a precise definition of the term *database* in this book prior to this point. What's more, I'm not going to give one now, either (the issue is a little more complicated than it might seem, as the previous paragraph might suggest). For practical purposes, however, it's probably simplest just to say as I did above that—from the point of view of the relational model, at least—a database is just a container for relvars. However, let me remind you

---

[6] It goes without saying that object databases, XML databases, and more generally nonrelational databases of any kind, do all violate it, necessarily. Unfortunately, so too do SQL databases, usually (see Part III of this book), unless an appropriate discipline is followed.

that, given that each relvar has a predicate, and given that each tuple in one of those relvars corresponds to a true instantiation of the corresponding predicate, then (as we saw in Chapter 6) we can usefully think of the database at any given time as representing *a collection of true propositions. End of remark.*

RELATIONAL ASSIGNMENT

The fourth relational model component—*a relational assignment operator for assigning relation values to such relation variables*—follows on from the second and third. The point is simple: The assignment operator ":=", like the equality comparison operator "=", must be available in connection with every type (for without it we would have no way of assigning values to a variable of the type in question), and of course relation types are no exception to this rule. The operators INSERT, DELETE, and UPDATE (also D_INSERT and I_DELETE) are permitted and indeed useful, but strictly speaking they're only shorthands. What's more, support for relational assignment (a) must include support for *multiple* relational assignment in particular (see the remark on this subject at the end of the section "Database Constraints" in Chapter 6) and (b) must abide by both *The Assignment Principle* and **The Golden Rule**, where:

- *The Assignment Principle* (see Chapter 1) states that after assignment of a value *v* to a variable *V*, the comparison *v* = *V* must give TRUE.

- **The Golden Rule** (see Chapter 6) states that all integrity constraints must be satisfied at statement boundaries.

RELATIONAL OPERATORS

The fifth and last component of the model is *a relationally complete, but otherwise open ended, collection of generic relational operators for deriving relation values from other relation values.* That collection of operators is, of course, the relational algebra, or something logically equivalent to the algebra. As explained in Chapter 4, the operators are generic, in the sense that they apply, in effect, to all possible relations (meaning, for example, that we don't need one join operator to join, say, suppliers and shipments and some completely different join operator to join, say, departments and employees). Precisely which operators must be supported isn't specified, but at least they're required to possess in their totality the property of *relational completeness*, which I now explain.

    Relational completeness is a basic measure of the expressive power of a language. What it means, loosely, is this: If a language is relationally complete, then (a) "all possible queries" can be expressed in that language, and (b) what's more, any such query can be formulated as *a single expression* in that language. Thus, queries of arbitrary complexity can be formulated without having to resort to branching or iterative loops.[7] A little more precisely, we can say that if some language *L* is complete in this sense, then expressions in *L* permit the definition of every relation that can be defined by means of expressions of the relational algebra. Language *L* is thus at least as powerful as (better: at least as *expressive* as) the relational algebra. Observe that it's basically relational completeness that allows interactive users—at least in principle, though possibly not in practice—to access the database directly, without having to go through the potential bottleneck of the IT department.

> *A remark on relational calculus:* Actually, in the paper where he first defined the notion of relational completeness—see Appendix E—Codd said a language was relationally complete if and only if it was at least as powerful as the relational *calculus*, not the relational algebra. The relational calculus is an alternative to the relational algebra; it's another formalism, based on predicate logic rather than set theory, that (a) can be used as a basis for formulating queries, constraints, and the like, and (b) is expressively equivalent to the algebra. (By *expressively equivalent* here, I mean that for every expression of the algebra there's a logically equivalent expression of the calculus, and for every expression of the calculus there's a logically equivalent expression of the algebra.)
>
> I don't want to get into details of the relational calculus here. Suffice it to say that the choice between algebra and calculus is in some respects just a matter of taste; some people prefer the algebra, some the calculus. (It's also true that some problems can be more easily formulated in the algebra and some in the calculus; it's not as if either is clearly superior to the other. To repeat, they're equivalent.) If you're interested and want to know more, further details can be found in Appendix D. *End of remark.*

Now, there seems to be a widespread misconception concerning the purpose of the algebra. To be specific, many people seem to think it's meant just for formulating queries—but it's not; rather, it's for formulating *relational expressions*. Those expressions in turn serve many purposes, including queries but certainly not limited to queries alone. Here are some other important ones:

- Defining a set of tuples to be inserted into, deleted from, or updated in, some relvar (or, more generally, defining the set of tuples to be assigned to some relvar)

- Defining integrity constraints (though here the relational expression in question will be just a subexpression of some boolean expression, typically though not invariably an IS_EMPTY invocation, in **Tutorial D**)

- Defining security constraints (see below for further discussion)

---

[7] Note that none of the examples in previous chapters did involve any such branching or iterative loops.

■ Defining views (again, see below for further discussion)

■ Serving as a basis for further theoretical investigations into such areas as optimization and database design[8]

And so on (this isn't an exhaustive list).

Security

As we saw in Chapter 1, security constraints (or security controls, as I called them in that chapter) have to do with ensuring that user requests are legitimate. In other words, user requests must be constrained to (a) just those operations the user in question is allowed to carry out on (b) just those portions of the database he or she is allowed to access. Clearly, therefore, we need a language in which to define security constraints. Now, it tends to be easier in practice to state what's allowed rather than what's not allowed; security languages therefore typically support the definition, not of security constraints as such, but rather of *authorities*, which are effectively the opposite of security constraints (if something is authorized, it's not constrained). I'll content myself here with just giving a couple of more or less self-explanatory examples:[9]

```
AUTHORITY SX1
    GRANT RETRIEVE { SNO , SNAME } , DELETE
    ON    S
    WHERE CITY = 'London'
    TO    Jim , Fred , Mary ;

AUTHORITY SX2
    GRANT RETRIEVE , UPDATE { STATUS , CITY }
    ON    S
    TO    Dan , Misha ;
```

An extensive discussion of security matters in general—i.e., not just authorities as such—can be found in my book *An Introduction to Database Systems* (8th edition, Addison-Wesley, 2004).

Views

Consider the following query ("Get suppliers in London"):

---

[8] I note in passing that optimization and database design both now have a rich literature of their own. But in both cases the huge amount of effort that has gone into investigating them would simply not have been possible, absent the solid and rigorous logical framework provided by the relational model. (Further discussion of database design in particular can be found in Chapter 9.)

[9] **Tutorial D** currently includes no security features, but these examples can be regarded as being in the spirit of that language. SQL does include such features, but the specifics are beyond the scope of this book.

```
S WHERE CITY = 'London'
```

Suppose this particular query is used repeatedly, over and over again. Then we can simplify matters somewhat by defining a corresponding *virtual relvar* or *view*:

```
VAR LS VIRTUAL ( S WHERE CITY = 'London' ) ;
```

Now the query can be expressed more simply as just:

```
LS
```

Or if we want a slightly more complicated variant on the original query, say "Get suppliers in London with status 10":

```
LS WHERE STATUS = 10
```

Let's focus on this latter example for a moment. The basic idea is this: When we define the view, the DBMS "remembers" that definition by storing it in what's called the *catalog*.[10] Then, when it processes the query, the DBMS looks up the view definition in the catalog and uses what it finds there to replace the *view reference* (i.e., "LS") in the query by the associated *view defining expression*, thus:

```
( S WHERE CITY = 'London' ) WHERE STATUS = 10
```

This expression can now be evaluated in exactly the same way relational expressions always are evaluated.

As this simple example should be sufficient to suggest, the view mechanism allows the user to behave exactly as if the view in question were a regular ("base") relvar, thereby making life a little simpler for the user in certain respects. (There's an obvious analogy here with the familiar notion of *macros* in a programming language system.) Points arising:

- First, views work precisely because of the relational closure property! That's because it's a logical consequence of that property that if (a) a relvar reference *R* is allowed to appear at some point within some relational expression *rx* and (b) that reference *R* is to a relvar of type *RT*, then (c) an expression that evaluates to a relation of that same type *RT* is allowed to appear in *rx* in place of that relvar reference *R*. Thus it follows, as a particular instance of this rule, that we can replace the view reference LS in the expression LS WHERE STATUS = 10 by the view defining expression (viz., S WHERE CITY = 'London').

---

[10] The catalog for a given database is a set of system defined relvars, kept in the database itself, that describe the database in question. That descriptive information ("metadata," as it's sometimes called) includes such things as details regarding the attributes and keys for a given relvar and details of integrity constraints and authorities.

■ The second point is this. Recall Fig. 1.2 ("database system architecture") from Chapter 1. Well, views effectively add another layer to that architecture, as shown in Fig. 7.1.

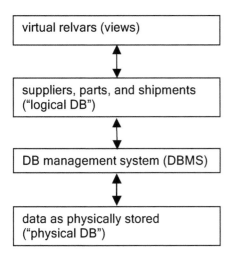

Fig. 7.1: Database system architecture with views

Recall now that I said in Chapter 1 that the separation between the logical and physical databases is what allows us to achieve the goal of data independence. Well, now I can be a little more precise about the matter. To be specific, that separation (between logical and physical databases) allows us to achieve what's more usually called *physical* data independence, which means we can change the way the data is physically stored and accessed without having to make corresponding changes in the way the data is perceived by the user. And the separation between views and the (base) relvars in terms of which those views are defined allows us to achieve what's called *logical* data independence, which means we can change the way the data is *logically* stored and accessed without having to make corresponding changes in the way the data is perceived by the user.

For further discussion of views in general, see *SQL and Relational Theory* or (for a considerably more detailed exposition) another book by myself, *View Updating and Relational Theory: How to Update Views* (O'Reilly, 2013).

CONCLUDING REMARKS

This brings us to the end of the first part of the book, which has been exclusively concerned with the relational model as such and hence with what it means for a DBMS to be relational. In Part III, by contrast, we'll take a look at the standard "relational" language SQL, concentrating in particular on how—or perhaps I should say, to what extent—the various relational features we've been discussing can be realized in that language. Before then, however, we need to examine certain topics (viz., transactions and database design) that, as I put it in the preface, (a) you do need to have at least an elementary understanding of in order to appreciate what databases are all about in general, but (b) don't really have much to do with the relational model as such (though they do both build on that model as a foundation). That's the purpose of Part II of the book, which follows immediately.

Part II

TRANSACTIONS

AND

DATABASE DESIGN

Chapter 8

Transactions

For tyme ylost may nought recovered be
—Geoffrey Chaucer: *Troilus and Criseyde* (c. 1385)

The transaction concept is only tangentially relevant to most users. Well, this isn't *quite* true—if you're a programmer writing database applications, then you certainly need to know what the implications of transactions are for the way you write your code. But you don't need to know much more than that. And if you're an interactive user, you probably don't even need to know that much. On the other hand (as I've said several times previously, more or less), if you want to be able to lay honest claim to having at least a broad understanding of what database technology is all about, then you do need to have, among other things, a basic appreciation of what transaction management entails.

As I've also said previously, transaction management isn't really a relational topic as such. However, it's interesting to note that the original research—the research, that is, that put the concept on a sound scientific footing—was all done in a specifically relational context.[1]

WHAT'S A TRANSACTION?

A transaction is a program execution, or part of a program execution, that constitutes *a logical unit of work*. It begins when a BEGIN TRANSACTION statement is executed and ends when either a COMMIT statement or a ROLLBACK statement is executed, where:

- BEGIN TRANSACTION is normally (and desirably) explicit.

- COMMIT signifies successful termination, and is also normally explicit.

- ROLLBACK signifies unsuccessful termination, and is often implicit.

---

[1] The seminal paper was "The Notions of Consistency and Predicate Locks in a Data Base System," by K. P. Eswaran, J. N. Gray, R. A. Lorie, and I. L. Traiger (*CACM 19*, No. 11, November 1976). The standard work on the subject is *Transaction Processing: Concepts and Techniques*, by Jim Gray and Andreas Reuter (Morgan Kaufmann, 1993).

Thus, any given program execution involves a *sequence* of transactions running one after another[2] (where the number of transactions in the sequence might be just one, of course). See Fig. 8.1.

```
time
begin transaction
         .....
commit or rollback
           .....
                     begin transaction
                              .....
                     commit or rollback
                                .....
                                          begin transaction
                                                   .....
                                          commit or rollback
                                                     .....                etc.
```

Fig. 8.1: Program execution is a sequence of transactions

RECOVERY

It's important to understand that all database updates must be done within the context of some transaction. The reason is that transactions aren't just a unit of work, they're also a unit of *recovery*. Let me explain. The standard example involves a banking application of some kind and a transaction that transfers a money amount, say $100, from one account to another. Here's the code—well, pseudocode—for such a transaction:

```
BEGIN TRANSACTION ;
    UPDATE account 123 : { BALANCE := BALANCE - 100 } ;
    IF error THEN ROLLBACK ;
    UPDATE account 321 : { BALANCE := BALANCE + 100 } ;
    IF error THEN ROLLBACK ;
COMMIT ;
```

As you can see, what's presumably meant to be a single atomic operation—"transfer $100 from account number 123 to account number 321"—in fact involves two separate updates to the database.[3] What's more, the database is actually in an incorrect state between those two updates, in the sense that it fails to reflect the true situation in the real world; clearly, a real world transfer

---

[2] Another way of saying this is: BEGIN TRANSACTION isn't allowed if a transaction is currently in progress.

[3] Actually it could be just one update in **Tutorial D**, thanks to the availability of the multiple assignment operator (see Chapter 6). For the purposes of the present discussion, it's necessary to assume that such an operator isn't available (or isn't being used, at any rate). Indeed, it's worth stating explicitly that multiple assignment wasn't even considered as a possibility when the original theoretical work was done on transactions.

of dollars from one account to another shouldn't affect the total number of dollars in the accounts concerned, but in the example the sum of $100 temporarily goes missing, as it were, between the two updates. Thus, the logical unit of work that's a transaction doesn't necessarily involve just a single database update. Rather, it involves a sequence of several such operations, in general, and the intent of that sequence is to transform a correct state of the database into another correct state, without necessarily preserving correctness at all intermediate points.

Note: At the risk of confusing you, let me now point out that, while the state of the database between the two updates in the example is certainly incorrect, it isn't *inconsistent*—it doesn't violate any known integrity constraints.[4] As I pointed out in Chapter 6, correctness implies consistency, but the converse isn't so: Incorrectness doesn't imply inconsistency. Thus, it would be more accurate to say the intent of a transaction is to transform a *consistent* state of the database into another *consistent* state, without necessarily preserving *consistency* at all intermediate points. I'll have more to say on this particular issue in the subsection "The ACID Properties" below.

Anyway, it's clear that what mustn't be allowed to happen in the example is for the first update to be done and the second not, because that would leave the database overall in an incorrect state. Ideally, we would like an ironclad guarantee that both updates will succeed. Unfortunately, it's impossible to provide any such guarantee—there's always a chance things will go wrong, and go wrong moreover at the worst possible moment. For example, a system crash might occur between the two updates, or an arithmetic overflow might occur on the second of them. But proper transaction management does provide the next best thing to such a guarantee; specifically, it guarantees that if the transaction executes some updates and then a failure occurs before the transaction reaches its planned termination, then those updates will be "rolled back" (i.e., undone). Thus the transaction *either* executes in its entirety *or* is totally canceled (meaning it's made to look as if it never executed at all). In this way, a sequence of operations that's fundamentally not atomic can be made to look as if it were atomic from an external point of view. And the COMMIT and ROLLBACK operations are the key to achieving this effect:

- *Successful termination:* COMMIT "commits" the transaction's updates (i.e., causes them to be installed in the database) and terminates the transaction.

- *Unsuccessful termination:* ROLLBACK "rolls the database back" to the state it was in when the transaction began (thereby undoing the transaction's updates) and terminates the transaction.

- *Implicit ROLLBACK:* The code in the dollar transfer example includes explicit tests for errors and forces an explicit ROLLBACK if it detects one. But we obviously can't assume,

---

[4] What's more, there's no reasonable integrity constraint we could write that would be violated by the dollar transfer in the example (right?).

nor would we want to assume, that transactions always include explicit tests for all possible errors that might occur. Therefore, the system will force an *implicit* ROLLBACK for any transaction that fails to reach its planned termination for any reason, where "planned termination" means either an explicit COMMIT or an explicit ROLLBACK. Moreover, if there's a system crash (in which case the transaction will fail through no fault of its own), then, when the system restarts, it will typically try to run the transaction again.

In the example, therefore, if the transaction gets through the two updates successfully, it executes a COMMIT to force those updates to be installed in the database. If it detects an error on either one of those updates, however, it executes a ROLLBACK instead, to undo all of the updates (if any) it has made so far. And if a totally unlooked-for error occurs, such as a system crash, then the system will force a ROLLBACK anyway on the transaction's behalf.

The Recovery Log

You might be wondering how it's possible to undo an update. Basically, the answer is that the system maintains a *log* in persistent storage (usually on disk), in which details of all updates—in particular, values of updated objects before and after each update, sometimes called *before-* and *after-images*—are recorded.[5] Thus, if it becomes necessary to undo some particular update, the system can use the corresponding log record to recover the original value of the updated object (that is, to restore the updated object to its previous value). Of course, in order for this process to work, the log record for a given update must be physically written to the log before that update is physically written to the database.[6] This protocol is known as *the write ahead log rule*.

> *Aside:* Of course, there's rather more to the write ahead log rule than that, as I'm sure you'd expect. To be more specific, the rule requires, among other things, (a) all other log records for a given transaction to be physically written to the log before the COMMIT record for that transaction is physically written to the log, and (b) COMMIT processing for a given transaction not to complete until the COMMIT record for that transaction has been physically written to the log. *End of aside.*

It follows from all of the above that (as noted at the beginning of this section) transactions aren't just a unit of work, they're also a unit of recovery. Which brings us to our next topic, viz., the so called *ACID properties* of transactions.

---

[5] You can think of "objects" here as tuples if you like, though in practice they're likely to be something more physical, such as disk pages.

[6] By "physically written" here, I mean the record in question isn't just waiting in main memory somewhere to be written out at some later time—rather, it has actually been forced out to persistent storage.

The ACID Properties

ACID is an acronym, standing for *atomicity – consistency – isolation – durability*, which are four properties that transactions in general are supposed to possess. Briefly:

■ *Atomicity:* Transactions are all or nothing.

■ *Consistency:* Transactions transform a consistent state of the database into another consistent state, without necessarily preserving consistency at all intermediate points.

■ *Isolation*: Any given transaction's updates are concealed from all other transactions until the given transaction commits.

■ *Durability:* Once a transaction commits, its updates survive in the database, even if there's a subsequent system crash.

As we've seen, the atomicity and durability properties mean the transaction is a unit of work and a unit of recovery, respectively; what's more, the consistency property means it's also a unit of *integrity*—but see the paragraph immediately following—and the isolation property means it's a unit of *concurrency* as well. Now, we've seen how the atomicity and durability properties are achieved; however, the other two require a little more explanation.

Actually I don't want to say too much more about the consistency property, other than to point out that it's more than a little suspect, because it assumes that integrity constraints aren't checked until commit time ("deferred checking"). And while it's true that some integrity checking, both in the SQL standard and in certain commercial DBMSs, is indeed deferred in this sense, the fact remains that to defer checking in this way is logically incorrect (as was mentioned briefly in Chapter 6, and as *SQL and Relational Theory* explains in detail).[7] That's why, again as we saw in Chapter 6, the relational model requires all constraint checking to be immediate— implying that, at least so far as the relational model is concerned, the "unit of integrity" is not the transaction but the *statement*.

So that leaves the isolation property. Here there's quite a bit more to say, and it deserves a section or two of its own.

CONCURRENCY

Most of the time in this chapter so far, I've been tacitly assuming there's just one transaction running in the system at any given time. But now suppose there are two or more, running concurrently. Then, as indicated in Chapter 1, controls are needed in order to ensure that those

---

[7] It's ironic, therefore, that in the literature "the C property" is often said to stand not for consistency but for *correctness*.

transactions—which we assume, reasonably enough, to be totally independent of one another—don't interfere with each other in any way. For example, consider the scenario illustrated in Fig. 8.2. That figure is meant to be read as follows: First, transaction *TX1* updates some object *p*; subsequently, transaction *TX2* retrieves that same (but now updated) object *p*; finally, transaction *TX1* is rolled back. At that point, transaction *TX2* has seen, and therefore become dependent on, an update that in effect never occurred.

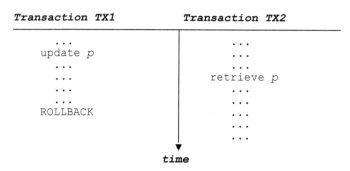

Fig. 8.2: Transaction *TX2* is dependent on an uncommitted update

The scenario illustrated in Fig. 8.3 is arguably even worse: Here, transactions *TX1* and *TX2* both retrieve the same object *p*; subsequently, transaction *TX1* updates that object *p*; and then transaction *TX2* also updates that same object *p*, thereby overwriting *TX1*'s update (at which point *TX1*'s update is said to be "lost").[8]

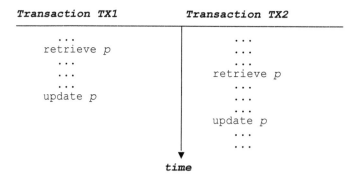

Fig. 8.3: Transaction *TX1*'s update is lost

Now, what has happened in both Fig. 8.2 and Fig. 8.3 is that one transaction has effectively interfered with another, concurrent, transaction, to produce an overall incorrect result. By the

---

[8] Such a situation isn't exactly unknown in real life, incidentally. Have you ever found someone else already sitting in your airline seat?

way, the problems illustrated in those figures—dependence on an uncommitted update in Fig. 8.2 and loss of an update in Fig. 8.3—aren't the only problems that can occur, absent suitable controls, if transactions are allowed to run concurrently; however, they're probably the easiest ones to understand. But the point is: We do need those controls. And the kind of control most commonly found in practice—though not the only kind possible—is called *locking*.

LOCKING

The basic idea behind locking is simple: When transaction *TX1* needs an assurance that some object it's interested in won't be updated while its back is turned, as it were, it *acquires a lock* on that object (in a manner to be explained). The effect of acquiring that lock is to "lock other transactions out of" the object in question (again, in a manner to be explained), and thereby in particular to prevent them from updating it. *TX1* is thus able to continue its processing in the certain knowledge that the object in question won't be updated by any other transaction, at least until such time as *TX1 releases* the lock in question (which of course it won't do until it has finished with it).

Typically, two kinds of locks are supported, "shared" or S locks (also called read locks) and "exclusive" or X locks (also called write locks). Loosely speaking, S locks are compatible with one another, but X locks aren't compatible with anything. To elaborate: Let *TX1* and *TX2* be distinct but concurrent transactions. Then:

- So long as *TX1* holds an X lock on object p, no request from *TX2* for a lock of either type on p can be granted.

- So long as *TX1* holds an S lock on object p, no request from *TX2* for an X lock on p can be granted, but a request from *TX2* for an S lock on p *can* be granted.

Thus, any number of transactions can hold an S lock on p at the same time, but at most one transaction can hold an X lock on p at any given time—and in this latter case, no other transaction can hold any lock on p at all at the time in question.

The system now uses the mechanism just described in order to enforce a protocol that will guarantee that problems such as those illustrated in Figs. 8.2 and 8.3 can't occur. Here in outline is how that protocol works:[9]

- A transaction's request to retrieve some object p causes an implicit request for an S lock on that object p.

---

[9] The formal name for the protocol is *strict two-phase locking*. In practice, real systems typically adopt various improvements to the protocol as described here. Details of what's possible in this connection are beyond the scope of this book, however.

■ A transaction's request to update some object *p* causes an implicit request for an X lock on that object *p*. *Note:* If the transaction in question already holds an S lock on *p* (as indeed it very likely will in practice), then that implicit lock request is treated as a request to *upgrade* that S lock to an X lock.

■ In both cases, if the implicit lock request can't be granted (because some other transaction currently holds a conflicting lock on the object in question), then the requesting transaction enters a wait state, waiting for that conflicting lock to be released.

■ Finally, COMMIT and ROLLBACK both cause all locks held by the terminating transaction to be released.

Now let's see how the foregoing protocol solves the problems illustrated in Figs. 8.2 and 8.3. Fig. 8.4 is a modified version of Fig. 8.2, showing what happens to the interleaved execution of transactions *TX1* and *TX2* from that figure under the protocol. First, *TX1* updates the object *p*, acquiring as it does so an X lock on *p*. Subsequently, *TX2* attempts to retrieve that same (but now updated) object *p*; however, *TX2*'s implicit request for an S lock on *p* can't be granted at that point, and so *TX2* goes into a wait state. Then *TX1* is rolled back and its X lock on *p* is released. Now *TX2* can come out of the wait state and acquire its requested S lock on *p*; but *p* is now as it was before *TX1* ran, and so *TX2* is no longer dependent on an uncommitted update.

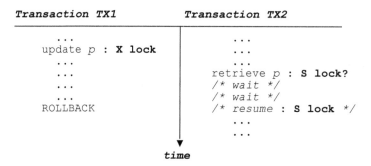

Fig. 8.4: Transaction *TX2* is no longer dependent on an uncommitted update

To refer back to the so called ACID properties for a moment, observe how the locking protocol has served to "isolate" transactions *TX1* and *TX2* from each other in Fig. 8.4.

I turn now to Fig. 8.5, which is a similarly modified version of Fig. 8.3. First, *TX1* retrieves the object *p*, acquiring as it does so an S lock on *p*. Subsequently, *TX2* retrieves that same object *p* and also acquires an S lock on it. *TX1* then attempts to update *p*; that attempt causes a request for an X lock, which can't be granted, and so *TX1* goes into a wait state. Then *TX2* also attempts to update *p*, and for analogous reasons also goes into a wait state. Neither transaction can now proceed, so there's certainly no question of any update being lost. On the other hand, no useful work is being done, either!—in other words, we've solved the lost update problem by reducing it to another problem (but at least we've solved the original problem). The new problem is called *deadlock*.

```
Transaction TX1                Transaction TX2

        ...                            ...
   retrieve p : S lock                 ...
        ...                            ...
        ...                     retrieve p : S lock
        ...                            ...
   update p : X lock?                  ...
   /* wait */                          ...
   /* wait */              update p : X lock?
   /* wait */              /* wait */
   /* wait */              /* wait */

                    time
```

Fig. 8.5: No update is lost, but deadlock occurs

The typical solution to the deadlock problem involves (a) choosing one of the deadlocked transactions—typically the youngest one, meaning the one that began most recently—as the "victim" and rolling it back, thereby releasing its locks, and then (b) starting the victim again as a new transaction.

A REMARK ON SQL

Since I don't plan to say any more about transactions in subsequent chapters (in Part III of this book in particular), let me close this chapter by noting that everything I've been saying about transactions in general applies to SQL systems in particular (more or less!). Thus, SQL does support explicit BEGIN TRANSACTION, COMMIT, and ROLLBACK statements (so does **Tutorial D**, incidentally).[10] It also has no explicit reliance on locking as such—that is, it has no explicit syntax for requesting or releasing locks—which means the system is free to use some mechanism other than locking, if it chooses, as a basis for concurrency control. (Again, the same is true of **Tutorial D**.) But what SQL does have is all kinds of additional features, concepts, and statements having to do with transactions in general that (a) **Tutorial D** most certainly doesn't have and (b) are far beyond the scope of an introductory book of this nature. One "simple" example of such a feature is the ability to have a transaction begin implicitly, without requiring execution of an explicit BEGIN TRANSACTION statement—but there's much, much more to the matter than that. *Caveat lector.*

---

[10] Actually SQL has START TRANSACTION in place of BEGIN TRANSACTION.

EXERCISES

8.1   (From *An Introduction to Database Systems*, 8th edition, Addison-Wesley, 2004.) The
term *schedule* is used to refer to the overall sequence of database retrieval and update operations
that occurs when some set of transactions run interleaved (i.e., concurrently). The schedule
below represents the sequence of operations in a schedule involving transactions *T1, T2, ..., T12*
(*a, b, ..., h* are objects in the database):

```
time t00      . . . . . . . . .
time t01    (T1)    : RETRIEVE a ;
time t02    (T2)    : RETRIEVE b ;
   ...      (T1)    : RETRIEVE c ;
   ...      (T4)    : RETRIEVE d ;
   ...      (T5)    : RETRIEVE a ;
   ...      (T2)    : RETRIEVE e ;
   ...      (T2)    : UPDATE e ;
   ...      (T3)    : RETRIEVE f ;
   ...      (T2)    : RETRIEVE f ;
   ...      (T5)    : UPDATE a ;
   ...      (T1)    : COMMIT ;
   ...      (T6)    : RETRIEVE a ;
   ...      (T5)    : ROLLBACK ;
   ...      (T6)    : RETRIEVE c ;
   ...      (T6)    : UPDATE c ;
   ...      (T7)    : RETRIEVE g ;
   ...      (T8)    : RETRIEVE h ;
   ...      (T9)    : RETRIEVE g ;
   ...      (T9)    : UPDATE g ;
   ...      (T8)    : RETRIEVE e ;
   ...      (T7)    : COMMIT ;
   ...      (T9)    : RETRIEVE h ;
   ...      (T3)    : RETRIEVE g ;
   ...      (T10)   : RETRIEVE a ;
   ...      (T9)    : UPDATE h ;
   ...      (T6)    : COMMIT ;
   ...      (T11)   : RETRIEVE c ;
   ...      (T12)   : RETRIEVE d ;
   ...      (T12)   : RETRIEVE c ;
   ...      (T2)    : UPDATE f ;
   ...      (T11)   : UPDATE c ;
   ...      (T12)   : RETRIEVE a ;
   ...      (T10)   : UPDATE a ;
   ...      (T12)   : UPDATE d ;
   ...      (T4)    : RETRIEVE g ;
time t36      . . . . . . . . .
```

Assume that RETRIEVE *p* (if successful) acquires an S lock on *p*, and UPDATE *p* (if
successful) promotes that lock to X level. Assume also that all locks are held until end of
transaction. At time *t36*, which transactions are waiting for which other transactions? Are there
any deadlocks at that time?

ANSWERS

8.1 At time *t36* no transactions are doing any useful work at all! Transactions *T1, T5, T6,* and *T7* have all terminated (*T1, T6,* and *T7* successfully, *T5* unsuccessfully). There's one deadlock, involving transactions *T2, T3, T9,* and *T8*; in addition, *T4* is waiting for *T9, T12* is waiting for *T4,* and *T10* and *T11* are both waiting for *T12.* We can represent the situation by means of a graph (the *wait-for graph*), in which (a) the nodes represent transactions; (b) a directed edge from node *Ti* to node *Tj* indicates that *Ti* is waiting for *Tj*; and (c) the edge from note *Ti* to node *Tj* is labeled with the name of the database object and the kind of lock that *Ti* is waiting for (see Fig. 8.6 below). Observe that a cycle in the graph corresponds to a deadlock.

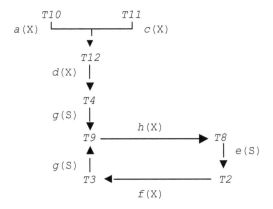

Fig. 8.6: Wait-for graph for Exercise 8.1

Chapter 9

Database Design

I don't do design, normally

—Anon.: *Where Bugs Go*

As noted in Chapter 7, Codd's introduction of the relational model paved the way for research into numerous aspects of database management. One such aspect was, and still is, database design; in fact, design theory is now an extremely rich field, with an extensive literature of its own. That theory concerns itself with questions such as the following: What exactly is it that constitutes, or characterizes, a "good" database design? And how can such a "good" design be achieved? Of course, we can only scratch the surface of such matters here; but, just as with transactions (the subject of the previous chapter), a certain degree of familiarity with database design—or database design theory, rather—is essential to a basic understanding of what database technology in general is all about.

So design theory is certainly part of relational theory in general; however, it isn't part of the relational model as such. Rather, it's a separate theory that builds on top of that model. In fact, the relational model as such doesn't care how well—or how badly!—the database is designed (neither does **Tutorial D**, a fortiori, and the same goes for SQL): So long as the database is at least relational, meaning it abides by *The Information Principle*, then all of the concepts of the relational model do still apply, and in particular all of the operators of the relational algebra do still work. Thus, if the database is badly designed, it's the user that suffers, not the relational model as such.[1]

By the way, our running example, the suppliers-and-parts database (with its three relvars S, P, and SP), *is* well designed. And I hope you agree the design in question is pretty obvious, too; in fact, it's essentially common sense. Indeed, much of design theory is just glorified common sense, in a way. Well ... that's not really fair; it would be better to say it's *formalized* common sense. Formalization is important, because if something can be formalized, it can be mechanized; in other words, we can get the machine to do the work. But further discussion of that particular point here would take us much too far afield. If you want to investigate further, I'm afraid I'll have to point you to another book of mine, *Database Design and Relational Theory: Normal Forms and All That Jazz* (O'Reilly, 2012).

---

[1] Actually the DBMS can suffer too, though perhaps to a lesser extent.

NONLOSS DECOMPOSITION

Recall from Chapter 2 that relations are always normalized (i.e., in *first normal form* or 1NF), which simply means that every tuple in the relation in question conforms to the pertinent heading. Observe now that this definition applies specifically to *relations*—but we can extend it in an obvious way to apply to relvars as well, thus:

> **Definition:** Relvar *R* is in **first normal form** (1NF) if and only if every relation *r* that can legally be assigned to *R* is in 1NF—i.e., if and only if every relation *r* that can legally be assigned to *R* is such that each tuple *t* of *r* contains (a) exactly one value (of the appropriate type) in every attribute position and (b) nothing else.

Of course, every relvar is in 1NF by this definition. But the reason for the definition is that it provides a base on which to build, as it were. That is, we can define a series of "higher" normal forms—second normal form (2NF), third normal form (3NF), and so on—such that if a relvar is in one of those higher normal forms, it possesses certain desirable properties that a relvar that's only in 1NF doesn't.

Let's take a look at an example that's only in 1NF and not in one of those higher normal forms. Fig. 9.1 shows a sample value for a relvar I've called SPCT, with attributes SNO, PNO, QTY, CITY, and STATUS, where the attributes have the usual meanings (but note that CITY in particular means *supplier* city), and the relvar predicate is:

Supplier SNO supplies part PNO in quantity QTY, has status STATUS, and is located in city CITY.

SPCT

SNO	PNO	QTY	CITY	STATUS
S1	P1	300	London	20
S1	P2	200	London	20
S1	P3	400	London	20
S1	P4	200	London	20
S1	P5	100	London	20
S1	P6	100	London	20
S2	P1	300	Paris	10
S2	P2	400	Paris	10
S3	P2	200	Paris	30
S4	P2	200	London	20
S4	P4	300	London	20
S4	P5	400	London	20

Fig. 9.1: Relvar SPCT—sample value

A glance at the figure is sufficient to show what's bad about this design—it's *redundant*, in the sense that certain pieces of information are recorded repeatedly; to be specific, the fact that a given supplier has a certain city and the fact that a given supplier has a certain status both appear many times, in general. What's more, these redundancies lead, either directly or indirectly, to certain "update anomalies" (as they're usually called). For example:

- *INSERT anomaly:* We can't insert the fact that the city for supplier S5 is Athens until that supplier supplies a part.

- *DELETE anomaly:* If we delete the only tuple for supplier S3, we lose the fact that the city for that supplier is Paris (i.e., the delete "deletes too much," as it were).

- *UPDATE anomaly:* If we change the city for supplier S1 from London to Rome in the tuple for S1 and P1 but not in any other tuple, we introduce an obvious inconsistency. *Note:* Of course, we wouldn't be able to perform such an UPDATE if there's an integrity constraint in effect to say that each supplier has just one city—but for the moment, at least, let's assume there isn't. I'll have more to say on this specific issue in the next section.

To repeat, the foregoing design is obviously bad.[2] And the solution to the problem is obvious, too: We need to replace relvar SPCT by two separate relvars, one being our usual suppliers relvar S—except that for simplicity I'm ignoring supplier names[3]—and the other being our usual shipments relvar SP. As Fig. 9.2 clearly shows, the effect of this change is to remove the redundancies and thereby to avoid the update anomalies.

S

SNO	STATUS	CITY
S1	20	London
S2	10	Paris
S3	30	Paris
S4	20	London
S5	30	Athens

SP

SNO	PNO	QTY
S1	P1	300
S1	P2	200
S1	P3	400
S1	P4	200
S1	P5	100
S1	P6	100
S2	P1	300
S2	P2	400
S3	P2	200
S4	P2	200
S4	P4	300
S4	P5	400

Fig. 9.2: Relvars S (simplified) and SP—sample values

---

[2] To be fair, at least part of the reason it's so easy to see it's bad is that the example is extremely simple. Spotting the redundancies and anomalies in a more realistic example might not be so easy.

[3] And I'll continue to do so throughout this chapter, until further notice.

Observe now that the two replacement relvars S and SP are both projections of relvar SPCT.[4] What's more, if we join those projections back together again, we get back to where we started. Thus, what this example shows—or at least strongly suggests—is this: The higher normal forms (2NF, 3NF, and so on) are all about (a) decomposing a relvar via projection in such a way that (b) redundancies are removed and (c) the original relvar is equal to the join of the projections in question. Because of point (c) in particular, the decomposition process is said to be *nonloss* (of course, it's very important that we don't lose any information in that process). And because, as we'll see, the result of the decomposition is relvars in some higher normal form, the process is also known as *further normalization*, or, more usually, just *normalization* for short. Also, because of points (a) and (c) taken together, when we talk about the normalization process in general, we can say that projection is the *decomposition* operator and join is the corresponding *recomposition* operator. As you can see, therefore, design theory—or the part of design theory we're talking about here, at any rate—is, as I claimed earlier, critically dependent on certain features of the relational model: to be specific, it depends on the operators projection and join.

> *A remark on terminology:* Strictly speaking, the terms *projection* and *join* ought to be in quotation marks throughout the previous paragraph. That's because, as we know from Part I of this book, those operators really apply to relations, not relvars. Of course, we can and do say things like "*R* is the join of *R1* and *R2*," where *R* and *R1* and *R2* are relvars; but what we usually mean when we say such a thing is that the relation *r* that's the current value of *R* is equal to the join of the relations *r1* and *r2* that are the current values of *R1* and *R2*, respectively. But now we're using such a manner of speaking to mean something slightly different. To be specific, when we say in the normalization context that *R* is the join of *R1* and *R2*, we mean it's *always* true that the relation *r* that's the value of *R*, at any given time, is equal to the join of the relations *r1* and *r2* that are the values of *R1* and *R2*, respectively, at that same time. (I'm sorry if you find this confusing, but sometimes it's important to be precise about such matters.) *End of remark.*

FUNCTIONAL DEPENDENCIES

I noted in the previous section that there ought really to be an integrity constraint in effect to say that each supplier has just one city. Formally speaking, that constraint is an example of a *functional dependency*. Functional dependencies are an extremely important notion (they've been described as "not quite fundamental, but very nearly so"). Here's a definition:

> **Definition:** Let *X* and *Y* be subsets of the heading of relvar *R*. Then the **functional dependency** (FD)

---

[4] Except that (in order to show how the decomposition avoids the insert anomaly in particular) I've shown a tuple for supplier S5 in the "projection" S, even though there was no such tuple in SPCT.

```
X → Y
```

holds in *R* if and only if, whenever two tuples of *R* have the same value for *X*, they also have the same value for *Y*. *X* and *Y* are the *determinant* and the *dependant*, respectively, and the FD overall can be read as "*X* functionally determines *Y*" or "*Y* is functionally dependent on *X*," or more simply just as "*X* arrow *Y*."

By way of example, the FD {SNO} → {CITY} holds in relvar SPCT ("for one supplier number, there's one corresponding city"). In fact, of course, the FD {SNO} → {STATUS} holds in relvar SPCT as well, and so we can combine these two FDs into one and say simply that the FD

```
{ SNO } → { CITY , STATUS }
```

holds in that relvar. Note the braces, by the way; *X* and *Y* in the definition are subsets of the heading of *R*, and are therefore *sets* (of attributes), even when, as in the case of {SNO} → {CITY}, they happen to be *singleton* sets. By the same token, *X* and *Y* values are *tuples*, even when, as in that same example, they happen to be tuples of degree one.[5] And if these remarks ring a bell with you, they should, because the situation is very similar to something you should be very familiar with by now: viz., the fact that keys too are sets of attributes, and key values are tuples (see the answer to Exercise 3.2 in Chapter 3 if you need to refresh your memory here).

Talk of keys brings me to my next point. Let relvar *R* have key *K*. Then I hope it's obvious that the FD

```
K → { A }
```

holds in *R* for every attribute *A* of *R*. For if two tuples of *R* have the same value for *K*, they must be the very same tuple, and so they must certainly have the same value for *A*. Another way of saying the same thing is as follows: The FD

```
K → X
```

holds in *R* for all subsets *X* of the heading of *R*. Thus, "FDs out of keys"—i.e., FDs where the determinant is a key—always hold, in every relvar. Loosely speaking, we can say that *if any other FDs (i.e., FDs not out of keys) hold, then the design is bad*. Observe in the case of relvar SPCT that we did indeed have some FDs not out of keys; to be specific, the FDs {SNO} → {CITY} and {SNO} → {STATUS} both held, and {SNO} wasn't a key for that relvar.

---

[5] Recall from the answer to Exercise 2.7 in Chapter 2 that it does make sense to talk about the degree of a tuple.

Irreducible FDs

There's one more concept I need to introduce before I can get on to the higher normal forms as such. Observe first that if the FD $X \to Y$ holds in relvar R, then the FD $X' \to Y'$ also holds in R for all supersets X' of X and all subsets Y' of Y (just so long as X' is still a subset of the heading, of course). In other words, you can always add attributes to the determinant or subtract them from the dependant, and what you get will still be an FD that holds in the relvar in question. For example, the FD

```
{ SNO } → { CITY , STATUS }
```

holds in relvar SPCT as we've seen, and so the FD

```
{ SNO , PNO } → { CITY }
```

does so too (I've added attribute PNO to the determinant and subtracted attribute STATUS from the dependant). Now, if the FD $X' \to Y'$ holds but the FD $X \to Y'$ doesn't hold for any proper subset X of X', then $X' \to Y'$ is *irreducible*. For example, in relvar SPCT,

```
{ SNO , PNO } → { QTY }
```

is irreducible, but

```
{ SNO , PNO } → { CITY }
```

isn't (because the FD $\{SNO\} \to \{CITY\}$ holds in that relvar as well).

SECOND NORMAL FORM

Now I can give a precise definition of 2NF:

> **Definition:** Relvar R is in **second normal form** (2NF) if and only if, for every key K of R and every nonkey attribute A of R, the FD $K \to \{A\}$ (which holds in R, necessarily) is irreducible. *Note:* A nonkey attribute of relvar R is an attribute of R that's not part of any key of R.

And now I can explain that the problem with relvar SPCT was precisely that it was in 1NF (because all relvars are in 1NF) but not in 2NF. To be specific, (a) {SNO,PNO} is a key; (b) the FDs {SNO ,PNO} → {CITY} and {SNO ,PNO} → {STATUS} therefore hold; but (c) those FDs are reducible. And it's those FDs that are the source of the redundancies in relvar SPCT.

Given that SPCT isn't in 2NF, the principles of further normalization would suggest that we decompose it—in a nonloss way, of course—into projections that are (of course, that's exactly what I did when I first introduced this example). And there's an important theorem, Heath's Theorem, that can help in this regard:

Heath's Theorem: Let relvar *R* have heading *H* and let *X*, *Y*, and *Z* be subsets of *H* such that the set theory union of *X*, *Y*, and *Z* is equal to *H*. Let *XY* denote the set theory union of *X* and *Y*, and similarly for *XZ*. If the FD *X* → *Y* holds in *R*, then *R* is equal to the join of its projections on *XY* and *XZ*, and so it can be nonloss decomposed into those projections.

As a special case of the theorem, let relvar *R* have heading {*A,B,C*}—i.e., let *A*, *B*, and *C* be individual attributes as such, instead of sets of attributes—and let the FD {*A*} → {*B*} hold in *R*. Then Heath's Theorem tells us *R* can be nonloss decomposed into *R1* and *R2* as follows:

```
R1 { A , B } KEY { A }
R2 { A , C } ..... FOREIGN KEY { A } REFERENCES R1
```

I'll conclude this section by giving an alternative definition for 2NF, one that can be proved to be equivalent to the one I gave previously (though I omit such a proof here) but can sometimes be more useful:

Definition: Relvar *R* is in **second normal form** (2NF) if and only if, for every nontrivial FD *X* → *Y* that holds in *R*, at least one of the following is true: (a) *X* is a superkey; (b) *Y* is a subkey; (c) *X* is not a subkey.

This definition requires some explanation! First, an FD is *trivial* if and only if it can't possibly fail to hold. In relvar SPCT, for example, the following FDs are both trivial:

```
{ SNO , PNO } → { SNO }

{ SNO }        → { SNO }
```

In fact, it's easy to see that an FD is trivial if and only if the right side (the dependant) is a subset of the left side (the determinant).

Second, a *superkey* for relvar *R* is a subset *SK* of the heading of *R* that has the key uniqueness property but not necessarily the key irreducibility property (see Chapter 3). Note, therefore, that all keys are superkeys, but "most" superkeys aren't keys (and a superkey that isn't a key is a *proper* superkey). Note too that if *SK* is a superkey for *R*, then the FD *SK* → {*A*} holds in *R* for all attributes *A* of *R*, necessarily. *Exercise:* How many superkeys does our usual parts relvar P have? (*Answer:* 16. This count includes both the key {PNO} and the entire heading. Note that the heading for an arbitrary relvar *R* is always a superkey for *R*.)

Third, a *subkey* for relvar *R* is a subset of a key of *R*. Thus, all keys are subkeys, but "most" subkeys aren't keys (and a subkey that isn't a key is a *proper* subkey). *Exercise:* How many subkeys does our usual shipments relvar SP have? (*Answer:* 4. This count includes both the key {SNO,PNO} and the empty subset { } of the heading. Note that the empty subset is always a subkey for any arbitrary relvar *R*.)

> *A remark on KEY specifications:* Let the relvar definition for relvar *R* contain the KEY specification KEY {*K*}. Now, we would of course typically say that such a specification means that *K* is a key for *R*. Strictly speaking, however, all it really means is that *K* is a *superkey* for *R*! The point is this: While the system can and certainly will enforce the uniqueness property implied by that KEY specification, it can't in general enforce the corresponding irreducibility property as well. With respect to the parts relvar P, for example, we know—because we know what the relvar mean (i.e., we know the corresponding predicate)—that the combination {PNO,CITY} doesn't have the irreducibility property (though of course it does have the uniqueness property). To repeat, we know that—but the system doesn't. So if we were to specify KEY {PNO,CITY}, instead of KEY {PNO}, for that relvar, the system wouldn't—*couldn't*—enforce the constraint that part numbers as such, as opposed to PNO-CITY combinations, were unique. In other words, as I've said, when we specify KEY {*K*} as part of the definition of relvar *R*, the system can and will guarantee that {*K*} is a superkey, but not necessarily a key as such, for *R*. *End of remark.*

THIRD NORMAL FORM

On now to third normal form (3NF). I'll introduce this one with another example. Suppose the additional FD CITY} → {STATUS} holds in our usual suppliers relvar S (see Fig. 9.3, where (a) I've changed the status for supplier S2 in order to conform to this new FD and (b) I've also reinstated the supplier name attribute SNAME).

SNO	SNAME	STATUS	CITY
S1	Smith	20	London
S2	Jones	30	Paris
S3	Blake	30	Paris
S4	Clark	20	London
S5	Adams	30	Athens

Fig. 9.3: Relvar S with {CITY} → {STATUS}—sample value

This revised version is in 2NF, as you can check for yourself. However, it's not in 3NF—see the definition below—and therefore suffers from redundancy, as you can see (to be specific, the fact that a given city has a given status appears many times, in general).

Definition: Relvar R is in **third normal form** (3NF) if and only if, for every nontrivial FD $X \to Y$ that holds in R, either (a) X is a superkey or (b) Y is a subkey.

To see that the version of relvar S illustrated in Fig. 9.3 isn't in 3NF, observe that (a) the FD {CITY} $\to$ {STATUS} holds in that relvar, as we know; (b) that FD is certainly nontrivial; (c) {CITY} isn't a superkey and {STATUS} isn't a subkey; and so (d) the relvar isn't in 3NF. And it's that FD that's the source of the redundancies in that relvar.

Given that the relvar isn't in 3NF, the principles of normalization would suggest that we decompose it (in a nonloss way, of course) into projections that are. Applying Heath's Theorem, we obtain two projections, one on SNO, SNAME, and CITY, and the other on CITY and STATUS. *Exercise:* Check that this decomposition (a) complies with the conditions of Heath's Theorem, (b) is nonloss, and (c) does remove the redundancies.

By the way, if you compare the foregoing definition of 3NF with the second of the two definitions I gave for 2NF, you'll see immediately that every 3NF relvar is necessarily in 2NF. (The converse is false, of course.) This state of affairs is usually stated in the following simplified form: *3NF implies 2NF.*

BOYCE/CODD NORMAL FORM

Finally we come to Boyce/Codd normal form (BCNF), which is really *the* normal form with respect to FDs.[6] Here's the definition:

Definition: Relvar R is in **Boyce/Codd normal form** (BCNF) if and only if, for every nontrivial FD $X \to Y$ that holds in R, X is a superkey.

Note first that it's immediate from this definition that BCNF implies 3NF, meaning that every BCNF relvar is necessarily in 3NF. (Again the converse is false, of course.) It's also immediate that the only FDs that hold in a BCNF relvar are either trivial ones (we can't get rid of those, obviously) or "FDs out of superkeys" (we can't get rid of those, either). Or as some people like to say: *Every fact is a fact about the key, the whole key, and nothing but the key*—though I must immediately add that this informal characterization, attractive though it is, isn't really accurate, because it assumes among other things that there's just one key.

---

[6] By rights BCNF should have been called *fourth normal form* (indeed, it almost was). Unfortunately, by the time it was widely understood and its true significance generally appreciated, another normal form, beyond the scope of the present book, had been defined and labeled "fourth."

By way of an example of a relvar that's in 3NF but not BCNF, consider a revised version of the shipments relvar—let's call it SNP—that has an additional attribute SNAME, representing the name of the applicable supplier. Suppose also that supplier names are necessarily unique (i.e., no two suppliers ever have the same name at the same time; note that I explicitly do *not* make this assumption elsewhere in this book). Here then are some sample SNP tuples:

SNO	SNAME	PNO	QTY
S1	Smith	P1	300
S1	Smith	P2	200
S1	Smith	P3	400
..	.....	..	...
S2	Jones	P1	300
S2	Jones	P2	400
..	.....	..	...

Once again we observe some redundancy: Every tuple for supplier S1 tells us S1 is named Smith, every tuple for supplier S2 tells us S2 is named Jones, and so on; likewise, every tuple for Smith tells us Smith's supplier number is S1, every tuple for Jones tells us Jones's supplier number is S2, and so on. And the relvar isn't in BCNF. First of all, it has two keys, {SNO,PNO} and {SNAME,PNO}.[7] Second, every subset of the heading—{QTY} in particular—is (of course) functionally dependent on both of those keys. Third, however, the FDs {SNO} → {SNAME} and {SNAME} → {SNO} also hold; these FDs are certainly not trivial, nor are they FDs out of superkeys, and so the relvar isn't in BCNF (though it is in 3NF, because in both cases the dependant is a subkey).

Finally, the normalization discipline says: If relvar *R* isn't in BCNF, then decompose it into projections that are. In the case of relvar SNP, either of the following decompositions will achieve this objective:

- Projecting on {SNO,SNAME} and {SNO,PNO,QTY}

- Projecting on {SNO,SNAME} and {SNAME,PNO,QTY}

CONCLUDING REMARKS

To repeat, BCNF is *the* normal form with respect to FDs; thus, 2NF and 3NF really aren't very important in themselves, except as stepping stones on the way to BCNF. To put it another way, BCNF is clearly the important one in practice; database designers should generally strive to ensure that all of their relvars are in (at least) BCNF. Note too that BCNF is conceptually

---

[7] That's why I didn't show any double underlining when I showed the sample tuples: There are two keys, and there doesn't seem to be any good reason to make either of them primary or (in effect) "more equal than the other."

simpler than 2NF and 3NF, inasmuch as its definition makes no mention of such things as irreducible FDs, nonkey attributes, or subkeys.

Given that all of these things are so, why do we bother with 2NF and 3NF at all? Why did I even bother to mention them in this chapter? In fact, there are several answers to these questions:

- A study of 2NF and 3NF helps pave the way for acquiring an understanding of the higher normal forms, as well as of design theory in general (including FDs in particular).

- That same study also gives some insight into the history of the design theory field (the reason those normal forms are called "second" and "third" reflects, of course, the order in which they were originally defined).

- Last, 2NF and 3NF also give some insight into what can go wrong if we don't make sure that our relvars are in BCNF. BCNF says, in essence, "the only FDs are FDs out of keys." How can this requirement be violated? Simplifying somewhat, there are basically two ways: (a) There can be an FD out of a proper subkey (in which case the relvar isn't in 2NF), or (b) there can be an FD out of a nonkey (in which case the relvar isn't in 3NF).

A couple of final points to close this chapter:

- BCNF is the final normal form with respect to FDs, but it's certainly not the final normal form!—there are several higher ones (at least six or seven of them). However, BCNF is certainly one of the most important from a pragmatic point of view.

- Normalization is important, but there's much more to design theory than just normal forms, as I show in the book mentioned earlier, *Database Design and Relational Theory: Normal Forms and All That Jazz* (O'Reilly, 2012).

EXERCISES

9.1 In the body of the chapter, I said that relvar SPCT (see Fig. 9.1) suffered from the following insert anomaly: "We can't insert the fact that the city for supplier S5 is Athens until that supplier supplies a part." Of course, we also can't insert the fact that the status for supplier S5 is 30 until, again, that supplier supplies a part. But why exactly are these things so?

9.2 How many FDs hold in our usual shipments relvar SP? Which ones are trivial? Which ones are irreducible?

9.3   As noted in the body of the chapter, an FD is really just a special kind of integrity constraint. Write **Tutorial D** CONSTRAINT statements to express the FDs {SNO} → {SNAME} and {SNAME} → {SNO} that hold in relvar SNP (see the section "Boyce/Codd Normal Form").

9.4   Give examples from your own work environment of (a) a relvar not in 2NF; (b) a relvar in 3NF but not in 2NF; (c) a relvar in BCNF but not in 3NF.

9.5   Consider the version of the suppliers relvar S discussed in the section "Third Normal Form" (see Fig. 9.3). What update anomalies arise in connection with that relvar?

9.6   (From *An Introduction to Database Systems*, 8th edition, Addison-Wesley, 2004.) A certain database is to contain information about the departments, employees, etc., in a certain company, where:

- The company has a set of departments.

- Each department has a set of employees, a set of projects, and a set of offices.

- Each employee has a job history (set of jobs the employee has held).

- For each such job, the employee also has a salary history (set of salaries received while employed on that job).

- Each office has a set of phones.

The database is to contain the following information:

- For each department: Department number (unique), budget, and the department manager's employee number (unique)

- For each employee: Employee number (unique), current project number, office number, and phone number; also, title of each job the employee has held, plus date and salary for each distinct salary received in that job

- For each project: Project number (unique) and budget

- For each office: Office number (unique), floor area, and phone number (unique) for all phones in that office

Design an appropriate set of relvars to represent this information. State any assumptions you make regarding functional dependencies.

ANSWERS

9.1   Because there's no part number *p* and no quantity *q* such that *Supplier S5 supplies part p in quantity q, has status 30, and is located in city Athens* is a true proposition. In other words, there's no instantiation for supplier S5 of the predicate for relvar SPCT that evaluates to TRUE.

9.2   The complete set of FDs—what's known, formally, as the *closure*, though it has nothing to do with the closure property of the relational algebra—for relvar SP contains 31 FDs:

```
{ SNO , PNO , QTY } → { SNO , PNO , QTY }
{ SNO , PNO , QTY } → { SNO , PNO }
{ SNO , PNO , QTY } → { SNO , QTY }
{ SNO , PNO , QTY } → { PNO , QTY }
{ SNO , PNO , QTY } → { SNO }
{ SNO , PNO , QTY } → { PNO }
{ SNO , PNO , QTY } → { QTY }
{ SNO , PNO , QTY } → { }

{ SNO , PNO }        → { SNO , PNO , QTY }
{ SNO , PNO }        → { SNO , PNO }
{ SNO , PNO }        → { SNO , QTY }
{ SNO , PNO }        → { PNO , QTY }
{ SNO , PNO }        → { SNO }
{ SNO , PNO }        → { PNO }
{ SNO , PNO }        → { QTY }
{ SNO , PNO }        → { }

{ SNO , QTY }        → { SNO , QTY }
{ SNO , QTY }        → { SNO }
{ SNO , QTY }        → { QTY }
{ SNO , QTY }        → { }

{ PNO , QTY }        → { PNO , QTY }
{ PNO , QTY }        → { PNO }
{ PNO , QTY }        → { QTY }
{ PNO , QTY }        → { }

{ SNO }              → { SNO }
{ SNO }              → { }

{ PNO }              → { PNO }
{ PNO }              → { }

{ QTY }              → { QTY }
{ QTY }              → { }

{ }                  → { }
```

The only ones that aren't trivial are these four:

```
{ SNO , PNO }  →  { SNO , PNO , QTY }
{ SNO , PNO }  →  { SNO , QTY }
{ SNO , PNO }  →  { PNO , QTY }
{ SNO , PNO }  →  { QTY }
```

The only irreducible ones are the following eleven:

```
{ SNO , PNO }  →  { SNO , PNO , QTY }
{ SNO , PNO }  →  { SNO , PNO }
{ SNO , PNO }  →  { SNO , QTY }
{ SNO , PNO }  →  { PNO , QTY }
{ SNO , PNO }  →  { QTY }

{ SNO , QTY }  →  { SNO , QTY }

{ PNO , QTY }  →  { PNO , QTY }

{ SNO }           →  { SNO }

{ PNO }           →  { PNO }

{ QTY }           →  { QTY }

{ }               →  { }
```

9.3 CONSTRAINT C9A COUNT (SNP { SNO , SNAME }) = COUNT (SNP { SNO }) ;

CONSTRAINT C9B COUNT (SNP { SNO , SNAME }) = COUNT (SNP { SNAME }) ;

9.4 *No answer provided.*

9.5 *INSERT anomaly:* We can't insert the fact that a given city has a certain status until some supplier is located in that city. *DELETE anomaly:* If we delete the only tuple for a given city, we lose the fact that the city in question has a certain status. *UPDATE anomaly:* If we change the status for a given city in one tuple but not in another, we introduce an inconsistency. (How does decomposition to 3NF avoid these anomalies?). *Subsidiary exercise:* Repeat this entire exercise for relvar SNP from the section "Boyce/Codd Normal Form."

9.6 The most important FDs, both those implied by the wording of the exercise and those corresponding to reasonable assumptions (stated explicitly below), are as follows. The attribute names are intended to be self-explanatory.

```
{ DEPTNO }              →  { DBUDGET , MGRNO }
{ MGRNO }               →  { DEPTNO }
{ PROJNO }              →  { PBUDGET , DEPTNO }
{ EMPNO }               →  { PHONENO , PROJNO }
{ EMPNO , DATE }        →  { JOB , SALARY }
{ PHONENO }             →  { OFCNO }
{ OFCNO }               →  { AREA }
```

Assumptions:

■ No employee is the manager of more than one department at a time.

■ No employee works in more than one department at a time.

■ No employee works on more than one project at a time.

■ No employee has more than one office at a time.

■ No employee has more than one phone at a time.

■ No employee has more than one job at a time.

■ No project is assigned to more than one department at a time.

■ No office is assigned to more than one department at a time.

■ Department numbers, employee numbers, project numbers, office numbers, and phone numbers are all "globally unique."

Here then is a possible collection of BCNF relvars (in outline):[8]

```
DEPT { DEPTNO , DBUDGET , MGRNO }
     KEY { DEPTNO }
     KEY { MGRNO }
     FOREIGN KEY { MGRNO } REFERENCES
             EMP { EMPNO } RENAME { EMPNO AS MGRNO }
```

---

[8] Note the FOREIGN KEY specification for relvar DEPT in particular.

```
EMP { EMPNO , PROJNO , PHONENO }
     KEY { EMPNO }
     FOREIGN KEY { PROJNO } REFERENCES PROJ
     FOREIGN KEY { PHONENO } REFERENCES PHONE

SALHIST { EMPNO , DATE , JOB , SALARY }
     KEY { EMPNO , DATE }
     FOREIGN KEY { EMPNO } REFERENCES EMP

PROJ { PROJNO , PBUDGET, DEPTNO }
     KEY { PROJNO }
     FOREIGN KEY { DEPTNO } REFERENCES DEPT

OFC { OFCNO , AREA , DEPTNO }
     KEY { OFCNO }
     FOREIGN KEY { DEPTNO } REFERENCES DEPT

PHONE { PHONENO , OFCNO }
     KEY { PHONENO }
     FOREIGN KEY { OFCNO } REFERENCES OFFICE
```

Observe that these relvars, although they're indeed all in BCNF, still involve some redundancy. For example, the fact that a given employee held a given job on a given date will appear *n* times in relvar SALHIST, where *n* is the number of different salaries earned by that employee while holding that job. Also, the projection of PROJ on PROJNO and DEPTNO is at all times equal to the projection on those same attributes of the join of EMP and PHONE and OFC. This state of affairs shows that normalization to BCNF, although generally desirable, isn't sufficient in itself to eliminate all redundancies.

Part III

SQL

Chapter 10

SQL Tables

[The] natural sequel of an unnatural beginning
—Jane Austen: Persuasion (1818)

Recall from Chapter 1 that my plan for this book (for Parts I and III, at least) looked like this:

- First, I wanted to explain the relational model as such, using a language expressly designed for that purpose called **Tutorial D**.

- Then I wanted to show how terms and concepts from the relational model are realized in concrete form in the SQL language specifically.[1] (Please note, therefore, that I'm not trying to cover the whole of SQL in this book; rather, I just want to cover what might be called the relational aspects—what I referred to in the preface as the core features—of that language.)

I also claimed in Chapter 1 that, precisely because of the foregoing plan, this book wasn't going to look much like most of the books and presentations currently available in the marketplace that purport to be an introduction to relational databases. What's more, I don't think the chapters in this part of the book are going to look much like the usual introductory books and presentations on SQL either, come to that.

Incidentally, I do believe that learning the relational model first and SQL second is much easier than doing it the other way around. Part of the reason for this state of affairs is that doing it the other way around typically requires rather a lot of *un*learning (and as I said in the preface, unlearning can be very difficult, as we all know).

A LITTLE HISTORY

The SQL language was originally defined in IBM's Research Division in the early 1970s. The first paper on the subject to be published outside IBM appeared in the proceedings of the ACM SIGMOD Workshop on Data Description, Access, and Control (May 1st–3rd, 1974), under the

---

[1] The name SQL is officially pronounced "ess cue ell," though as noted in Chapter 1 the pronunciation "sequel" is often heard. In this book I assume the official pronunciation, thereby writing things like "an SQL table" (not "a SQL table").

title "SEQUEL: A Structured English Query Language," by Donald Chamberlin and Raymond Boyce.[2] (The name was subsequently changed to SQL—"Structured Query Language"—for legal reasons.[3] Of course, the earlier name accounts for the "sequel" pronunciation still commonly encountered.) It's interesting to note, incidentally, that SEQUEL (or SQL) was explicitly intended to be different from both the relational calculus and (perhaps to a lesser extent) the relational algebra, though it did subsequently grow to incorporate features of both.

The language was implemented in IBM Research as the interface to an ambitious and would-be industrial strength prototype called System R. Then it was reimplemented in the IBM products SQL/DS and DB2[4]—both of which first became generally available in the early 1980s—as well as in various nonIBM products, most notably Oracle (which first became generally available in 1979, before IBM's own products did). In 1986 the American National Standards Institute (ANSI) developed a standard version of the language, very closely based on the IBM dialect and known, somewhat informally, as SQL/86. Then in 1987 the International Organization for Standardization (ISO), of which ANSI is the United States member organization, adopted SQL/86 as an international standard. That international standard has since gone through numerous editions, or versions: SQL/89, SQL:1992, SQL:1999, SQL:2003, SQL:2008, and—the version current at the time of writing—SQL:2011. Here's the formal reference:

> International Organization for Standardization (ISO), *Database Language SQL*, Document ISO/IEC 9075:2011.

Please note that, barring explicit statements to the contrary, all references to SQL in this book should be understood as referring to the foregoing standard version specifically. Of course, your mileage may vary, as they say—no commercial product supports the standard in its entirety, while at the same time every product does support a variety of proprietary features that are peculiar to that particular product and aren't part of the standard at all. On the other hand, since I'm limiting myself in what follows to SQL's core features, it's reasonable to expect that those features, at least, are supported—by which I mean, of course, supported in accordance with what the standard dictates—in whatever your favorite SQL product happens to be.

Incidentally, it's worth mentioning that the official standard has become a positively enormous document (or set of documents, rather). First of all, it consists of a number of separate "Parts," as follows:

Part 1:   Framework
Part 2:   Foundation

---

[2] The Boyce of Boyce/Codd normal form, in fact (see Chapter 9).

[3] To repeat, *SQL* originally stood for "Structured Query Language," but nowadays—at least as far as the standard is concerned—it's just a name, and it doesn't stand for anything at all.

[4] Actually SQL/DS was heavily based on the System R code; by contrast, DB2 truly was a complete reimplementation.

I don't intend to elaborate on these various Parts here, except to say that Part 2 by itself (which deals with the core of the language) consists of nearly 1500 pages, including several pages of "possible problems" and "language opportunities" [*sic*]. I'll leave it to you to meditate on the significance of all of these various facts and figures.

BASIC CONCEPTS

The basic data construct in SQL is not a relation as such but, rather, an *SQL table* (with rows and columns in place of tuples and attributes). Thus, an SQL version of the suppliers-and-parts database consists of three tables. (*Note:* It goes without saying that I'll be using the term *table*, unqualified, in this part of the book to mean an SQL table specifically, barring explicit statements to the contrary.) And the basic operational construct is the *SELECT – FROM – WHERE expression*, which is used to derive "new" tables from "old" ones. Here, for example, is an SQL formulation of the query "Get supplier numbers and cities for suppliers with status greater than 10":

```
SELECT  SNO , CITY
FROM    S
WHERE   STATUS > 10
```

Now let's take a closer look.

PROPERTIES OF TABLES

Recall from Chapter 2 that relations possess the following properties:

- They never contain duplicate tuples.

- Their tuples are unordered, top to bottom.

- Their attributes are unordered, left to right.

■ They're always normalized.

We also saw at numerous points in Part I how important these relational properties were. So how do SQL tables measure up against them? The broad answer is: Not very well. I'll consider each in turn.

Relations never contain duplicate tuples: But SQL tables can contain duplicate rows—in fact, by default they do, unless explicit steps are taken to prohibit them. Right away, therefore, you can see that an SQL table is not, in general, the same thing as a relation.

The tuples of a relation are unordered, top to bottom: And the rows of an SQL table are likewise unordered, top to bottom—so on this point, at least, SQL and the relational model are in agreement.

The attributes of a relation are unordered, left to right: But the columns of an SQL table do have a left to right ordering, always. In other words, in an SQL table, in contrast to relations, there *is* such a thing as "the first column," "the second column" (and so on). Again, therefore, you can see that an SQL table is not, in general, the same thing as a relation.[5]

Relations are always normalized: Recall first that *normalized* here just refers to first normal form; it simply means that every tuple in the relation in question contains exactly one value (of the applicable type) for each attribute, and nothing else besides. But SQL tables can contain rows with *nothing at all* in one or more column positions—and so yet again you can see that an SQL table is not, in general, the same thing as a relation. By way of example, Fig. 10.1 shows an SQL table for suppliers, in which there's no STATUS value for supplier S3 and no CITY value for supplier S5.

S

SNO	SNAME	STATUS	CITY
S1	Smith	20	London
S2	Jones	10	Paris
S3	Blake		Paris
S4	Clark	20	London
S5	Adams	30	

Fig. 10.1: An SQL suppliers table, with nulls

By the way, do please note carefully that although I've had to use blank spaces in Fig. 10.1 to mark the places where values are missing, the pertinent rows do *not* contain blank spaces in

---

[5] Actually we could say an SQL table is *never* the same thing as a relation, except possibly if the table in question has just one column.

those positions—rather, as I said before, they don't contain anything at all. SQL would say those positions "are null." Now, it's difficult to talk coherently about SQL's nulls; indeed, if you ever try to do so, you'll be led very quickly and inevitably to the conclusion that they make no logical sense at all. So I'm not even going to attempt such an explanation here; instead, I'll content myself with the following brief observations.

- SQL's nulls are intended to address the problem—which, let me hasten to add, is certainly a genuine problem, and one that definitely needs a solution—that information in the real world is often incomplete. For example, in the real world we often need to deal with things like "present address unknown," "speaker to be announced," and so on. So the problem is indeed a real problem. Unfortunately, however, SQL's nulls don't solve that problem; in fact they make matters much worse, because they manage to introduce additional, and horrendous, complications and difficulties of their own.[6]

- In any case, SQL's nulls clearly violate the prescriptions of the relational model, if only because a null, by definition, isn't a value, and SQL tables with nulls therefore violate *The Information Principle.*[7] *Note:* Actually, SQL sometimes thinks null is a value, and sometimes it thinks it isn't; in other words, it's ambivalent about the issue. But nulls most certainly aren't values, and SQL's frequent attempts to treat them as if they were simply constitute another respect in which the language is deeply and logically flawed.

Further specifics are beyond the scope of this book. Suffice it to say that (as is shown in *SQL and Relational Theory*) you can never trust the answers you get from an SQL database with nulls. I regard this state of affairs as a complete showstopper! So my message has to be: *Don't use SQL nulls, nor any SQL feature related to them.* (And in this book, I'll ignore them totally from this point forward, except when I'm forced by circumstances to mention them in passing.)

More on Terminology

As you know, the relational model distinguishes very carefully between relation values ("relations") and relation variables ("relvars"). And an analogous distinction certainly exists in SQL, necessarily—but analogous terminology doesn't. That is, SQL doesn't use terms like "table value" and "table variable"; instead it uses the same term, *table* (unqualified), for both. In effect, therefore, it relies on that term being interpreted appropriately, according to context.

---

[6] For a lengthy discussion of several approaches to solving the problem—approaches that don't suffer from the difficulties that nulls give rise to—see *Database Explorations: Essays on The Third Manifesto and Related Topics* (Trafford, 2010), by Hugh Darwen and myself. A much briefer discussion of one of those approaches can be found in *SQL and Relational Theory* as well, where some of the specific complications caused by SQL's nulls are also described.

[7] But then so do SQL tables with duplicate rows, and so too do SQL tables with left to right column ordering—which is to say, *all* SQL tables (with the trivial exception, already noted, of tables with just one column, where that left to right ordering doesn't hurt).

SQL also has nothing corresponding to the relational terms *heading* and *body*. In fact (and more fundamentally), it doesn't really even have a proper notion of table type![8]

TABLE UPDATES

SQL has no explicit table assignment operator. But of course it does have INSERT, DELETE, and UPDATE statements (no D_INSERT or I_DELETE, though). By way of example, I show below SQL counterparts to the **Tutorial D** examples I gave in Chapter 2 (I repeat the **Tutorial D** formulations as well, for convenience—**Tutorial D** first, then SQL, in each case):

```
INSERT SP RELATION                                   /* Tutorial D */
       { TUPLE { SNO 'S5' , PNO 'P1' , QTY 250 } ,
         TUPLE { SNO 'S5' , PNO 'P3' , QTY 450 } } ;

INSERT INTO SP ( SNO , PNO , QTY )                   /* SQL        */
       VALUES ( 'S5' , 'P1' , 250 ) ,
              ( 'S5' , 'P3' , 450 ) ;

DELETE SP WHERE QTY < 150 ;                          /* Tutorial D */

DELETE FROM SP WHERE QTY < 150 ;                     /* SQL        */

UPDATE SP WHERE SNO = 'S2' : { QTY := 2 * QTY } ;    /* Tutorial D */

UPDATE SP                                            /* SQL        */
SET    QTY := 2 * QTY
WHERE  SNO = 'S2';
```

EQUALITY COMPARISONS

In Chapter 1, I said the operators supported in connection with any given type *T* must include the equality comparison operator, because without it we couldn't even tell whether a given value *v* is an element of a given set *S*.[9] I also said the comparison $v1 = v2$ must give TRUE if and only if *v1* and *v2* are the very same value (and are thus of the same type, necessarily), and hence that if some operator *Op* is such that $Op(v1) \neq Op(v2)$, then $v1 = v2$ must give FALSE. How does SQL match up to these requirements?

Well, first let's consider the case where *T* is a table type specifically. As we've already seen, SQL doesn't really support such a type; a fortiori, therefore, there's no possibility of its supporting an equality operator in connection with such a type. *Note:* Actually there's quite a

---

[8] Don't be misled here by the fact that it does have something it calls, most inappropriately, "typed tables" (again, see *SQL and Relational Theory* for further explanation).

[9] Implying in particular, incidentally, that we couldn't even tell whether a given value *v* is a value of that given type *T*.

bit more to be said about this particular issue, but I'll defer further discussion to the section "Table Comparisons" in Chapter 11.

What about the case where T is some scalar type? Unfortunately, the picture here is rather complicated, and I can give only the briefest of brief summaries. First of all, SQL supports *coercions* (i.e., implicit type conversions), with the consequence among other things that "=" can give TRUE even when the comparands are of different types. Second, in the case of certain character string types in particular, it's possible for "=" to give TRUE even when the comparands are of the same type but clearly distinct (I'll give an example in just a moment). And it's also possible—for all types, not just for character string types—for "=" not to give TRUE even when the comparands aren't distinguishable; in particular, this happens when, but not only when, the comparands are both null. Also, for the system defined type XML, and possibly for certain user defined types as well, "=" isn't defined at all.

By way of a simple illustration of the foregoing, let the character string variables X and Y have as their values the strings 'AB' and 'AB ', respectively (note the trailing space in the second of these). Now, these two values are clearly distinct; yet, depending on circumstances, the comparison X = Y can give TRUE, even though the comparison CHAR_LENGTH (X) = CHAR_LENGTH (Y) certainly doesn't. (The comparands in this latter comparison evaluate to 3 and 2, respectively.) Note too that even if that comparison X = Y does gives TRUE, the comparison X| |X = Y| |Y doesn't![10] I leave the detailed implications of such bizarre behavior for you to think about; suffice it to say that the consequences can be quite unpleasant, as you would probably expect.

Finally, let me mention for completeness that SQL does support equality comparisons (also other kinds of comparisons) in connection with row types. However, the details are beyond the scope of this book; refer to *SQL and Relational Theory* for a detailed explanation.

TABLE DEFINITIONS

Now I can show the SQL definitions—CREATE TABLE statements, in SQL—for tables S, P, and SP. First table S:

```
CREATE TABLE S
     ( SNO    VARCHAR(5)   NOT NULL ,
       SNAME  VARCHAR(25)  NOT NULL ,
       STATUS INTEGER      NOT NULL ,
       CITY   VARCHAR(20)  NOT NULL ,
       UNIQUE ( SNO ) ) ;
```

Points arising:

---

[10] Neither does the comparison X LIKE Y, incidentally—in other words, in SQL, *v1* and *v2* can be equal but not "like" each other (!).

- Table S is, implicitly, a base table (analogous to a base relvar in **Tutorial D**). *Note:* SQL supports views too, as I'm sure you would expect, but the specifics are beyond the scope of this book.

- Lines 2-6 of the definition specify the columns of that table and certain integrity constraints that apply to that table. Each column is named, has a type, and—thanks to the specification NOT NULL—is constrained not to allow nulls. The column type can be any known SQL type; note, however, that SQL doesn't support a type exactly analogous to **Tutorial D**'s CHAR type (see Chapter 1), so I've shown columns SNO, SNAME, and CITY as being of type VARCHAR ("varying length character string"), with an arbitrarily chosen but required maximum length in each case. Of course, the order in which the columns are specified is significant, because it defines the left to right order of those columns within the table.

- The specification UNIQUE (SNO) is an SQL counterpart to the **Tutorial D** specification KEY{SNO}.

- By default, base tables are initially empty (it's possible to specify a nonempty initial value, but the details are beyond the scope of this book).

Important: Note carefully that there's nothing—no sequence of linguistic tokens—in the foregoing CREATE TABLE statement that can logically be labeled "an invocation of the TABLE type generator." (This fact might become more apparent when you realize that the specification UNIQUE(SNO), which defines a certain integrity constraint, doesn't have to come after the column definitions but can appear almost anywhere—e.g., between the definitions of columns SNO and SNAME. Not to mention the NOT NULL specifications on individual column definitions, which also define certain integrity constraints.) In other words, as I've already said, SQL doesn't support a table type generator, and it doesn't really have a proper notion of "table type" at all.

Here now are the definitions of tables P and SP, which I take to be pretty much self-explanatory:

```
CREATE TABLE P
      ( PNO    VARCHAR(6)    NOT NULL ,
        PNAME  VARCHAR(25)   NOT NULL ,
        COLOR  VARCHAR(10)   NOT NULL ,
        WEIGHT NUMERIC(5,1)  NOT NULL ,
        CITY   VARCHAR(20)   NOT NULL ,
        UNIQUE ( PNO ) ) ;
```

```
CREATE TABLE SP
      ( SNO VARCHAR(5) NOT NULL ,
        PNO VARCHAR(6) NOT NULL ,
        QTY  INTEGER } NOT NULL ,
        UNIQUE ( SNO , PNO ) ,
        FOREIGN KEY ( SNO ) REFERENCES S ( SNO ) ,
        FOREIGN KEY ( PNO ) REFERENCES P ( PNO ) ) ;
```

"Table Literals"

SQL doesn't use the term *table literal*, but it does support a construct, the VALUES expression, that provides some of the same functionality. Here's an example:

```
VALUES ( 'S1' , 'Smith' , 20 , 'London' ) ,
       ( 'S2' , 'Jones' , 10 , 'Paris'  ) ,
       ( 'S3' , 'Blake' , 30 , 'Paris'  ) ,
       ( 'S4' , 'Clark' , 20 , 'London' ) ,
       ( 'S5' , 'Adams' , 30 , 'Athens' )
```

(As a matter of fact, we've seen an example of a VALUES expression already, in the INSERT example in the section "Table Updates.")

By the way, note the dependence on left to right column ordering in the foregoing VALUES expression. Note too that a genuine table literal ought by rights to be allowed to appear anywhere a table expression is allowed to appear, but there are places in SQL where a table expression can appear but a VALUES expression can't (see the exercises in Chapter 14). That's why I said only that such expressions provide *some* table literal functionality.

SQL SYSTEMS vs. PROGRAMMING SYSTEMS

Once again recall the code fragment shown in Fig. 1.3 in Chapter 1, which I used to illustrate various familiar concepts from the world of programming: statements, types, variables, assignment, literals, and read-only operators (including comparison operators as a special case). Recall too that I claimed that all of these concepts were directly relevant to databases. Let's see how far we've come in this regard with respect to SQL specifically. In brief:

- **SQL statements:** We've seen the SQL INSERT, DELETE, and UPDATE statements, also the CREATE TABLE statement.

- **SQL types:** We've seen various COLUMN types—VARCHAR(n), INTEGER, and NUMERIC(p,q)—and I've briefly mentioned certain other types as well, including user defined types in particular. Unfortunately, we've also seen that tables as such *don't* have types, in SQL.

- **Table variables:** The concept exists in SQL but not the terminology.

■ **Table assignment:** INSERT, DELETE, and UPDATE are supported, but not table assignment as such.

■ **Table literals:** See the discussion of VALUES expressions in the previous section. *Note:* We've also seen examples of scalar literals (e.g., 'S1', 'Smith', 20, 'London'); as a matter of fact, we've seen examples of row literals as well—the parenthesized expression ('S1', 'Smith', 20, 'London') being a case in point.

■ **Table values:** The concept exists in SQL but not the terminology; the values of S, P, and SP at any given time are such values. So too is the value denoted by a VALUES expression, of course.

■ **Table read-only operators:** These are still to be discussed in detail (in Chapters 11 and 12), though we've seen one example already—the expression SELECT SNO, CITY FROM S WHERE STATUS > 10 in the section "Basic Concepts," which is SQL syntax for a certain projection of a certain restriction.

■ **Table comparison operators:** These too will be discussed in Chapter 11, as mentioned earlier (in the section "Equality Comparisons").

EXERCISES

Which of the following statements are true?

10.1 SQL tables have no ordering to their rows.

10.2 SQL tables have no ordering to their columns.

10.3 SQL tables never have any unnamed columns.

10.4 SQL tables never have two or more columns with the same name.

10.5 SQL tables never contain duplicate rows.

10.6 SQL tables are always in 1NF.

10.7 The types over which SQL columns are defined can be arbitrarily complex.

10.8 SQL tables themselves have types.

10.9 SQL tables can have pointer valued columns.

ANSWERS

Before going into details on the answers here, I'd like to call your attention up front to the fact that exactly two of the points mentioned (out of a total of nine) are ones on which SQL and the relational model are in agreement. I'll leave you to draw your own conclusions from this state of affairs.

10.1 SQL tables have no ordering to their rows: *True.*

10.2 SQL tables have no ordering to their columns: *False.*

10.3 SQL tables never have any unnamed columns: *False.* It's true that *base* tables never have any unnamed columns (the same goes for views, incidentally). Unfortunately, however, certain table expressions do indeed produce a result with columns that have no name. Here's a trivial example of such an expression, together with the table denoted by that expression (given our usual sample values, of course):

```
SELECT PNO , 2 * WEIGHT
FROM   P
```

PNO	
P1	24.0
P2	34.0
P3	34.0
P4	28.0
P5	24.0
P6	38.0

Note: What the standard actually says in regard to this issue is that a result column that apparently has no name is supposed to be given a name by the DBMS—a name that's unique within the containing table but is otherwise undefined. But this prescription on the part of the standard was, and is, essentially nothing more than a belated attempt to fix a situation that was already broken (and indeed had been broken right from the outset). Note too that those undefined names will certainly vary from one DBMS to another; what's more, discovering just what the names are in any given situation is a highly nontrivial matter. In practice, therefore, it's really not too far from the truth to say the columns in question simply don't have a name.

10.4 SQL tables never have two or more columns with the same name: *False.* Again, it's true that *base* tables never have two columns with the same name (and the same goes for views), but certain table expressions do indeed produce a result with two or more columns that have the same name (and even the same type). Here's a trivial example of such an expression, together with the table denoted by that expression (again, given our usual sample values):

```
SELECT  PNO , PNO
FROM    P
```

PNO	PNO
P1	P1
P2	P2
P3	P3
P4	P4
P5	P5
P6	P6

Note: A more realistic example might be as follows:

```
SELECT  *
FROM    S , P
```

This expression gives a result with two CITY columns. See Chapter 11 for further explanation.

10.5 SQL tables never contain duplicate rows: *False.* It's true that, in the case of base tables specifically, a UNIQUE specification will prevent duplicate rows from occurring—but such a specification is optional! As for the result of a table expression, see Chapter 11.

10.6 SQL tables are always in 1NF: *False.* A table can be said to be in 1NF only if it's a faithful representation of some relation, which SQL tables almost never are. *Note:* It's true that, in the case of base tables specifically, NOT NULL specifications will at least ensure that every row does have a value (of the appropriate type) in every column position, but such specifications are optional. What's more, certain table expressions can produce a result with nulls, even if there aren't any nulls in the input (see Chapter 12 for at least one example). And in any case, there's always that business of left to right column ordering—not to mention the possibility of unnamed columns and the possibility of duplicate column names.

10.7 The types over which SQL columns are defined can be arbitrarily complex. *True.*

10.8 SQL tables themselves have types: *False*.

10.9 SQL tables can have pointer valued columns: *True*. I didn't discuss this issue in the body of the chapter, but, sadly, a table in SQL is indeed allowed to have a column whose values are pointers to rows in some "target" table. The pointers are called *reference values*, and the columns that contain them are said to be of some *REF type*. Frankly, it's not clear why these features are included in SQL at all; certainly there seems to be no useful functionality that can be achieved with them that can't equally well—in fact, better—be achieved without them. But the fact remains that these features *are* included. Don't use them!

Chapter 11

S Q L   O p e r a t o r s   I

You know my methods. Apply them.
—Arthur Conan Doyle: *The Sign of Four* (1890)

Now we can begin to examine the question of how, or to what extent, SQL supports the various operators of the relational algebra. For obvious reasons, the structure of this chapter deliberately parallels that of Chapter 4 in Part I of the book. First, however, let me remind you that:

- SQL tables can contain duplicate rows—so you should take steps to prohibit them wherever you can (at least if you want the tables in question to be amenable to relational processing).

- SQL tables have a left to right ordering to their attributes—but try not to write code that relies on that ordering, because such code is (by definition) not relational.

- SQL tables can contain nulls—*but don't let them!*

Note: The book *SQL and Relational Theory* describes a discipline it refers to as "using SQL relationally." The idea is that if you abide by the recommendations in that book, then you can behave almost as if SQL truly were relational, and you can enjoy the benefits of working with what is, in effect, a truly relational system (or close to one, at any rate). And it probably goes without saying that the SQL discussions in the present book do abide by those recommendations, pretty much. As I've said before, I'm not trying to cover the whole of SQL here, I'm just trying to cover those aspects that are at least somewhat relational.

RESTRICT

Most of the time I plan to use the same examples in this chapter as I did in Chapter 4. So here's the query I used in that chapter to introduce the restrict operator: "Get part information for parts whose weight is less than 12.5 pounds." For purposes of comparison, let me first repeat the **Tutorial D** formulation:

```
P WHERE WEIGHT < 12.5
```

Here's an SQL formulation:

```
SELECT PNO , PNAME , COLOR , WEIGHT , CITY
FROM    P
WHERE   WEIGHT < 12.5
```

Points arising:

■ Unlike **Tutorial D**, SQL supports *dot qualified references*. In fact, the expression just shown is effectively shorthand for this one (note the dot qualifications in the SELECT and WHERE clauses):

```
SELECT P.PNO , P.PNAME , P.COLOR , P.WEIGHT , P.CITY
FROM    P
WHERE   P.WEIGHT < 12.5
```

I could have formulated the query with any or all of these dot qualifications shown explicitly, if I'd wanted to.

■ SQL also supports another shorthand, illustrated here:

```
SELECT P.*
FROM    P
WHERE   P.WEIGHT < 12.5
```

The expression "P.*" in the SELECT clause here is defined to be shorthand for a commalist of references to all of the columns in table P, in the left to right order in which they appear within that table. Precisely because of that reliance on left to right ordering, however, there are traps for the unwary in this notation, and I won't use it again in this book unless I have some specific point I want to make in connection with it. Here let me just note that (once again) the dot qualification is optional; that is, I could have written just "SELECT *" in place of "SELECT P.*".

■ Like **Tutorial D**, SQL allows WHERE clauses to contain boolean expressions that are more general than a simple restriction condition. We'll see some examples later.

PROJECT

Consider the query "For each part, get part number, color, and city." Again I'll repeat the **Tutorial D** formulation from Chapter 4 first, then show an SQL counterpart:

```
P { PNO , COLOR , CITY }

SELECT PNO , COLOR , CITY
FROM   P
```

Note: SQL has nothing analogous to **Tutorial D**'s ALL BUT feature.

Now we come to an extremely important point. The second projection example in Chapter 4 involved the query "What part color and city combinations currently exist?" Here's the **Tutorial D** formulation:

```
P { COLOR , CITY }
```

Now, the most obvious SQL "counterpart" to this **Tutorial D** expression is the following:

```
SELECT COLOR , CITY
FROM   P
```

But here's the result:

COLOR	CITY
Red	London
Red	London
Red	London
Green	Paris
Blue	Oslo
Blue	Paris

As you can see, *this result isn't a relation*: It contains duplicates, and it therefore doesn't satisfy any key constraints (observe the lack of double underlining in the picture). In other words, SQL SELECT expressions, unlike projection operations in the relational model, do *not* eliminate duplicates—at least, not unless they're explicitly asked to do so. And the way to ask them to do so is to specify the keyword DISTINCT immediately prior to the commalist of expressions in the SELECT clause, as in the following revised version of the example:

```
SELECT DISTINCT COLOR , CITY
FROM   P
```

Now the result looks like this:

COLOR	CITY
Red	London
Green	Paris
Blue	Oslo
Blue	Paris

Points arising:

- Specifying DISTINCT in the first example above wouldn't have been incorrect, but it would have had no effect (why, exactly?). In general, though, omitting DISTINCT means you're doing something nonrelational, and therefore I have to say: Don't do that.

- At this point in Chapter 4, in order to illustrate the closure property of the relational algebra, I gave an example involving both restriction and projection. The query was "Get part number, color, and city for parts whose weight is less than 12.5 pounds." Here for the record is an SQL formulation of this query (it's essentially similar to the SELECT expression I showed in the section "Basic Concepts" near the beginning of Chapter 10):

```
SELECT DISTINCT PNO , COLOR , CITY   /* DISTINCT could be omitted */
FROM    P
WHERE   WEIGHT < 12.5
```

UNION, INTERSECTION, AND DIFFERENCE

Consider the query "Get cities in which at least one supplier or at least one part is located." **Tutorial D** formulation:

```
S { CITY } UNION P { CITY }
```

SQL analog:

```
SELECT CITY FROM S
UNION
SELECT CITY FROM P
```

The odd thing here is that, with UNION (unlike with "projection"), SQL does eliminate duplicates by default.[1] But it's not wrong to specify DISTINCT explicitly, as here:

```
SELECT CITY FROM S
UNION   DISTINCT
SELECT CITY FROM P
```

You could even write this:

---

[1] To spell the point out: There won't be any duplicates in the result, even if the same row appears in both operand tables, and even if there are duplicates in either or both of those operand tables.

```
SELECT DISTINCT CITY FROM S
UNION   DISTINCT
SELECT DISTINCT CITY FROM P
```

Recall now that in the relational model, the operands to UNION are required to be of the same type (i.e., to have the same heading), and the result is then of the same type as well. However, SQL tables have no type, so this simple rule can't possibly apply, and it doesn't. In fact, the SQL rules regarding the operands and result of a UNION operation are quite complex—much too complex to describe in detail here. (Of course, the reason they're so complex is *precisely* because SQL has no table type notion.) Anyway, suffice it to say that so long as you specify the optional keyword CORRESPONDING immediately following UNION or UNION DISTINCT, then the SQL rules degenerate, more or less, to the relational rules. To be more precise about the matter, if tables *t1* and *t2* both have columns called *C1*, *C2*, ..., *Cn* (only), and if column *Ci* in *t1* and column *Ci* in *t2* are both of the same type ($i = 1, 2, ..., n$), then the expression

```
SELECT C1 , C2 , ... , Cn FROM t1
UNION   [ DISTINCT ] CORRESPONDING
SELECT C1 , C2 , ... , Cn FROM t2
```

will produce a result with no duplicate rows and with the same column names and types as each of *t1* and *t2*. In fact, so long as you do specify CORRESPONDING, you don't even have to specify the columns in the same left to right order in the two SELECT clause commalists.[2] But if you omit CORRESPONDING, then you're doing something nonrelational, and so I have to say again: Don't.

As for intersection (INTERSECT) and difference (EXCEPT), everything I've said above regarding union applies equally to these operators, mutatis mutandis. Thus, I don't think it's worth showing examples.

Formal Properties

Recall from Chapter 4 that the relational union operator possesses certain important formal properties: It's *commutative* (*r1* UNION *r2* and *r2* UNION *r1* are equivalent), *associative* (*r1* UNION (*r2* UNION *r3*) and (*r1* UNION *r2*) UNION *r3* are equivalent), and *idempotent* (*r* UNION *r* reduces to simply *r*). Similar remarks apply to the relational intersection operator, mutatis mutandis. But the SQL analogs of these operators are, in general, *not* commutative (thanks to left to right column ordering) and *not* idempotent (thanks to duplicate rows). They are, however, associative.

---

[2] As this remark suggests (a trifle obliquely), if you don't specify CORRESPONDING, then columns are considered to correspond if and only if they appear at the same ordinal position in the left to right ordering within the two SELECT clause commalists. Note, however, that even if you do specify CORRESPONDING, columns will appear in the result in the left to right order in which they're specified in the first of those two commalists. In other words, even here, we can't get away entirely from that left to right column ordering "feature" of SQL. But don't write code that relies on this fact!

RENAME

In Chapter 4, I used the following query to introduce the need for RENAME: "Get names such that at least one supplier or at least one part has the name in question." (As I said in that chapter, the example was very contrived, but it sufficed to illustrate the point I want to make.) **Tutorial D** formulation:

```
( ( S RENAME { SNAME AS NAME } ) { NAME }. )
  UNION
( ( P RENAME { PNAME AS NAME } ) { NAME } )
```

Here's an SQL analog:

```
SELECT SNAME AS NAME FROM S
UNION  CORRESPONDING
SELECT PNAME AS NAME FROM P
```

As you can see, therefore, SQL does in effect support the RENAME operator; it does so by means of AS specifications in the commalist of expressions in the SELECT clause. *Note:* I could have omitted the keyword CORRESPONDING in this example with impunity, since the operand tables each have just one column. But it's not wrong to include it.

EXERCISES I

11.1 Write SQL expressions for the following queries:

a. Get all shipments.

b. Get part numbers for parts supplied by supplier S2.

c. Get suppliers with status in the range 15 to 25 inclusive.

d. Get supplier numbers for suppliers with status lower than that of supplier S2.

e. Get part numbers for parts supplied by all suppliers in Paris.

11.2 Try writing SQL expressions for some queries of your own—preferably on a database of your own but, failing that, on the suppliers-and-parts database.

ANSWERS I

11.1 Note that **Tutorial D** formulations for these queries were given in the answer to Exercise 4.7 in Chapter 4.

a.
```
SELECT SNO , PNO , QTY
FROM   SP
```

b.
```
SELECT DISTINCT PNO
FROM   SP
WHERE  SNO = 'S2'
```

Note: We don't need to specify DISTINCT here—but why not?

c.
```
SELECT SNO , SNAME , STATUS , CITY
FROM   S
WHERE  STATUS >= 15 AND STATUS <= 25
```

d.
```
SELECT SNO
FROM   S
WHERE  STATUS <
     ( SELECT STATUS
       FROM   S
       WHERE  SNO = 'S2' )
```

Like its **Tutorial D** counterpart in Chapter 4, this answer requires a certain amount of explanation. First, note that we have here an illustration of the point that, in SQL just as in **Tutorial D**, the boolean expression in the WHERE clause can, in general, be more complicated than just a simple restriction condition. Second, the subexpression following the "<" symbol— which consists of a SELECT – FROM – WHERE expression enclosed in parentheses—is an example of an SQL *subquery*.[3] Conceptually, at least, that subquery is evaluated first, to return a table of one row and one column that looks like this, given our usual sample data values:[4]

STATUS
10

---

[3] Incidentally, it was this ability to nest one SELECT – FROM – WHERE expression inside another (to any depth, of course) that was the justification for the appearance of that "Structured" in the original name of the SQL (or SEQUEL) language.

[4] The lack of double underlining in pictures like this one is *not* a mistake. See *SQL and Relational Theory* for further discussion of this point.

A double coercion (i.e., implicit type conversion) now occurs: The table is coerced to the single row it contains, and that row in turn is coerced to the single scalar value it contains. (By contrast, **Tutorial D** required these type conversions to be performed explicitly, as you might recall.) That scalar value can then be plugged back into the original query, to yield:

```
SELECT  SNO
FROM    S
WHERE   STATUS < 10
```

And the desired overall result follows.

But there's something else going on here, too, that warrants some discussion. Here again is the original expression, but this time with all implicit dot qualifications made explicit:

```
SELECT  S.SNO
FROM    S
WHERE   S.STATUS <
      ( SELECT  S.STATUS
        FROM    S
        WHERE   S.SNO = 'S2' )
```

Well, I hope it's obvious that the two column references of the form "S.SNO" in lines 1 and 6 of this expression can't possibly denote the same thing, and the same is true for the two column references of the form "S.STATUS" in lines 3 and 4. In fact, SQL is following some kind of block scoping rules here—though the details of those rules are extremely complex, and a long way beyond the purview of the present book. However, we can make matters more explicit, and possibly clearer (?), by including AS specifications in the FROM clause to introduce names of our own to use as dot qualifiers, as illustrated here:[5]

```
SELECT  X.SNO
FROM    S AS X
WHERE   X.STATUS <
      ( SELECT  Y.STATUS
        FROM    S AS Y
        WHERE   Y.SNO = 'S2' )
```

The symbols X and Y in this revised formulation denote what are called, technically, *range variables*—they're variables (variables in the sense of logic, that is, not programming language variables) that "range over" table S, and, at any given point during evaluation of the overall expression, each of them denotes some row in that table (in general, not the *same* row). Observe that **Tutorial D** has no need of any such construct; in fact, range variables are a feature

---

[5] Note that the AS clauses discussed earlier (in the discussion of column renaming) appeared in the SELECT clause, not the FROM clause.

of the relational calculus (see Chapter 7 or Appendix D), while **Tutorial D** is, of course, b
the relational algebra.

```
e.  SELECT  PNO
    FROM    P
    WHERE   NOT EXISTS
          ( SELECT  *
            FROM    S
            WHERE   CITY = 'Paris'
            AND     NOT EXISTS
                  ( SELECT  *
                    FROM    SP
                    WHERE   S.SNO = SP.SNO
                    AND     SP.PNO = P.PNO ) ) ;
```

Now, this exercise—actually like its counterpart in Chapter 4—was somewhat unfair, because I don't think it can be answered using only the constructs discussed so far in this part of the book. Briefly, however, let me explain that (a) the SQL expression EXISTS *subquery* returns TRUE if and only if the table denoted by *subquery* contains at least one row;[6] (b) the two subqueries in the overall expression are of the *correlated* variety, meaning they include references to items defined in some outer expression; and (c) the problems I mentioned earlier in connection with the use of "SELECT *" don't arise in the context of an EXISTS expression, and so that construct can be used safely in such contexts. (By the way, it's also safe to omit DISTINCT from the SELECT clause in a subquery that represents the argument to an EXISTS invocation—why, exactly?)

11.2 *No answer provided.*

JOIN

SQL has several different ways, or styles, of representing a join operation. The sample join query I used in Chapter 4 was "For each shipment, get the part number and quantity and corresponding supplier details," for which a suitable **Tutorial D** formulation was:

```
SP JOIN S
```

The first SQL style I want to discuss is superficially fairly similar to that **Tutorial D** formulation:

```
SELECT * FROM SP NATURAL JOIN S
```

---

[6] SQL's EXISTS *operator* is its counterpart to the EXISTS *quantifier* of relational calculus (see Appendix D).

arising:

- style relies (as the **Tutorial D** style does also, mutatis mutandis) on the columns on ich the join is to be done having the same names and types in both operand tables—a discipline I strongly recommend you follow in practice, for reasons that *SQL and Relational Theory* explains in detail.

- The expression overall produces a result with columns as follows (in left to right order, of course, as always in SQL): SNO – PNO – QTY – SNAME – STATUS – CITY. In general, the result of SELECT * FROM *t1* NATURAL JOIN *t2* has, first, the joining columns, in the order in which they appear in *t1*, followed by the other columns of *t1* in the order in which they appear in *t1*, followed by the other columns of *t2* in the order in which they appear in *t2*.[7]

- Of course, "SELECT *" is, as explained earlier in the chapter, generally to be avoided. I use it here primarily so that we can see the forest for the trees, as it were, and so focus on the real topic of this section, viz., the join as such. In the recommended formulation, by contrast—

```
SELECT SNO , PNO , QTY , SNAME , STATUS , CITY
FROM   SP NATURAL JOIN S
```

—the join as such does tend to get a little lost (though writing the SELECT and FROM clauses on separate lines helps).

Alternative Formulations

Of course, SQL doesn't actually require you to follow the column naming discipline referred to above. Partly for that reason, I suppose (?), it provides a number of different ways of formulating the foregoing example. I'll show those different ways here for the record, but I don't propose to discuss them in detail:

```
SELECT SP.SNO /* or S.SNO */ , PNO , QTY , SNAME , STATUS , CITY
FROM   SP JOIN S
ON     SP.SNO = S.SNO      /* note the necessary dot qualifications */

SELECT SNO /* not S.SNO or SP.SNO! */ , PNO , QTY , SNAME , STATUS , CITY
FROM   SP JOIN S
USING  ( SNO )
```

---

[7] As I wrote in *SQL and Relational Theory:* Do you begin to see what a pain this left to right ordering business is?

```
SELECT SP.SNO /* or S.SNO */ , PNO , QTY , SNAME , STATUS , CITY
FROM    SP , S
WHERE   SP.SNO = S.SNO      /* note the necessary dot qualifications */
```

Formal Properties

Recall from Chapter 4 that the relational join operator is commutative, associative, and idempotent. By contrast, SQL's join is, in general, *not* commutative (thanks to left to right column ordering) and *not* idempotent (thanks to duplicate rows[8]). It is, however, associative.

Cartesian Product

An example of a cartesian product query is "Get all current supplier and part number pairs." **Tutorial D** formulation:

```
S { SNO } TIMES P { PNO }
```

As for SQL, there are at least two different ways of formulating this query:

```
SELECT SNO , PNO
FROM   S CROSS JOIN P
```

Or more simply:

```
SELECT SNO , PNO
FROM    S , P
```

I also considered this query in Chapter 4: "Get SNO-PNO pairs such that supplier SNO doesn't supply part PNO." **Tutorial D** formulation:

```
( S { SNO } TIMES P { PNO } ) MINUS SP { SNO , PNO }
```

SQL analog:

```
SELECT SNO , PNO
FROM    S , P
EXCEPT CORRESPONDING
SELECT SNO , PNO
FROM    SP
```

---

[8] Thanks also to nulls.

EVALUATING TABLE EXPRESSIONS

In one of his early papers Codd defined, in addition to natural join, an operator he called *θ-join*, where θ denoted any of the usual scalar comparison operators ("=", "≠", "<", and so on). Now, θ-join isn't a primitive operator; in fact, it's defined to be a restriction of a product (which is why I didn't bother to discuss it in Chapter 4). Here by way of example is an SQL formulation of the "not equals" join of suppliers and parts on cities (so θ here is "≠", or "<>" in SQL):

```
SELECT SNO , SNAME , STATUS , S.CITY AS SCITY ,
       PNO , PNAME , COLOR , WEIGHT , P.CITY AS PCITY
FROM   S , P
WHERE  S.CITY <> P.CITY
```

You can think of this expression as being evaluated in three steps, as follows:

1. The FROM clause is evaluated, to yield the product of tables S and P. *Note:* If we were doing this relationally, we would have to rename at least one of the CITY attributes before that product could be computed. SQL gets away with renaming them afterward because its tables have a left to right ordering to their columns, meaning it can distinguish the two CITY columns by their ordinal position. For simplicity, let's ignore this detail.

2. Next, the WHERE clause is evaluated, to yield a restriction of that product by eliminating rows in which the two city values are equal. *Note:* If θ had been "=" instead of "≠" (or "<>", rather, in SQL), this step would have been: Restrict the product by *retaining* just the rows in which the two city values are equal—in which case we would now have formed what's called the *equijoin* of suppliers and parts on cities. In other words, an equijoin is a θ-join for which θ is "=". *Exercise:* What's the difference between an equijoin and a natural join?

3. Finally, the SELECT clause is evaluated, to yield a "projection" of that restriction on the columns specified in the SELECT clause—"projection" in quotes because it won't actually eliminate duplicates, as true projection does, unless DISTINCT is specified. (Actually it's doing some renaming too, in this particular example, and we'll see in Chapter 12 that SELECT provides other functionality too, in general—but for now I want to ignore these details as well, for simplicity.)

At least to a first approximation, then, the FROM clause corresponds to a product, the WHERE clause to a restriction, and the SELECT clause to a projection; thus, the overall SELECT – FROM – WHERE expression denotes a projection of a restriction of a product. It follows that I've just given a loose, but reasonably formal, definition of the *semantics* of SQL's SELECT – FROM – WHERE expressions; equivalently, I've given a *conceptual algorithm* for evaluating such expressions. Now, there's no implication that the DBMS actually has to use that algorithm in order to evaluate such expressions; *au contraire*, it can use any algorithm it likes, just so long as whatever algorithm it does use is guaranteed to give the same result as the conceptual one. And there are often good reasons—usually performance reasons—for using a different algorithm, thereby (for example) evaluating the clauses in a different order or otherwise rewriting the original query. However, the DBMS is free to do such things *only if it can be proved that the algorithm it does use is logically equivalent to the conceptual one.* Indeed, one way to characterize the job of the optimizer is to find an algorithm that's guaranteed to be equivalent to the conceptual one but performs better. (Recall from Chapter 1 that the optimizer is the DBMS component that's responsible for deciding exactly how to implement user requests.)

TABLE COMPARISONS

Chapter 4 discussed the relational comparison operators "=", "≠", "⊆" (is included in), "⊂" (is properly included in), "⊇" (includes), and "⊃" (properly includes). SQL has no direct support for these operators, but workarounds are available. For example, consider the following relational comparison, expressed in **Tutorial D**:

```
S { SNO } ⊃ SP { SNO }
```

The meaning of this expression, considerably paraphrased, is: "Some suppliers supply no parts at all." Here's an SQL analog:

```
      EXISTS ( SELECT SNO FROM S
               EXCEPT CORRESPONDING
               SELECT SNO FROM SP )
AND
NOT EXISTS ( SELECT SNO FROM SP
               EXCEPT CORRESPONDING
               SELECT SNO FROM S )
```

Explanation: Recall from the answer to Exercise 11.1e that the SQL expression EXISTS *subquery* returns TRUE if and only if the table denoted by *subquery* contains at least one row. In the foregoing expression, therefore, the EXISTS portion says there must be at least one supplier number that appears in S and not in SP, and the NOT EXISTS portion says there mustn't be any supplier numbers that appear in SP and not in S. *Note:* We could omit the NOT EXISTS portion if we're prepared to rely on the fact that there's a foreign key constraint from SP to S. Also, we could omit the two CORRESPONDINGs with impunity, since in both cases the operand tables each have just one column. But it's not wrong to include them.

Incidentally, note that EXISTS and NOT EXISTS are effectively SQL's counterparts to **Tutorial D**'s IS_NOT_EMPTY and IS_EMPTY, respectively.

A remark on table equality: I've said that SQL has no direct support for the relational comparison operators in general, and that's true. However, "=" and "≠" are *almost* directly supported. Let me explain. *Warning:* This gets a little complicated!

First of all, the body, if I might be permitted to use that term, of an SQL table is not a set but a *bag*, in general—a bag of rows, to be specific. (Recall from Chapter 5 that a bag is like a set but permits duplicate elements.) Now, SQL does in fact support bags as such—the preferred SQL term is *multisets*—and those bags can contain elements of many different kinds;[9] bags of rows are just a special case. Now, a bag of rows in SQL isn't the same thing as a table in SQL, even though the two constructs might appear to be rather similar on their face, because the operators that apply to SQL tables are not, in general, available for SQL's row-bags (as I'll call them from this point forward for the purposes of this brief discussion). However, it is at least possible to convert an instance of either one of these constructs into an instance of the other.

Now, one significant difference between SQL row-bags and SQL tables is that equality comparisons on row-bags *are* directly supported, unlike equality comparisons on tables. So if we want to test whether two tables, say the projection of table S on CITY and the projection of table P on CITY, are equal, what we can do is convert those two tables into row-bags and do the equality test on those two row-bags.

Well, I hope you're OK with what I've said so far ... but now I'm probably going to confuse you when I tell you that the operator for converting a table to a row-bag is called—of all things!—*TABLE*. Thus, in order to test whether the projections of tables S and P on CITY are equal, what we can write is this:

```
TABLE ( SELECT DISTINCT CITY FROM S ) =
TABLE ( SELECT DISTINCT CITY FROM P )
```

At the risk of confusing you even further, let me now tell you that the rows in the row-bags produced by a TABLE operator invocation *have no column names*. Thus, the row-bags being compared in the foregoing example actually look like this:

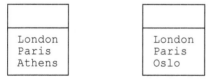

By the way, those DISTINCTs in the example are really necessary. For example, if the value London appeared exactly twice in the CITY column in table S and exactly three times

---

[9] The elements in any specific bag must all be of the *same* kind, however.

in the CITY column of table P (and if no other CITY value appeared at all in either table), then the corresponding projections would be equal but the corresponding row-bags, without duplicate elimination, wouldn't be. *End of remark.*

DISPLAYING RESULTS

Like the tuples of a relation, the rows of an SQL table are unordered, top to bottom. But when a table is displayed on paper or a video screen, then of course the rows do necessarily appear in some top to bottom sequence. What's more, it's helpful to the user if that sequence is meaningful, not just random (because humans are very good at recognizing and dealing with patterns like the ones represented by some meaningful ordering). For such reasons, SQL provides an ORDER BY operator, whose purpose is to convert a table as such into a sequence of rows.[10] For example:

```
SELECT  SNO , CITY
FROM    S
WHERE   CITY <> 'Athens'
ORDER   BY CITY
```

Of course, there's nothing in the relational algebra corresponding to ORDER BY, because ORDER BY isn't a relational operator, precisely because its result isn't a relation. Now, please don't misunderstand me here; I'm not saying ORDER BY isn't useful; however, I *am* saying it can't sensibly appear as part of a relational expression.

As a matter of fact, ORDER BY differs from operators of the relational algebra in another respect also: viz., it's not a *function*. All of the operators of the relational algebra described in this book—in fact, all read-only operators, in effect, as that term is usually understood—*are* functions, meaning there's always just one possible output for any given input. By contrast, ORDER BY can produce several different outputs from the same input. As an illustration of this point, consider the ORDER BY example shown above. Given our usual sample values, the expression overall can clearly return any of four distinct results, corresponding to the following sequences (I'll show just the supplier numbers, for simplicity):

- S1 , S4 , S3 , S5

- S1 , S4 , S5 , S3

- S4 , S1 , S3 , S5

- S4 , S1 , S5 , S3

---

[10] **Tutorial D** supports a similar operator, which it calls just ORDER.

A remark on functions: I've said that all of the operators of the relational algebra described in this book are functions. I note, however, that most of those operators have counterparts in SQL that aren't! This state of affairs is due to the fact that, as explained in Chapter 10, SQL sometimes defines the result of the comparison *v1* = *v2* to be TRUE even when *v1* and *v2* are distinct. For example, consider the character strings 'Paris' and 'Paris ', respectively (note the trailing spaces in the second of these). These values are clearly distinct, and yet SQL sometimes regards them as equal. As a consequence, certain SQL expressions are what the standard calls "possibly nondeterministic." Here's a simple example:

```
SELECT DISTINCT CITY FROM S
```

If one supplier has CITY value 'Paris' and another 'Paris ', then the result will include either 'Paris' or 'Paris ' (or possibly both), but which result we get might not be defined. We could even legitimately get one result on one day and another on another, even if the database hasn't changed at all in the interim. You might like to meditate on some of the implications of this state of affairs. *End of remark.*

EXERCISES II

11.3 When a table is displayed (e.g., on a screen), its rows appear in some top to bottom order—either an order explicitly specified via ORDER BY, or some arbitrary (system determined and unpredictable) order if ORDER BY is omitted. But what about the left to right order of columns in such a display?

11.4 Give SQL analogs of the following **Tutorial D** expressions:

a. `P { PNO } MINUS ( SP WHERE SNO = 'S2' ) { PNO }`

b. `( S { CITY } INTERSECT P { CITY } ) UNION P { CITY }`

c. `S { SNO } MINUS ( S { SNO } MINUS SP { SNO } )`

d. `SP MINUS SP`

e. `S INTERSECT S`

f. `( S WHERE CITY = 'Paris' ) UNION ( S WHERE STATUS = 20 )`

g. S JOIN SP JOIN P

h. ((S RENAME { CITY AS SC }) { SC }) JOIN
   ((P RENAME { CITY AS PC }) { PC })

11.5 Give an SQL formulation of the following query: Get pairs of supplier numbers, x and y say, such that suppliers x and y are located in the same city.

ANSWERS II

11.3 This isn't an issue in SQL: Since SQL tables have a left to right ordering to their columns anyway, the left to right display ordering can obviously be the same as the ordering within the table concerned (and I'm sure all SQL products follow this simple rule). It's also not really an issue for a relational language like **Tutorial D**, since by definition we're talking about something nonrelational here. Of course, a real relational system will necessarily have to have *some* rule for determining how results should be displayed; however, that rule won't be visible in the purely relational part of whatever language—**Tutorial D** or whatever—the system happens to support.

11.4 As usual the following solutions aren't the only ones possible.

a. SELECT PNO FROM P
  EXCEPT CORRESPONDING
  SELECT PNO FROM SP
  WHERE SNO = 'S2'

b. (SELECT CITY FROM S
    INTERSECT CORRESPONDING
    SELECT CITY FROM P)
  UNION CORRESPONDING
  SELECT CITY FROM P

Note the parentheses here. Of course, the foregoing expression could be simplified somewhat (exercise for the reader).

c. SELECT SNO FROM S
  EXCEPT CORRESPONDING
  (SELECT SNO FROM S
    EXCEPT CORRESPONDING
    SELECT SNO FROM SP)

Again the expression could be simplified (exercise for the reader).

```
d. SELECT * FROM SP
   EXCEPT CORRESPONDING
   SELECT * FROM SP
```

The result here is empty, of course. In fact, the expression overall is logically equivalent to this one:

```
SELECT * FROM SP WHERE FALSE
```

```
e. SELECT * FROM S
   INTERSECT CORRESPONDING
   SELECT * FROM S
```

The result here is identically equal to the current value of table S, of course. In fact, the expression overall is logically equivalent to this one:

```
SELECT * FROM S WHERE TRUE
```

(And that WHERE TRUE could optionally be omitted, too.)

```
f. SELECT * FROM S WHERE CITY = 'Paris'
   UNION  CORRESPONDING
   SELECT * FROM S WHERE STATUS = 20
```

The expression overall is logically equivalent to this one:

```
SELECT * FROM S WHERE CITY = 'Paris' OR STATUS = 20
```

```
g. SELECT * FROM S NATURAL JOIN SP NATURAL JOIN P
```

```
h. SELECT DISTINCT S.CITY AS SC , P.CITY AS PC FROM S , P
```

```
11.5 SELECT X.SNO AS XNO , Y.SNO AS YNO
     FROM   S AS X , S AS Y
     WHERE  X.CITY = Y.CITY
     AND    X.SNO < Y.SNO
```

Note the use of range variables X and Y in this solution. But do we need DISTINCT?

Chapter 12

SQL Operators II

Function is smothered in surmise
—William Shakespeare: *Macbeth* (1606)

In Chapter 5 I described certain additional relational operators, over and above the ones originally defined by Codd in the late 1960s and early 1970s. Specifically, I discussed (a) MATCHING and NOT MATCHING; (b) EXTEND; (c) image relations; and (d) aggregation, summarization, and related matters. Let's see what functionality SQL provides in these areas.

MATCHING AND NOT MATCHING

Here's the query I used in Chapter 5 to introduce the semijoin operator (MATCHING, in **Tutorial D**): "Get full supplier details for suppliers who supply at least one part." **Tutorial D** formulation:

```
S MATCHING SP
```

SQL has no direct analog of MATCHING as such, but IN with a subquery works:

```
SELECT SNO , SNAME , STATUS , CITY
FROM   S
WHERE  SNO IN
     ( SELECT SNO
       FROM   SP )
```

Recall from the answer to Exercise 11.1 in Chapter 11 that (simplifying slightly) a subquery in SQL is basically just a SELECT – FROM – WHERE expression enclosed in parentheses. As for the operator IN, the boolean expression

```
rx IN tx
```

is defined to return TRUE if the row *r* denoted by the row expression *rx* appears in the table *t* denoted by the table expression *tx*, and FALSE if it doesn't. In the example, therefore, the subquery is evaluated first and returns the following table:

```
SNO
─────
 S1
 S2
 S3
 S4
```

Then the outer query is evaluated, and it returns just that subset of table S where the supplier number is one of these four.

Actually the query under discussion—like just about every query, in fact!—can be formulated in a huge number of different ways in SQL. Here's another possible formulation, using EXISTS instead of IN:

```
SELECT  SNO , SNAME , STATUS , CITY
FROM    S
WHERE   EXISTS
      ( SELECT SNO
        FROM   SP
        WHERE  SP.SNO = S.SNO )
```

And here's another, using NATURAL JOIN:

```
SELECT  DISTINCT SNO , SNAME , STATUS , CITY
FROM    S NATURAL JOIN SP
```

Note that this last formulation effectively just spells out the definition of the semijoin of S with SP, in that order (see Chapter 5). *A word of caution:* Replacing that commalist of column names in the SELECT clause here by just "S.*" will *not* work, for a rather complicated reason that's explained in *SQL and Relational Theory*. Nor will replacing it by just "*" (for a different and more obvious reason).

Turning now to semidifference (NOT MATCHING in **Tutorial D**), here's the query I used in Chapter 5 to introduce that operator: "Get full supplier details for suppliers who supply no parts at all." **Tutorial D** formulation:

```
S NOT MATCHING SP
```

Again SQL has no direct analog, but NOT IN with a subquery works:

```
SELECT  SNO , SNAME , STATUS , CITY
FROM    S
WHERE   SNO NOT IN
      ( SELECT SNO
        FROM   SP )
```

Of course, the expression *rx* NOT IN *tx* is defined to be logically equivalent to the expression NOT (*rx* IN *tx*).

Alternatively, we could use NOT EXISTS:

```
SELECT SNO , SNAME , STATUS , CITY
FROM   S
WHERE  NOT EXISTS
     ( SELECT SNO
       FROM   SP
       WHERE  SP.SNO = S.SNO )
```

But there's no obvious way to use NATURAL JOIN for this query, unless we effectively just want to spell out the definition of the semidifference between S and SP in that order (again, see Chapter 5), thus:

```
SELECT SNO , SNAME , STATUS , CITY
FROM   S
EXCEPT CORRESPONDING
SELECT SNO , SNAME , STATUS , CITY
FROM   S NATURAL JOIN SP
```

EXTEND

Here's the query I used to introduce EXTEND in Chapter 5: "For each part, get full part information, together with the part weight in grams." **Tutorial D** formulation:

```
EXTEND P : { GMWT := WEIGHT * 454 }
```

SQL analog:

```
SELECT PNO , PNAME , COLOR , WEIGHT , CITY ,
                    ( WEIGHT * 454 ) AS GMWT
FROM   P
```

Note: The SQL SELECT clause really does cover a lot of territory ... In Chapter 11, we saw that SQL's analogs of the relational projection and renaming operators both relied on it; now we see that SQL's analog of EXTEND relies on it too, and later in this chapter we'll see it being used for still another purpose.

Be that as it may, my second EXTEND example in Chapter 5 was this:

```
( ( EXTEND P : { GMWT := WEIGHT * 454 } )
                    WHERE GMWT > 7000.0 )
                                { PNO , GMWT }
```

The query was "Get part number and gram weight for parts with gram weight greater than 7000 grams." Now, it's tempting to try the following as an SQL formulation of this query:

```
SELECT  PNO , ( WEIGHT * 454 ) AS GMWT
FROM    P
WHERE   GMWT > 7000.0
```

As I hope you can see, however, this formulation is incorrect. The reason is that GMWT is the name of a column of *the final result*; table P has no such column, the WHERE clause thus makes no sense, and the expression thereby fails at compile time. *Note:* The real problem here is that—as the **Tutorial D** formulation makes clear—we need to do the extension before the restriction, but SQL does the restriction before the extension. (Recall the conceptual algorithm I gave in Chapter 11 for evaluating SQL SELECT – FROM – WHERE expressions, where I showed that the sequence of evaluation is FROM first, then WHERE, then SELECT.)

Now, one fix for the foregoing problem is simply to replace the reference to GMWT in the WHERE clause by the corresponding defining expression, thus:

```
SELECT  PNO , ( WEIGHT * 454 ) AS GMWT
FROM    P
WHERE   ( WEIGHT * 454 ) > 7000.0
```

Of course, the subexpression WEIGHT * 454 now appears twice within the overall expression, and we just have to hope the optimizer will be smart enough to recognize that it need evaluate it just once per row instead of twice.

Alternatively, SQL does in fact allow the query to be formulated in a style that's a little closer to that of **Tutorial D** (and this time I'll show all of the otherwise implicit dot qualifications explicitly, for clarity):

```
SELECT  TEMP.PNO , TEMP.GMWT
FROM  ( SELECT PNO , ( WEIGHT * 454 ) AS GMWT
        FROM P ) AS TEMP
WHERE   TEMP.GMWT > 7000.0
```

Note the use of a subquery in the FROM clause in this example; note also the introduced name TEMP, which refers to the table that results from evaluating that subquery.[1]

Now I'd like to show some more of the **Tutorial D** EXTEND examples from Chapter 5, with an SQL analog in each case but little by way of further commentary:

```
1. EXTEND S : { TAG := 'Supplier' }
```

---

[1] Actually TEMP here isn't exactly a table name; rather, it's a *range variable*, as we saw in Chapter 11. Note further that it's an SQL rule that a subquery in the FROM clause *must* be accompanied by an AS specification that explicitly defines an associated range variable, even if that range variable is never explicitly referenced anywhere in the overall expression.

SQL analog:

```
SELECT SNO , SNAME , STATUS , CITY , 'Supplier' AS TAG
FROM   S
```

2. EXTEND (P JOIN SP) : { SHIPWT := WEIGHT * QTY }

   SQL analog:

```
SELECT PNO , PNAME , COLOR , WEIGHT , CITY , SNO , QTY ,
                            ( WEIGHT * QTY ) AS SHIPWT
FROM   P NATURAL JOIN SP
```

3. ((EXTEND P : { GMWT := WEIGHT * 454 }) { ALL BUT WEIGHT })
                                         RENAME { GMWT AS WEIGHT }

   Note that this expression represents a "what if" query. SQL analog:

```
SELECT PNO , PNAME , COLOR , ( WEIGHT * 454 ) AS WEIGHT , CITY
FROM   P
```

IMAGE RELATIONS

SQL has no direct equivalent to **Tutorial D's** image relations. As a consequence, queries for which image relations are helpful in **Tutorial D** tend to be quite awkward to express in SQL. I'll give just one example here. Recall the following **Tutorial D** expression, which represented the query "Get suppliers who supply all parts":

```
S WHERE ( !!SP ) { PNO } = P { PNO }
```

Here's one possible SQL formulation of this query:

```
SELECT SNO , SNAME , STATUS , CITY
FROM   S
WHERE  NOT EXISTS
     ( SELECT *
       FROM   P
       WHERE  NOT EXISTS
            ( SELECT *
              FROM   SP
              WHERE  S.SNO = SP.SNO
              AND    SP.PNO = P.PNO ) ) ;
```

In stilted English: "Get information for suppliers *s* such that there does not exist a part *p* such that there does not exist a shipment *sp* with the same supplier number as *s* and the same part number as *p*"—or, a little more colloquially, "Get suppliers such that there doesn't exist a part they don't supply" (note the double negation).

AGGREGATION AND SUMMARIZATION

Refer to Chapter 5 if you need to refresh your memory regarding the specifics of aggregation and summarization—there's really too much material to repeat it all here, where of course I want to focus on the corresponding SQL features anyway. Let me just remind you that:

■ Typical aggregate operators are COUNT, SUM, AVG, MAX, MIN, AND, OR, and XOR. Such operators are used primarily to derive a single value from the aggregate—i.e., the set or bag—of values of some attribute of some relation (or, in the case of COUNT, which is slightly special, from the aggregate that's the entire relation).

■ Aggregate operators have two main uses—they can be used in summarizations, and they can be used in what I referred to in Chapter 5 as "generalized restrictions." Recall also that image relations are almost always involved as well, in both cases.

Now, we already know SQL has no support for image relations, and I'm going to claim it has no proper support for aggregate operators, either. (This latter claim might come as a surprise if you happen to know something about SQL already.) But it does support both summarization and generalized restriction nevertheless; in fact, it has two features, GROUP BY and HAVING, that are explicitly intended for dealing with such matters. Let's take a closer look.

Summarization

I'll begin by reminding you of the **Tutorial D** formulation of the query "For each supplier, get the supplier number and a count of the number of parts that supplier supplies":

```
EXTEND S { SNO } : { PCT := COUNT ( !!SP ) }
```

Let me also remind you of the result, given our usual sample data values (note what happens with supplier S5 in particular):

SNO	PCT
S1	6
S2	2
S3	1
S4	3
S5	0

Here now is an SQL formulation of this query:

```
SELECT S.SNO , ( SELECT COUNT ( PNO )
                 FROM    SP
                 WHERE   SP.SNO = S.SNO ) AS PCT
FROM    S
```

Note the use of a subquery in the SELECT clause in this example (with an AS specification to provide a name for the corresponding result column). As in the answer to Example 11.1d in Chapter 11—where we first encountered the SQL subquery notion—a certain amount of explanation is required here! First of all, the subquery in this example is of the *correlated* variety (see the answer to Example 11.1e in Chapter 11), meaning that it includes a reference to something defined in the outer (or containing) expression, and meaning more particularly that—conceptually, at least—it needs to be evaluated repeatedly, once for each value of that "outer reference." (The outer reference in the example is the column reference S.SNO appearing in the WHERE clause in the subquery.) So you can imagine the expression overall being evaluated by examining the rows of the "outer table"—i.e., table S, in the example—one at a time in some sequence. Let's consider some row of table S, say the row for supplier S1. For that row, the subquery effectively reduces to the following:

```
( SELECT COUNT ( PNO )
  FROM    SP
  WHERE   SP.SNO = 'S1' )
```

Evaluating this expression returns a table of one row and one column that looks like this (note the lack of a column name):[2]

A double coercion (i.e., implicit type conversion) now occurs: This table is coerced to the single row it contains, and that row in turn is coerced to the single scalar value it contains. That scalar value then becomes—thanks to the specification AS PCT—the PCT value in the overall result row for supplier S1. This entire process is then repeated for each of the remaining rows of table S, to produce the overall final result shown earlier.

A remark on syntax: We've now seen subqueries in the SELECT clause, subqueries in the FROM clause, and subqueries in the WHERE clause. But have you noticed that those

---

[2] Again, the lack of double underlining in this picture is *not* a mistake.

subqueries sometimes return scalar values and sometimes tables? (As a matter of fact, sometimes they return neither scalars nor tables but *rows*, though I don't plan to give any detailed examples or discussion of this case in this book.) What do you think the SQL rule might look like for determining which kind of subquery, or which kind of interpretation of such a subquery, is intended in any given context? *End of remark.*

I should now explain that the foregoing SQL formulation of the original query is probably *not* what most SQL practitioners would have proposed for the query under discussion. Rather, most SQL practitioners would probably have written something like this:

```
SELECT SNO , COUNT ( PNO ) AS PCT
FROM   SP
GROUP  BY SNO
```

Explanation: Let *t* be the table that results from evaluating the FROM and WHERE clauses (in the example, *t* is just SP, since there's no WHERE clause, and omitting such a clause is equivalent to specifying WHERE TRUE). The GROUP BY clause is evaluated next, and it has the effect—conceptually, at any rate—of dividing *t* up into groups of rows, one such group for each distinct value of the specified "grouping columns" (in the example, there's one such group for each SNO value). Finally, the SELECT clause is evaluated, and it has the effect of constructing one row, consisting of the SNO value and the associated PCT value (i.e., the corresponding count), from each of those groups. But there's a trap here ... There's no row for supplier S5 in table SP, and so there's no group for supplier S5 in the result of the grouping operation, and so there's no row for supplier S5 in the final result. In other words, that result looks like this:

SNO	PCT
S1	6
S2	2
S3	1
S4	3

The fact is, GROUP BY, which was part of SQL (or SEQUEL, rather) right from the very beginning and was explicitly meant to help with queries like the one under discussion, (a) never needs to be used—after all, the first, and correct, SQL formulation of the query under discussion didn't use it—and (b) needs to be handled rather carefully if it *is* used, in order to avoid problems like the one just illustrated.

I haven't finished with this example—there's one further point I want to make. Consider again the following (correct) formulation:

```
SELECT  S.SNO  ,  (  SELECT  COUNT  (  PNO  )
                     FROM    SP
                     WHERE   SP.SNO = S.SNO )  AS PCT
FROM    S
```

Observe now that the construct "COUNT (PNO)" in the subquery here does *not* constitute an invocation of an aggregate operator! (That's why I claimed earlier that SQL has no proper aggregate operator support.) Because, if that construct did represent an aggregate operator invocation, we would be able to write an SQL assignment statement like this—

```
SET  PCT  =  COUNT  (  PNO  )  ;
```

—which clearly we can't (right?).

Now I want to move on to consider another example (a slightly modified version of the previous one). The query is "For each supplier, get the supplier number and the corresponding total shipment quantity." **Tutorial D** formulation:

```
EXTEND  S  {  SNO  }  :  {  TOTQ  :=  SUM  (  !!SP  ,  QTY  )  }
```

Here's the result (again note what happens with supplier S5 in particular):

SNO	TOTQ
S1	1300
S2	700
S3	200
S4	900
S5	0

The obvious SQL formulation is:

```
SELECT  S.SNO  ,  (  SELECT  SUM  (  QTY  )
                     FROM    SP
                     WHERE   SP.SNO = S.SNO )  AS TOTQ
FROM    S
```

But now there's another trap: The sum of shipment quantities for supplier S5 is, of course, the sum of an empty set. Now, the sum of an empty set is, logically and correctly, zero—but SQL says it's *null*,[3] and thus, in the example, produces the following incorrect result:

---

[3] In fact, in SQL, SUM, AVG, MAX, MIN, EVERY, and SOME—these last two being SQL's analogs of **Tutorial D**'s AND and OR aggregate operators, respectively—all return null if their argument is empty. (SQL has no analog of XOR.) COUNT, which does correctly return zero if its argument is empty, is the odd one out.

```
SNO   TOTQ

S1    1300
S2     700
S3     200
S4     900
S5
```

This example illustrates just one of the many situations where an SQL expression can return a table with nulls, even when there aren't any nulls in the input. Since (as always!) we definitely want to avoid nulls, what we need here is an operator that will replace a null as soon as it appears—before it has a chance to do any damage, as it were—by some genuine value. The operator we need is called COALESCE. Here's a revised version of the foregoing SQL expression that uses this operator:

```
SELECT S.SNO , ( SELECT COALESCE ( SUM ( QTY ) , 0 )
                FROM    SP
                WHERE   SP.SNO = S.SNO ) AS TOTQ
FROM    S
```

Explanation: In general, the expression COALESCE (*exp1,exp2,...,expn*), where "*exp1, exp2, ..., expn*" is a commalist of expressions all of the same type, returns the value of the first of those expressions (left to right) to denote a genuine value, not a null.[4] In the example, therefore, if a given supplier has at least one shipment, the corresponding sum will be computed correctly; but if some supplier has no shipments at all, SQL will return a null, which the COALESCE will then immediately replace by a zero.

"Generalized Restriction"

I used the term *generalized restriction* (rather sloppily) in Chapter 5 to refer to an expression of the form *r* WHERE *bx*, such that the boolean expression *bx* involves an aggregate operator invocation and, almost invariably, an image relation reference as well (at least in **Tutorial D**). Here's an example ("Get suppliers with fewer than three shipments"):

```
S WHERE COUNT ( !!SP ) < 3
```

And here's the result:

---

[4] Of course, there had better be such an expression, because otherwise the COALESCE invocation itself will return null.

SNO	SNAME	STATUS	CITY
S2	Jones	10	Paris
S3	Blake	30	Paris
S5	Adams	30	Athens

Here now is an SQL formulation (note the subquery in the WHERE clause):

```
SELECT SNO , SNAME , STATUS , CITY
FROM    S
WHERE ( SELECT COUNT ( PNO )
        FROM    SP
        WHERE   SP.SNO = S.SNO ) < 3
```

Once again, however, this formulation is probably not what most SQL practitioners would have proposed for the query under discussion. Rather, most SQL practitioners would probably have written something like this:

```
SELECT SNO , SNAME , STATUS , CITY
FROM    S NATURAL JOIN SP
GROUP   BY SNO
HAVING COUNT ( PNO ) < 3
```

Explanation: The HAVING clause is effectively "a WHERE clause for groups"; that is, it causes certain groups to be eliminated from further consideration, just as WHERE allows certain rows to be eliminated from further consideration. (Note that an SQL expression that involves HAVING will almost always involve GROUP BY as well.) But once again there's a trap … The groups for suppliers S2 and S3 both pass the HAVING test, and so those suppliers are represented in the final result (by contrast, the groups for suppliers S1 and S4 both fail that test); but as for supplier S5 … Well, there's no group for supplier S5, because there's no row for supplier S5 in the result of S NATURAL JOIN SP, and so supplier S5 isn't represented in the result! In other words, that result looks like this:

SNO	SNAME	STATUS	CITY
S2	Jones	10	Paris
S3	Blake	30	Paris

The fact is, HAVING, which (like GROUP BY) was explicitly meant to help with queries like the one under discussion, (a) never needs to be used, and (b) needs to be handled rather carefully if it *is* used (like GROUP BY again, in fact, in both respects).

I turn now to another example ("Get suppliers for whom the total shipment quantity is less than 1000"). **Tutorial D** formulation:

```
S WHERE SUM ( !!SP , QTY ) < 1000
```

SQL formulation (note the COALESCE, which is needed to ensure, again, that supplier S5 appears in the result):

```
SELECT SNO , SNAME , STATUS , CITY
FROM   S
WHERE ( SELECT COALESCE ( SUM ( QTY ) , 0 )
        FROM    SP
        WHERE   SP.SNO = S.SNO ) < 1000
```

Finally, here's a slightly more complicated example ("Get supplier number and total shipment quantity for suppliers where the total quantity is greater than 250"). **Tutorial D** formulation:

```
( EXTEND S { SNO } : { TOTQ := SUM ( !!SP , QTY } ) WHERE TOTQ > 250
```

SQL formulation:

```
SELECT TEMP.SNO , TEMP.TOTQ
FROM ( SELECT SNO , ( SELECT COALESCE ( SUM ( QTY ) , 0 )
                      FROM    SP
                      WHERE   SP.SNO = S.SNO ) AS TOTQ
       FROM    S ) AS TEMP
WHERE   TEMP.TOTQ > 250
```

EXERCISES

12.1 Give SQL analogs of the following **Tutorial D** expressions:

a. `P MATCHING S`

b. `S NOT MATCHING ( SP WHERE PNO = 'P2' )`

c. `EXTEND P : { SCT := COUNT ( !!SP ) }`

d. `P WHERE SUM ( !!SP , QTY ) < 500`

ANSWERS

12.1 As usual, the following solutions aren't the only ones possible.

a.
```
SELECT  PNO , PNAME , COLOR , WEIGHT , CITY
FROM    P
WHERE   CITY IN ( SELECT CITY
                  FROM   S )
```

b.
```
SELECT  SNO , SNAME , STATUS , CITY
FROM    S
WHERE   SNO NOT IN ( SELECT SNO
                     FROM   SP
                     WHERE  PNO = 'P2' )
```

c.
```
SELECT  PNO , PNAME , COLOR , WEIGHT , CITY ,
                            ( SELECT COUNT ( SNO )
                              FROM   SP
                              WHERE  SP.PNO = P.PNO ) AS SCT
FROM    P
```

d.
```
SELECT  PNO , PNAME , COLOR , WEIGHT , CITY
FROM    P
WHERE   ( SELECT COALESCE ( SUM ( QTY ) , 0 )
          FROM   SP
          WHERE  SP.PNO = P.PNO ) < 500
```

Chapter 13

SQL Constraints

The Golden Rule will keep the database
In the Golden State, which is a state of grace

—Anon.: *Where Bugs Go*

Recall from Chapter 6 that an integrity constraint, or just a constraint for short, is, loosely, a boolean expression that must evaluate to TRUE (because otherwise there would be something wrong with the database). Also recall **The Golden Rule**, which says that all integrity constraints must be satisfied at statement boundaries; in other words, the individual statement is "the unit of integrity," and no statement—in particular, no update statement—must ever leave the database in an inconsistent state. In this chapter, we'll take a look at the relevant features of SQL.

DATABASE CONSTRAINTS

Database constraints in SQL are defined by means of CREATE ASSERTION, which is SQL's counterpart to **Tutorial D**'s CONSTRAINT statement. In Chapter 6, I discussed five possible "business rules" and showed how they could be formulated using CONSTRAINT statements; now let's see what CREATE ASSERTION analogs of those CONSTRAINT statements might look like. *Note:* For purposes of comparison, I'll show the original **Tutorial D** formulations as well.

1. Supplier status values must be in the range 1 to 100 inclusive. In **Tutorial D**:

```
CONSTRAINT CX1 IS_EMPTY ( S WHERE STATUS < 1 OR STATUS > 100 ) ;
```

Here's an SQL analog:

```
CREATE ASSERTION CX1
       CHECK ( NOT EXISTS ( SELECT * FROM S
                            WHERE STATUS < 1 OR STATUS > 100 ) ) ;
```

As this example shows, a CREATE ASSERTION statement consists of (a) the keywords CREATE ASSERTION, followed by (b) a constraint name, followed by (c) the keyword CHECK, followed by (d) a boolean expression in parentheses that must evaluate to TRUE.

Now, you might recall that there's another way to formulate this constraint in **Tutorial D**:

```
CONSTRAINT CX1 AND ( S , STATUS ≥ 1 AND STATUS ≤ 100 ) ;
```

Well, we can do the same kind of thing in SQL with CREATE ASSERTION:[1]

```
CREATE ASSERTION CX1
        CHECK ( ( SELECT COALESCE ( EVERY ( STATUS >= 1 AND
                                            STATUS <= 100 ) , TRUE )
                  FROM   S ) ) ;
```

2. Suppliers in London must have status 20. In **Tutorial D**:

```
CONSTRAINT CX2 IS_EMPTY ( S WHERE CITY = 'London' AND STATUS ≠ 20 ) ;
```

SQL analog:

```
CREATE ASSERTION CX2
        CHECK ( NOT EXISTS ( SELECT * FROM S
                             WHERE CITY = 'London' AND STATUS <> 20 ) ) ;
```

3. Supplier numbers must be unique. In **Tutorial D**:

```
CONSTRAINT CX3 COUNT ( S ) = COUNT ( S { SNO } ) ;
```

SQL analog:

```
CREATE ASSERTION CX3
        CHECK ( ( SELECT COUNT ( SNO ) FROM S ) =
                ( SELECT COUNT ( DISTINCT SNO ) FROM S ) ) ;
```

Several points arise from this example:

■ First of all, note the construct COUNT (DISTINCT SNO) in the last line here. This is the first example of such a construct we've seen in this book. What it means, loosely, is that the COUNT operator is to be applied to the *projection*—the true relational projection, I mean, with duplicates eliminated—of S on SNO. To illustrate the difference, consider the case of COUNT (STATUS) vs. COUNT (DISTINCT STATUS); given our usual data values, the first of these returns the value five, while the second returns the value three.

---

[1] The COALESCE I show here might not be necessary in practice, though it's not wrong. See *SQL and Relational Theory* for further discussion.

■ Second, it's not immediately obvious that the foregoing SQL formulation is valid; indeed, something rather mysterious is happening here. As you can see, the boolean expression in the CHECK specification involves an equality comparison in which the comparands are denoted by subqueries. Now, subqueries are supposed to evaluate to tables; thus, it appears we're trying to compare two tables for equality—yet we saw in Chapter 11 that SQL doesn't support such comparisons. So what exactly is going on? I won't attempt to clear up this mystery here; I'll just leave it as something for you to think about.

■ Third, there's in fact a simpler way of stating this constraint in SQL, as follows:

```
CREATE ASSERTION CX3
       CHECK ( UNIQUE ( SELECT SNO FROM S ) ) ;
```

The SQL UNIQUE operator returns TRUE if and only if the rows in its argument table are all distinct. Thus, the UNIQUE invocation in the example returns TRUE if and only if no two rows in table S have the same supplier number.

■ In practice, of course, we would state the constraint in this example—viz., that supplier numbers must be unique—not by means of an explicit CREATE ASSERTION statement as such, but rather by specifying UNIQUE (SNO) as part of the definition of table S.[2] But it's interesting to note that such a specification is really nothing more than shorthand for something that can be expressed, albeit more longwindedly, using explicit CREATE ASSERTION syntax.

4. Suppliers with status less than 20 mustn't supply part P6. In **Tutorial D**:

```
CONSTRAINT CX4
     IS_EMPTY ( ( S JOIN SP ) WHERE STATUS < 20 AND PNO = 'P6' ) ;
```

SQL analog:

```
CREATE ASSERTION CX4
       CHECK ( NOT EXISTS ( SELECT * FROM S NATURAL JOIN SP
                       WHERE STATUS < 20 AND PNO = 'P6' ) ) ;
```

This is the first example in the list to involve (or, rather, interrelate) two distinct base tables, viz., S and SP. In general, of course, a constraint might interrelate any number of such tables. And the significant point about such constraints for our purposes is this: In general, SQL

---

[2] Just for interest (?), let me tell you how the standard explains the semantics of that UNIQUE (SNO) specification on table S (I've adapted the standard's own generic phrasing to apply to the specific case at hand): "The constraint UNIQUE(SNO) is not satisfied if and only if EXISTS(SELECT * FROM S WHERE NOT(UNIQUE(SELECT SNO FROM S))) is true." I hope that's perfectly clear.

will require the corresponding constraint checking to be *deferred*, typically to commit time. Thus SQL, most unfortunately, sometimes fails to support **The Golden Rule**.

5. Every supplier number in SP must also appear in S. In **Tutorial D**:

```
CONSTRAINT CX5 SP { SNO } ⊆ S { SNO } ;
```

SQL analog:

```
CREATE ASSERTION CX5
        CHECK ( NOT EXISTS ( SELECT SNO FROM SP
                             EXCEPT CORRESPONDING
                             SELECT SNO FROM S ) :
```

This example also interrelates two base tables. More to the point, of course, we would specify this constraint in practice not by means of an explicit CREATE ASSERTION statement as shown, but rather by means of an appropriate FOREIGN KEY specification as part of the definition of table SP. But as with Example 3 above, it's interesting to note that such a specification is really nothing more than shorthand for something that can be expressed, albeit more longwindedly, using explicit CREATE ASSERTION syntax.

A remark on base table and column constraints: As the foregoing examples should have been sufficient to suggest, any constraint that can be formulated by means of a CONSTRAINT statement in **Tutorial D** can be formulated by means of a CREATE ASSERTION statement in SQL.[3] But SQL has a feature according to which any such constraint can alternatively be specified as part of the definition of some base table—i.e., as a *base table constraint*. (**Tutorial D** supports such a possibility in connection with key and foreign key constraints but not with any others.) What's more, SQL also has a feature by which certain constraints—for example, NOT NULL constraints and key constraints for keys that involve just one column—can be formulated as a *column constraint* (which is a constraint that's specified, not just as part of the definition of some base table, but as part of the definition of some specific column of some base table). But these features are basically just syntactic frills, and further details of them are beyond the scope of this book. *End of remark.*

---

[3] Except that SQL constraints are supposed not to contain "possibly nondeterministic expressions" (see Chapter 11 for an explanation of this term), a rule that, if true, could cause serious problems in practice—especially since almost all table expressions are considered by the standard to be "possibly nondeterministic" if they contain a subexpression of some character string type (a fairly common state of affairs, one might have thought). See *SQL and Relational Theory* for further discussion.

TYPE CONSTRAINTS

I mentioned a couple of times in passing in Chapter 10 that SQL does allow users to define their own types. Now, it's axiomatic—or at least, so one would think—that part of the definition of some user defined type *T* must surely be a specification of the values that go to make up that type *T*. By way of example, suppose we wanted the quantity column (QTY) in table SP to be, not of the system defined type INTEGER as I've been assuming throughout this book so far, but rather of some user defined type. For simplicity, let's agree to use that same name, QTY, to refer to that user defined type, as well as to the column of that type in table SP. Then we surely want a way of saying that the only legal quantities—i.e., the only legal values of type QTY—are, let's say, integers in the range 1–5000, inclusive. In **Tutorial D**, then, the definition of that type QTY might look like this, in outline:

```
TYPE QTY ... CONSTRAINT Q > 1 AND Q < 5000 ... ;
```

The symbol *Q* here denotes an arbitrary value of the type (i.e., an arbitrary quantity, in effect).[4]

Observe now that **Tutorial D** uses the keyword CONSTRAINT in this connection: not unreasonably, because what we're doing in the example is *constraining* QTY values to lie in a certain range. In other words, we've defined a *type constraint*, which is, precisely, a specification of the legal values that constitute some given type. *Note:* The constraints discussed in Chapter 6 (also in this chapter, prior to the present discussion) are called *database* constraints precisely in order to distinguish them from type constraints. In practice, though, the unqualified term *constraint* is usually taken to mean a database constraint specifically, unless the context demands otherwise.

Now, I didn't mention type constraints at all in Chapter 6 because, first, they're not really part of relational theory as such (rather, they're part of the associated type theory); second, I more or less took it for granted that a system that allowed users to define their own types would necessarily allow users to define the values that made up those types. I was wrong. SQL doesn't.

Let me spell the point out: SQL would allow us to define quantities as a type, called QTY; it would allow us to say that quantities are represented by integers; but it would *not* allow us to say that legal values of that type lie in a certain range, say 1–5000 inclusive. Thus, e.g., a quantity of one billion—1,000,000,000—is apparently legal, in SQL! (So too is a quantity of -1,000,000,000, come to that.)

Of course, we can compensate for SQL's lack of support for type constraints (at the cost of considerable effort) by using CREATE ASSERTION, as follows. Let *Q* be a column of type QTY and let *T* be the base table that contains it. Then we can write:

---

[4] This explanation is considerably oversimplified, but it's adequate for present purposes.

```
CREATE ASSERTION CXQ
        CHECK ( NOT EXISTS ( SELECT * FROM T
                             WHERE   Q < QTY ( 1 )
                             OR      Q > QTY ( 5000 ) ) ) ;
```

(The expressions QTY(1) and QTY(5000) here are QTY literals.) Understand, however, that such a CREATE ASSERTION would have to be specified for every such column Q and every such table T.

EXERCISES

13.1 Write CREATE ASSERTION statements for the suppliers-and-parts database for the following "business rules":

a. All red parts must weigh less than 50 pounds.

b. No two suppliers can be located in the same city.

c. At most one supplier can be located in Athens at any one time.

d. There must be at least one London supplier.

e. Supplier S1 and part P1 must never be in different cities.

13.2 Does your favorite SQL DBMS support CREATE ASSERTION?

13.3 If your answer to the previous question is no, does it support any other kinds of declarative constraints?

13.4 What can you do about constraints that can't be declaratively stated?

13.5 Why do you think SQL requires the constraint checking for constraints such as constraint CX4 to be "deferred"?

ANSWERS

13.1 a.
```
        CREATE ASSERTION CXA
                CHECK ( NOT EXISTS ( SELECT * FROM P
                                     WHERE COLOR = 'Red' AND WEIGHT >= 50 ) ) ;
```

b.   CREATE ASSERTION CXB
                 CHECK ((SELECT COUNT (SNO) FROM S) =
                         (SELECT COUNT (CITY) FROM S)) ;

c.   CREATE ASSERTION CXC
                 CHECK ((SELECT COUNT (SNO) FROM S
                         WHERE CITY = 'Athens') < 2) ;

d.   CREATE ASSERTION CXD
                 CHECK (EXISTS (SELECT * FROM S
                         WHERE CITY = 'London')) ;

e.   CREATE ASSERTION CXE
                 CHECK ((SELECT COUNT (CITY)
                         FROM (SELECT CITY FROM S
                         WHERE   SNO = 'S1'
                         UNION   CORRESPONDING
                         SELECT CITY FROM P
                         WHERE   PNO = 'P1') AS POINTLESS) < 2) ;

13.2 The answer here is probably no. In fact, integrity constraints constitute one area where the standard is better than most if not all of the current crop of products—though it's certainly not perfect.

13.3 Most products do support UNIQUE constraints; PRIMARY KEY constraints (which are little more than a syntactic variation on UNIQUE constraints); FOREIGN KEY constraints; and certain other simple "base table" constraints. These latter are, typically, constraints that can be checked for a given row by examining just that single row in isolation; in other words, the boolean expression in the constraint question is limited to being a restriction condition on the base table in question. (In SQL terms, the constraints in question aren't allowed to contain a subquery.)

13.4 Somebody somewhere has to write some appropriate application code (possibly in the form of a "trigger"). See *SQL and Relational Theory* for further discussion.

13.5 In essence, the reason is that SQL fails to support a counterpart to **Tutorial D's** multiple assignment (see Chapter 6), which would allow the user to update two or more tables in a single statement. Consider constraint CX4, for example, and the following UPDATE:

```
UPDATE S
SET    STATUS = 10
WHERE  SNO = 'S1' ;
```

If the constraint is checked at this point, the UPDATE will fail. But if the checking is deferred until after the following DELETE—

```
DELETE
FROM    SP
WHERE   SNO = 'S1'
AND     PNO = 'P6' ;
```

—then the pair of updates taken together will succeed. The fact remains, however, that if checking is deferred in this manner, then the database is inconsistent throughout the interval from the time the UPDATE is done to the time the DELETE is done, and SQL has thereby violated **The Golden Rule**. Observe in particular that if the program doing the updates were to ask the question "Does any supplier with status less than 20 supply part P6?" during that interval, it would get the answer *yes*.

   Note: The odd thing is that SQL does in fact support multiple assignment! For example, the following SQL statement assigns the values of variables X, Y, and Z to variables A, B, and C, respectively.

```
SET ( A , B , C ) = ( X , Y , Z ) ;
```

(Actually this is a *row* assignment, technically speaking.) The trouble is, the target variables in such an assignment aren't allowed to be table variables as such.[5] What makes the situation even odder is that SQL does perform certain multiple *table* assignments, at least implicitly— e.g., when it's performing a "cascade delete" (see the answer to Exercise 3.4 in Chapter 3).

---

[5] Perhaps this isn't so surprising, given that SQL doesn't have a proper notion of table variables at all.

Chapter 14

SQL vs. the Relational Model

Between the idea
And the reality ...
Falls the Shadow

—T. S. Eliot: *The Hollow Men* (1925)

Well, it should be very clear from the last few chapters that SQL and the relational model aren't the same thing—or, to state the matter more precisely, it should be clear that SQL, considered as a concrete relational language, fails in all too many ways to realize the ideas and potential of the abstract relational model. Indeed, SQL suffers from both sins of omission and sins of commission: There are aspects of the relational model it doesn't support properly (or at all), and there are constructs it does support that don't correspond to anything relational. (Of course, I'm limiting my attention here, as elsewhere throughout the book, to what I've been calling the "core features" of SQL.) Some examples of omissions are proper support for equality; proper support for table types; and proper support for the operators of the relational algebra. And some examples of nonrelational features are nulls, duplicate rows, and left to right column ordering.

Now, my principal aim in this book has been to describe and explain the relational model, not SQL. But given SQL's ubiquitous nature—more particularly, given the fact that, for better or worse, every database professional does need to come to grips with it—I think it's important for such professionals to have some idea of the multifarious ways in which SQL departs from the prescriptions of the abstract model. In fact, I believe strongly that such professionals should have a good working knowledge of the relational model per se, and an awareness of the discrepancies between that model and SQL can only help in this regard. Hence this chapter.

SOME GENERALITIES

To repeat something I said in Chapter 10, I do believe that learning the relational model first and SQL second is much easier than doing it the other way around, in part because doing it the other way around can require a lot of unlearning. (This state of affairs accounts for the structure of the book, as I explained in Chapter 1.) Actually, though, I don't believe anyone really knows SQL anyway: not if "knowing" a language means knowing it in its entirety. SQL is so huge, so complex, so ad hoc, and so unorthogonal—not to mention the fact that it's riddled with so many logical gaps, inconsistencies, and flat out contradictions[1]—that I honestly believe that, in the final analysis, it's unteachable. Indeed, I've been impressed by the fact that, on more than one occasion, I've applied to various SQL experts for the answer to some technical question (I'm referring here to members or past members of the SQL standard committee) and have had to be "put on hold," sometimes for several days, before getting an answer. The answers, even when they were forthcoming (which wasn't always), weren't always correct, either.

Anyway, I hope you can see from all of the above why people like myself refuse to regard today's mainstream "relational" products as relational at all. Instead, they're *SQL* products: The basic data object they support is the SQL table, not a relation, and the operators they support are operators that work on SQL tables, not relations. The sad (not to say curious) thing is, I really believe a truly relational DBMS would be vastly superior to a mere SQL DBMS—superior not only from the point of view of usability, but superior in that it would be easier to implement and would provide better optimizability, and hence better performance, as well. Let me elaborate briefly:

- Regarding *usability:* It's undeniably true that SQL is much more complex than the relational model, and yet it provides no useful additional functionality. In fact, it provides strictly less functionality than the relational model, because it isn't relationally complete (refer to Chapter 7 if you need to refresh your memory regarding this concept).

- Regarding *optimizability and performance:* Here I first need to explain that one of the things the optimizer does is *expression transformation.* That is, it transforms the expression representing the user's original request into another expression that's logically equivalent to the original, in the sense that it's guaranteed to evaluate to the same result, but has better performance characteristics, or at least so we hope. (I've touched on this notion briefly elsewhere in this book—e.g., in Chapter 1.) And the point is this: While there are many such transformations that work for relations, there aren't so many that work for tables with duplicate rows; and there are far fewer if column ordinal position also has to be taken into account; and there are far fewer still if nulls have to be taken into account as well. In other words, those nonrelational features—duplicate rows, left to right column ordering, nulls—all (a) serve as significant optimization inhibitors, thereby affecting performance, and (b) actually make the optimizer more complicated, and therefore harder to implement, as well.

Note: I'd like to mention two further points briefly here. First, you need to understand that "no two SQLs are equal." As I pointed out in Chapter 10:

---

[1] For evidence in support of these claims (regarding inconsistencies and the rest), I refer you to Appendix D of the book *A Guide to the SQL Standard* (4th edition, Addison-Wesley, 1997), by Hugh Darwen and myself.

- No commercial product supports the standard in its entirety (in fact no product could possibly do so, given the inconsistencies and the like that I mentioned above).

- At the same time, every product does support a variety of proprietary features that are peculiar to that particular product and aren't part of the standard at all.

- Moreover, the standard explicitly leaves certain issues to be resolved by the particular product in question. (An example is the name to be given to a result column that would otherwise have no name, as discussed in the answer to Exercise 10.3 in Chapter 10.) Do you think those products always resolve those issues in exactly the same way?

The other point I feel obliged to mention is that, considered purely as a formal programming language, SQL is badly designed by just about any measure. The fact is, there are certain well-established principles of good language design—I have in mind here such things as *generality, parsimony, completeness, similarity, extensibility, openness,* and *orthogonality*[2]—but there seems to be little evidence that SQL was designed in accordance with any of them.

Of course, it's interesting to speculate as to why the marketplace chose to run with SQL instead of the relational model. (I have my own thoughts in this connection, but I choose not to air them here.) But the fact is that it did, and for now, at any rate, we all have to live with the consequences of that choice. Given that this is so, the idea of applying some discipline to the (a) the design of SQL tables and (b) the use of SQL operators, with the aim of making the overall system behave almost as if it were truly relational, is an attractive one. Indeed, as I mentioned in Chapter 11, such a discipline is in large part what *SQL and Relational Theory* is all about. Unfortunately, however, adopting such a discipline can be a little painful, owing to the design of both the SQL language and current SQL products; certainly it doesn't seem to be followed very widely in practice. But I recommend it strongly nevertheless.

SOME SQL DEPARTURES FROM THE RELATIONAL MODEL

In this section I list, mainly for purposes of reference and with little by way of additional commentary, some of the ways in which SQL departs from the relational model. Now, I know there are those who will quibble over individual items in the list; it's not easy to compile a list of this nature, especially if it's meant to be orthogonal (i.e., if an attempt is made to keep the various items all independent of one another). But I don't think such quibbling is important. What's important is the cumulative effect, which I think is quite frankly overwhelming.[3]

---

[2] This list is taken from Chapter 9, "Little Languages," of Jon Bentley's book *More Programming Pearls: Confessions of a Coder* (Addison-Wesley, 1988).

[3] I'd also like to remind you here of Wittgenstein's dictum, much appealed to by Hugh Darwen and myself in technical writings and mentioned here and there in the present book, to the effect that *all logical differences are big differences*.

Without further ado, then:

■ SQL fails to distinguish adequately between table values and table variables.

■ SQL tables aren't the same as relations (or relvars), because they either permit or require, as the case may be, (a) duplicate rows; (b) nulls; (c) left to right column ordering; (d) anonymous columns; (e) duplicate column names; (f) pointers; and—at least in certain products, though not in the standard as such—(g) hidden columns. *Note:* Possibilities (a), (b), (c), (f), and (g) all represent violations of *The Information Principle*. Possibilities (d) and (e)—i.e., anonymous columns and duplicate column names, respectively—can occur only in tables resulting from evaluation of some operational expression; they can't occur in base tables, nor in views. Strictly speaking, therefore, if we take *The Information Principle* to mean exactly what it says (see Chapter 7), then possibilities (d) and (e) don't violate it, because the tables in which such things occur aren't actually part of the database. But note the weirdness here: SQL lets us derive results that can't then be stored back directly as base tables in the database from which they're derived! Thus, I think possibilities (d) and (e) certainly violate the spirit, if not the letter, of *The Information Principle*.

■ SQL has no proper table literals. The closest approximation to such a construct is the VALUES expression—incidentally, note the appropriation, or usurpation, here of a very general term ("values") for a very specific purpose—and such expressions can't be used in every context where a literal ought to be allowed. (In this connection, see Exercise 14.2 at the end of the chapter.)

■ SQL often seems to think views aren't tables. The following text is taken, lightly edited, from *SQL and Relational Theory:*

> The SQL standard, as well as most other SQL documentation, typically—quite ubiquitously, in fact—talks in terms of "tables and views." Clearly, anyone who talks this way is under the impression that tables and views are different things, and probably also that "tables" always means base tables specifically, and probably also that base tables are physically stored and views aren't. But the whole point about a view is that it *is* a table (or, as I would prefer to say, a relvar); that is, we can perform the same kinds of operations on views as we can on regular relvars (at least in the relational model), because views *are* "regular relvars."

In mathematics, the whole point about a subset is that it's a set; indeed, the whole point about set theory operations (e.g., union) in general is that the result of performing them on any given set(s) is a set. And the situation in the relational model is precisely analogous: The result of any relational expression is a relation, and that goes for the expressions used to define views in particular. Thus, anyone in the SQL world who thinks a view is something different from a table isn't thinking relationally, and is thereby likely to make mistakes.

■ SQL tables (views included!—see the previous point) must have at least one column. For an explanation of this point (which accounts, incidentally, for SQL's not being relationally complete), see Appendix B.

■ SQL has no explicit table assignment operator.

■ SQL has no explicit multiple table assignment a fortiori (nor does it have an INSERT / DELETE / UPDATE analog).

■ SQL violates *The Assignment Principle* in numerous ways, some but not all of them having to do with nulls (others have to do with character string types, and others with "possibly nondeterministic" expressions).

■ SQL violates **The Golden Rule** in numerous ways, some but not all of them having to do with nulls; in particular, deferred integrity checking constitutes such a violation.

■ SQL has no proper "table type" notion.

■ SQL has no "=" operator for tables; in fact, it has no table comparison operators at all.

■ SQL explicitly allows proper superkeys to be declared as keys.

■ SQL's union, intersection, and join operators aren't commutative.

■ SQL's union, intersection, and join operators aren't idempotent.

■ SQL's intersection operator isn't a special case of its join operator (duplicates and nulls are the culprit here).

■ SQL's join operator isn't even precisely defined (the problem here being, precisely, that the "body" of an SQL table is a bag, not a set, of rows).

■ SQL has no proper aggregate operators.

■ SQL makes all kinds of logical mistakes, both syntactic and semantic, in connection with empty sets.

■ Numerous SQL table expressions are "possibly nondeterministic."

■ SQL supports various row level operators (cursor updates, row level triggers).

■ Although the SQL standard doesn't, the dialects of SQL supported in certain commercial products do sometimes refer to certain physical level constructs (e.g., indexes).

■ SQL's view definitions include mapping information as well as structural information.[4] *Note:* For a detailed discussion of the significance of both this point and the next, see my book *View Updating and Relational Theory: Solving the View Update Problem* (O'Reilly, 2013).

■ SQL's support for view updating is weak, ad hoc, and incomplete.

■ SQL fails to distinguish properly between types and representations. (This problem occurs chiefly but not exclusively in connection with SQL's subtyping mechanism, further details of which are beyond the scope of this book.)

■ SQL doesn't support type constraints.

■ SQL's "structured types" are sometimes encapsulated and sometimes not. *Note:* Structured types have to do with the mechanism by which SQL users can define their own types. Detailed discussion is beyond the scope of this book.

■ SQL fails to distinguish properly between types and type generators.

■ Although the SQL standard does support type BOOLEAN, most if not all commercial SQL products don't.

■ SQL's support for "=" is seriously deficient. To be more specific, the "=" operator (a) can give TRUE even when the comparands are clearly distinct; (b) can fail to give TRUE even when the comparands aren't clearly distinct; (c) can have user defined, and hence arbitrary, semantics (in the case of user defined types); (d) isn't supported at all for the system defined type XML; and (e) in certain products though not the standard, isn't supported for certain other types (typically BLOB and CLOB) as well.

■ SQL is based on three-valued logic (sort of), whereas the relational model is based on classical two-valued logic.

---

[4] To be fair, this criticism applies to **Tutorial D** also, at least in its present incarnation.

- As previously noted, SQL isn't relationally complete.

- SQL has no straightforward support for image relations, nor for RENAME, XUNION ("exclusive union"), MATCHING, NOT MATCHING, D_UNION, I_MINUS, D_INSERT, I_DELETE, and various other relational operators not discussed in this book.

The foregoing list is not exhaustive.

EXERCISES

14.1 Which of the following are legal as standalone SQL expressions (i.e., expressions not nested inside other expressions) and which not, syntactically speaking? (*A* and *B* here are table names, and you can assume the tables they denote satisfy the requirements for the operator in question in each case.) *Note:* This exercise is somewhat unfair, since we haven't covered enough of SQL in this book to answer all of it—but I think it's worth attempting anyway; I think you'll find it instructive. At least let me explain that the SQL construct "TABLE *T*" (where *T* is a simple table name, not a more general table expression) is defined to be shorthand for the expression "(SELECT * FROM *T*)". Perhaps I should remind you too that, in the relational world, intersection is a special case of natural join.

a. `A NATURAL JOIN B`

b. `A INTERSECT B`

c. `SELECT * FROM A NATURAL JOIN B`

d. `SELECT * FROM A INTERSECT B`

e. `SELECT * FROM ( A NATURAL JOIN B )`

f. `SELECT * FROM ( A INTERSECT B )`

g. `SELECT * FROM ( SELECT * FROM A INTERSECT SELECT * FROM B )`

h. `SELECT * FROM ( A NATURAL JOIN B ) AS C`

i. `SELECT * FROM ( A INTERSECT B ) AS C`

j. `TABLE A NATURAL JOIN TABLE B`

k. `TABLE A INTERSECT TABLE B`

l. `SELECT * FROM A INTERSECT SELECT * FROM B`

m. `( SELECT * FROM A ) INTERSECT ( SELECT * FROM B )`

n. `( SELECT * FROM A ) AS AA INTERSECT ( SELECT * FROM B ) AS BB`

What do you conclude from this exercise?

14.2 If $x + y$ is a numeric expression, and x has the value 3, we can substitute the literal 3 for the variable reference x, giving $3 + y$ (and this expression is logically equivalent to the original one). What happens to the SQL expressions, or would-be expressions, in Exercise 14.1 if we substitute a "table literal" (i.e., appropriate VALUES expression) for A or B?

ANSWERS

14.1 A formal BNF grammar for SQL table expressions, which is of course what's needed in order to answer this exercise fully, can be found in *SQL and Relational Theory* (where the exercise was taken from).

a. `A NATURAL JOIN B` : **Illegal.**

b. `A INTERSECT B` : **Illegal.**

c. `SELECT * FROM A NATURAL JOIN B` : **Legal.**

d. `SELECT * FROM A INTERSECT B` : **Illegal.**

e. `SELECT * FROM ( A NATURAL JOIN B )` : **Legal.**

f. `SELECT * FROM ( A INTERSECT B )` : **Illegal.**

g. `SELECT * FROM ( SELECT * FROM A INTERSECT SELECT * FROM B )` : **Illegal.**

h. `SELECT * FROM ( A NATURAL JOIN B ) AS C` : **Illegal.**

i. `SELECT * FROM ( A INTERSECT B ) AS C` : **Illegal.**

j. `TABLE A NATURAL JOIN TABLE B` : **Illegal.**

k. `TABLE A INTERSECT TABLE B` : **Legal.**

l.   `SELECT * FROM A INTERSECT SELECT * FROM B` : **Legal.**

m.   `( SELECT * FROM A ) INTERSECT ( SELECT * FROM B )` : **Legal.**

n.   `( SELECT * FROM A ) AS AA INTERSECT ( SELECT * FROM B ) AS BB` : **Illegal.**

As for what you conclude from this exercise, only you can answer that, but I know what I do.

14.2 The effects are as follows: Expression b. was previously illegal but becomes legal; expressions c., e., k., l., and m. were legal but become illegal; and the others were all illegal anyway and remain so. What do you conclude from *this* exercise?

APPENDIXES

Appendix A

A Tutorial D Grammar

I never use a big, big D—
—W. S. Gilbert: HMS Pinafore (1878)

This appendix gives for purposes of reference a simple BNF grammar for **Tutorial D** relational expressions and assignments. Details of nonrelational expressions, including aggregate operator invocations in particular, are omitted, and so are definitional operations such as those used to define base relvars and constraints. The following are also omitted:

- SUMMARIZE, because (as explained in Chapter 5) this operator is somewhat deprecated

- Aspects of the language not discussed in the body of the book

Also, the grammar is simplified in certain respects. In particular, it makes no attempt to say where image relations can and can't be used, nor does it pay any attention to operator precedence rules. (As a result of this latter point, certain constructs permitted by the grammar—for example, the expression *r1* MINUS *r2* MINUS *r3*—are potentially ambiguous. Additional syntax rules are needed to resolve such issues, but such rules are omitted here. Of course, parentheses can always be used to guarantee a desired order of evaluation anyway.) A few further points of detail:

- All syntactic categories of the form *<... name>* are assumed to be *<identifier>*s and are defined no further here.

- Although the category *<bool exp>* is left undefined, it might help to recall that a relational comparison in particular is a special case.

- As usual, all of the various commalists mentioned are allowed to be empty.

Expressions

```
<relation exp>
    ::=   <with exp> | <nonwith exp>

<with exp>
    ::=   WITH ( <temp assign commalist> ) : <relation exp>
```

Note: A *<temp assign>* is syntactically identical to a *<relation assign>*, except that an introduced "temporary" name can appear wherever a *<relvar name>* can appear.

```
<nonwith exp>
    ::=   <image relation ref> | <relation op> | ( <relation op> )

<image relation ref>
    ::=   !!<relvar name> | !!( <relation exp> ) | ( <image relation ref> )

<relation op>
    ::=   <relation selector> | <monadic op> | <dyadic op>

<relation selector>
    ::=   RELATION [ <heading> ] { <tuple exp commalist> }
        | TABLE_DUM | TABLE_DEE
```

Note: In the first *<relation selector>* format, the optional *<heading>* can be omitted only if the *<tuple exp commalist>* is nonempty. TABLE_DUM and TABLE_DEE are shorthand for the *<relation selector>*s RELATION { } { } and RELATION { } { TUPLE { }}, respectively (see Appendix B).

```
<heading>
    ::=   { <attribute commalist> }

<attribute>
    ::=   <attribute name> <type name>

<monadic op>
    ::=   <relvar name> | <rename> | <where> | <project> | <extend>

<rename>
    ::=   <relation exp> RENAME { <renaming commalist> }

<renaming>
    ::=   <attribute name> AS <attribute name>

<where>
    ::=   <relation exp> [ WHERE <bool exp> ]

<project>
    ::=   <relation exp> { [ ALL BUT ] <attribute name commalist> }

<extend>
    ::=   EXTEND <relation exp> : { <attribute assign commalist> }

<attribute assign>
    ::=   <attribute name> := <exp>
```

Note: An alternative form of *<attribute assign>*, syntactically identical to a *<relation assign>* except that the pertinent *<attribute name>* (a) can appear wherever a *<relvar name>* is allowed and (b) must appear in place of the target *<relvar name>* (in both cases, within that *<relation assign>*), is also supported if the attribute in question is relation valued.

```
<dyadic op>
   ::=    <relation exp> <dyadic op name> <relation exp>

<dyadic op name>
   ::=    UNION | D_UNION | INTERSECT | MINUS | I_MINUS
        | JOIN | TIMES | MATCHING | NOT MATCHING

<relation comp>
   ::=    <relation exp> <relation comp op> <relation exp>

<relation comp op>
   ::=    = | ≠ | ⊆ | ⊂ | ⊇ | ⊃
```

Assignments

```
<relation assignment>
   ::=    [ WITH ( <temp assign commalist> ) : ]
                          <relation assign commalist> ;

<relation assign>
   ::=    <relvar name> := <relation exp>
        | <insert> | <d_insert>| <delete> | <i_delete>| <update>

<insert>
   ::=    INSERT <relvar name> <relation exp>

<d_insert>
   ::=    D_INSERT <relvar name> <relation exp>

<delete>
   ::=    DELETE <relvar name> <relation exp>
        | DELETE <relvar name> [ WHERE <bool exp> ]

<i_delete>
   ::=    I_DELETE <relvar name> <relation exp>

<update>
   ::=    UPDATE <relvar name> [ WHERE <bool exp> ] :
                          { <attribute assign commalist> }
```

Appendix B

TABLE_DUM and TABLE_DEE

Tweedledum and Tweedledee
Agreed to have a battle;
For Tweedledum said Tweedledee
Had spoiled his nice new rattle.
Just then flew by a monstrous crow
As big as a tar-barrel;
Which frightened both the heroes so,
They quite forgot their quarrel.

—old English nursery rhyme, quoted by Lewis Carroll in
Through the Looking-Glass and What Alice Found There (1871)

As noted in Chapter 3, the empty set—the set that contains no elements—is a subset of every set. It follows in particular that the empty heading is a valid heading, and hence that a tuple with an empty set of components is a valid tuple. Such a tuple is of type TUPLE { }; indeed, it's sometimes referred to explicitly as a *0-tuple*, in order to emphasize the fact that it has no components and is of degree zero. It's also sometimes called an *empty tuple*. In **Tutorial D**, it's denoted thus:

```
TUPLE { }
```

Note: The syntactic construct TUPLE { } thus does double duty in **Tutorial D**. However, the intended interpretation is always clear (and unambiguous) from context.

It follows further from the above that a relation too can have an empty heading. Such a relation is of type RELATION { }, and its degree is zero. In **Tutorial D**, such a relation can be denoted thus:

```
RELATION { } body
```

Here the braces denote the empty heading, and *body* is either { } or {TUPLE{ }}—see the explanation immediately following, also Appendix A.

Let *r* be a relation of degree zero, then. How many such relations are there? The answer is: Just two. First, *r* might of course be empty (meaning it contains no tuples)—remember from the answer to Exercise 3.3 in Chapter 3 that there's exactly one empty relation of any given type.

Second, if *r* isn't empty, then the tuples it contains must all be 0-tuples. But there's only one 0-tuple!—equivalently, all 0-tuples are duplicates of one another—and so *r* can't possibly contain more than one of them. So there are indeed just two relations with no attributes: one with just one tuple, and one with no tuples at all. What's more (perhaps surprisingly), these two relations are of considerable practical, as well as theoretical, significance: so much so, in fact, that we have pet names for them—we call them TABLE_DUM and TABLE_DEE, or DUM and DEE for short (DUM is the empty one, DEE is the one with one tuple).

Note: **Tutorial D** supports the keywords TABLE_DUM and TABLE_DEE explicitly, although in fact they're both really just shorthand. To be specific, TABLE_DUM is shorthand for the relation selector invocation

```
RELATION { } { }
```

Likewise, TABLE_DEE is shorthand for the relation selector invocation

```
RELATION { } { TUPLE { } }
```

(again, see Appendix A).

Now, what makes TABLE_DEE and TABLE_DUM so special is the fact that they can be interpreted as TRUE and FALSE, respectively, as I now explain. By way of illustration, consider the projection of the suppliers relvar S on SNO:

```
S { SNO }
```

Let *r* be the result of this projection (given our usual sample data values, *r* contains five tuples). Now consider the projection of that relation *r* on the empty set of attributes:

```
r { }
```

Clearly, projecting any *tuple* on no attributes at all yields an empty tuple; thus, projecting relation *r* on no attributes at all yields a result containing an empty tuple for every tuple in *r*. But as we saw above, all empty tuples are duplicates of one another. Thus, projecting relation *r* (as defined above on no attributes at all yields a relation with no attributes and just one (empty) tuple, or in other words TABLE_DEE.

> *Aside:* Note how the foregoing paragraph appeals to the fact—which I take to be intuitively obvious—that it does make sense to define a version of the familiar projection operator that applies to tuples instead of relations. To be specific: Let *t* be a tuple with heading *H*, and let *X* be a subset of *H*. Then the (tuple) projection of *t* on *X* is a tuple with heading *X*: namely, that subset of *t* that consists of just those components of *t* that correspond to attributes mentioned in *X*. *Note:* Other relational operators for which it

makes sense to define tuple analogs include EXTEND, RENAME, and UNION. See *SQL and Relational Theory* for further discussion. *End of aside.*

Now recall from Chapter 6—see in particular the answer to Exercise 6.4—that every relvar, and in fact every relational expression, has an associated *predicate.* For relvar S, that predicate looks something like this:

Supplier SNO is under contract, is named SNAME, has status STATUS, and is located in city CITY.

For the projection *r* of S on SNO, it looks like this:

There exists some name SNAME and there exists some status STATUS and there exists some city CITY such that supplier SNO is under contract, is named SNAME, has status STATUS, and is located in city CITY.

And for the projection *r*{ } of *r* on the empty set of attributes, it looks like this:

There exists some supplier number SNO and there exists some name SNAME and there exists some status STATUS and there exists some city CITY such that supplier SNO is under contract, is named SNAME, has status STATUS, and is located in city CITY.

Observe now that this last predicate, although it might look rather complicated at first glance, is in fact a proposition: It evaluates to TRUE or FALSE, unconditionally.[1] In the case at hand, *r*{ } is TABLE_DEE and the predicate (proposition) clearly evaluates to TRUE. But suppose no suppliers at all were represented in the database at this time. Then relvar S would be empty, the projection S{SNO} would yield an empty relation *r*, the projection *r*{ } would be TABLE_DUM, and the predicate (proposition) in question would evaluate to FALSE.

So TABLE_DUM means FALSE (or *no*) and TABLE_DEE means TRUE (or *yes*). They have the most fundamental meanings of all! By the way, a good way to remember which is which is this: DEE and *yes* both have an "E"; DUM and *no* don't.

Now, it would take us too far beyond the scope of this book to go into much more detail on these matters, so I'll content myself here with just a few further remarks. First let me give a concrete (and practical) example of DEE and DUM in action, as it were. Consider the query "Does any supplier in Athens supply any parts?" Observe that this is a yes/no query (that is, the answer is either yes or no). Here's a **Tutorial D** formulation:

---

[1] In general, in fact, a predicate always degenerates to a proposition if the set of parameters to that predicate happens to be the empty set. Note that such is exactly the situation in the example under discussion. To be specific, in the predicate for the projection *r*{ }, the symbols SNO, SNAME, STATUS, and CITY no longer denote parameters as such, they denote *bound variables* instead (see Appendix D).

```
( ( S WHERE CITY = 'Athens' ) MATCHING SP ) { }
```

This expression, since it finishes up by taking a projection on no attributes, clearly evaluates to either TABLE_DUM or TABLE_DEE. If the result is TABLE_DUM, it means no, no supplier in Athens does supply any parts; if the result is TABLE_DEE, it means yes, at least one supplier in Athens does supply at least one part.

So what about SQL? Well, SQL says, quite correctly, that the result of any query is a table; unfortunately, however, it forgot to support the tables that mean yes and no.[2] So yes/no queries can't be done directly in SQL. Indeed, the best we can do in SQL with the foregoing example is something like the following. First we can ask *how many* suppliers in Athens supply any parts:

```
SELECT COUNT ( SNO ) AS X
FROM   S
WHERE  CITY = 'Athens'
AND    SNO IN
     ( SELECT SNO
       FROM   SP )
```

Then we can extract the value of column X from the single row in the table that results from this query. And if that value is zero, it means no supplier in Athens supplies any parts, while if it's nonzero it means at least one supplier in Athens does supply at least one part.

The other point I want to make is this (it's a more general and more fundamental point, in a way): These two special relations TABLE_DUM and TABLE_DEE (especially TABLE_DEE) play a role in the relational algebra that's analogous to the role played by zero in conventional arithmetic. And we all know how important zero is; in fact, it's hard to imagine an arithmetic without zero (the ancient Romans tried, but it didn't get them very far). Well, it should be equally hard to imagine a relational algebra without TABLE_DEE.

Let me give one specific illustration of the foregoing. First, it's well known that, in logic, TRUE is the identity with respect to AND (I mentioned this fact in passing in Chapter 5); that is, if p is an arbitrary proposition, then the expressions p AND TRUE and TRUE AND p both reduce to simply p. Similarly, 0 is the identity with respect to "+", and 1 is the identity with respect to "*", in ordinary arithmetic; that is, for all numbers x, the expressions $x + 0$, $0 + x$, $x * 1$, and $1 * x$ all reduce to simply x. Well, in the same kind of way, TABLE_DEE is the identity with respect to JOIN in the relational algebra; that is, the join of any relation r with TABLE_DEE is simply r.[3] In particular, therefore, just as the AND of no propositions is TRUE, and the sum of no numbers is zero, and the product of no numbers is one, so the join of no relations is TABLE_DEE.

---

[2] It also forgot to support the empty row—most of the time, but not quite always! See *SQL and Relational Theory* for an explanation of this point.

[3] As I explained in Chapter 4, join degenerates to cartesian product if the operands have no attributes in common. It follows that join always degenerates to cartesian product if one of the operands is either TABLE_DEE or TABLE_DUM, and it further follows that the join we're talking about here is in fact a cartesian product.

Let me say too that once you're aware of the existence of these two special relations, you'll find them cropping up all over the place. In fact, they represent just one specific, and important, manifestation of the concept of *nullology*, which was something I mentioned briefly in footnote 1 in Chapter 3. *Note:* As I also mentioned in that same footnote, nullology has nothing to do with SQL-style nulls! Nullology is the study of the empty set, and it's both theoretically respectable and of considerable practical utility. SQL's nulls do *not* enjoy theoretical respectability, and in practice should be avoided like the plague.

In closing, perhaps I should say just a little more about the pet names TABLE_DUM and TABLE_DEE. First, for the benefit of non English speakers, I should explain that (as the epigraph to this appendix indicates) they're basically just wordplay on Tweedledum and Tweedledee, who were originally characters in a children's nursery rhyme and were subsequently incorporated into Lewis Carroll's *Through the Looking-Glass*. Second, the names are perhaps a little unfortunate, given that these two relations are precisely the ones that can't reasonably be depicted as tables! (Note that I didn't even try to draw pictures of these relations in our discussions earlier; in fact, this is the one place where the idea of thinking of relations as tables breaks down completely.) But we've been using those names for so long now in the relational world that we're probably not going to change them.

Appendix C

Set Theory

The Joy of Sets

—Anon.: *Where Bugs Go*

An understanding of set theory can be very helpful in dealing with databases; indeed, as mentioned in Chapter 7, the relational model is directly based on certain aspects of that theory. In this appendix, therefore, I offer a brief tutorial on set theory basics.

WHAT'S A SET?

I'll begin with a definition:

> **Definition:** A **set** S is a collection of distinct **elements**, or **members**, such that, given an arbitrary object x, it can be determined whether or not x is contained in S (i.e., is an element of S). *Note the terminology:* A set is said to **contain** its members.

Here's an example:

```
{ 2 , 3 , 5 , 7 }
```

As this example suggests, the standard "on paper" representation of a set is as a commalist, enclosed in braces, of symbols denoting the elements of the set in question. Points arising:

- Sets never contain duplicate elements. Thus, if duplicate symbols appear in the "on paper" representation (which by convention they usually don't), they can simply be ignored. For example, the following—

```
{ 2 , 2 , 3 , 5 , 5 , 5 , 7 , 7 }
```

—is another possible, albeit unlikely, "on paper" representation of the set {2,3,5,7}.

- Sets have no ordering to their elements. Thus, for example, the following—

```
{ 7 , 2 , 5 , 3 }
```

—is another possible "on paper" representation of that same set.

- A set can contain no elements at all, in which case it's the (unique) *empty set*, written { }, or sometimes Ø.

- There's another unique set called the *universal set*, which is the set that contains all of the elements of interest (all of the elements of interest, that is, in whatever the context at hand happens to be; in the foregoing example, it might be positive integers). It's sometimes referred to as *the universe* (or *domain*) *of discourse*.

- The elements of a set can be anything at all, even other sets. *Note:* This statement is somewhat oversimplified, but it's good enough for the purposes of this appendix.

- The number of elements in a set is the *cardinality* of the set in question. Note that the cardinality of the empty set is zero.

Now, there are several ways of specifying any given set. First, the set can be specified by simply *enumerating* its elements, as in the example already discussed:

```
{ 2 , 3 , 5 , 7 }
```

Note, however, that such enumeration is possible only if the set in question is finite. Set theory in general does permit infinite sets; in the computing context, however, sets are necessarily finite, and so I'll have nothing more to say regarding infinite sets as such in this appendix.

Second, a set can be specified in terms of a *predicate*—for example:

```
{ x : x is a prime AND x < 10 }
```

This specification defines the set in question to be the collection of all objects x such that x is a prime number less than ten (the colon ":" in the specification can be read as "where" or "such that"). Of course, the set in this example is identical to the one specified by enumeration above.

Third, a set can be specified by *substitution*—for example:

```
{ x² : x is a prime AND x < 10 }
```

This specification defines the set in question to be the collection of all objects y such that y is equal to x^2 and x in turn is a prime number less than 10; in other words, it species the set {4,9,25,49}. *Note:* Specification by means of a predicate, as in the previous example, can of course be regarded as just a special case of specification by means of substitution.

Now I can define the set membership operator "∈" (which is derived from the Greek letter *epsilon* and is sometimes referred to by that name):

Definition: The expression $x \in S$ returns TRUE if and only if the object x is a member of the set S. Conversely, the expression $x \notin S$ returns FALSE if and only if the object x is not a member of the set S. *Note:* The expression $x \in S$ can be read as "x appears in S," or "x belongs to S," or just "x is an element of S." Similarly for the expression $x \notin S$, of course.

For example, $5 \in \{2,3,5,7\}$ returns TRUE, while $8 \in \{2,3,5,7\}$ returns FALSE. By the way, note the logical difference between an object x and the *singleton set* $\{x\}$ that contains just that object x as its sole member.

I'll close this introductory section with another definition:

Definition: Set theory is a branch of mathematics, closely related to predicate logic, that deals with the nature of sets. In particular, it formalizes the concept of a set in terms of certain axioms: for example, **the axiom of extension**, which states that two sets are equal if and only if they contain exactly the same members.

Incidentally, observe the crucial role played in this theory by the notion of equality. To start with, the definition of set membership is crucially dependent on it (after all, how could we say whether the expression $5 \in \{2,3,5,7\}$ returns TRUE without the ability to test whether 5 is equal to each of the elements of that set in turn? Second, the axiom of extension in turn is crucially dependent on it, too (obviously so, in fact).

SUBSETS AND SUPERSETS

Let $S1$ and $S2$ be sets, not necessarily distinct. Then we have:

Definition: $S2$ is a **subset** of $S1$ (in symbols, $S2 \subseteq S1$) if and only if every element of $S2$ is an element of $S1$. $S1$ is a **superset** of $S2$ (in symbols, $S1 \supseteq S2$) if and only if $S2$ is a subset of $S1$.

Points arising:

■ Every subset of a set is a set; every superset of a set is a set.

■ Every set is both a subset and a superset of itself.

■ The empty set is a subset of every set; the universal set is a superset of every set.

The next definition is equivalent to the previous one but introduces some new terminology:

Definition: *S2* is **included in** *S1* (in symbols, *S2* ⊆ *S1*) if and only if every element of *S2* is an element of *S1*. *S1* **includes** *S2* (in symbols, *S1* ⊇ *S2*) if and only if *S2* is is included in *S1*.

Points arising:

- Every set is included in and includes itself.

- The empty set is included in every set; the universal set includes every set.

- The term *set inclusion* is usually taken, a trifle arbitrarily, to refer to the "⊆" operator, not the "⊇" operator.

- *Terminology:* Don't confuse "⊆" and "∈"!—a set *includes* its subsets but *contains* its elements. Be aware, however, that the literature isn't entirely consistent on this point; indeed, sometimes it's difficult to be consistent, at least in English prose, because there are occasions where the stylistic conventions of the language are such as to demand use of the "wrong" word. *Caveat lector.*

- Observe that we can now define sets *S1* and *S2* to be *equal* (i.e., to be in fact the very same set—in symbols, *S1* = *S2*) if and only if the expressions *S1* ⊆ *S2* and *S1* ⊇ *S2* both return TRUE.

Now, we've seen that to say *S2* is a subset of *S1* doesn't exclude the possibility that *S2* and *S1* are one and the same set. If we do want to exclude that possibility, we need to talk in terms of *proper* subsets. Here are the pertinent definitions:

Definition: *S2* is a **proper** subset of *S1* (in symbols, *S2* ⊂ *S1*)—equivalently, *S2* is **properly** included in *S1*—if and only if *S2* is a subset of *S1* and *S2* and *S1* are distinct (i.e., there exists an element of *S1* that isn't an element of *S2*). *S1* is a **proper** superset of *S2* (in symbols, *S1* ⊃ *S2*)—equivalently, *S1* **properly** includes *S2*—if and only if *S2* is a proper subset of *S1*.

For example, let *S1* be {2,3,5} and let *S2* be {2,5}. Then *S2* is a proper subset of *S1*; it's also a subset of itself, but not a proper one (*no* set is a proper subset of itself).
And one further definition:

Definition: The **power set** *P(S)* of a given set *S* is the set of all subsets of that set *S*.

For example, let *S* be the following set:

{ 2 , 3 , 5 }

Then *P(S)* is the set:

{ { } , { 2 } , { 3 } , { 5 } ,
        { 2 , 3 } , { 3 , 5 } , { 5 , 2 } , { 2 , 3 , 5 } }

Observe that the cardinality of this power set is 8 (=2^3). In general, in fact, if the cardinality of *S* is *n*, then the cardinality of *P(S)* is 2^n (don't forget that the empty set and *S* itself are both subsets of *S*, necessarily).

Exercises

Let S be the following set:

{ 2 , 3 , { 2 , 5 } , 5 , { 3 , 7 } , 7 , { 2 , { 3 , 7 } } }

C.1   What's the cardinality of *S*?

C.2   What's the truth value of the expression {3,7} ∈ *S*?

C.3   What's the truth value of the expression {3,7} ⊆ *S*?

C.4   What's the truth value of the expression {2,3,7} ∈ *S*?

C.5   What's the truth value of the expression {2,3,7} ⊆ *S*?

C.6   What's the truth value of the expression { } ⊆ *S*?

C.7   What's the cardinality of *P(S)*?

C.8   Can there exist a set *X* such that *P(X)* = *X* is true?

Answers

C.1   7.

C.2   TRUE.

C.3   TRUE.

C.4   FALSE.

C.5   TRUE.

C.6   TRUE (of course!).

C.7 $2^7 = 128$.

C.8   No. Let X have cardinality n; then $P(X)$ has cardinality 2^n. Since 2^n is always strictly greater than n (even when n is zero), $P(X)$ and X can never be equal; thus, the answer to the question has to be no, even if X is empty. *Note:* If $n = 0$, $2^n = 2^0 = 1$.

SET OPERATORS

The set theory operators union and intersection are surely familiar to most readers,[1] but I'll define them here for the record:

> **Definition:** The **union** of sets *S1* and *S2* (in symbols, *S1* ∪ *S2*, sometimes pronounced "*S1* cup *S2*") is the set of objects *x* such that *x* is an element of *S1* or *S2* or both:
>
> ```
> { x : x ∈ S1 OR x ∈ S2 }
> ```

> **Definition:** The **intersection** of sets *S1* and *S2* (in symbols, *S1* ∩ *S2*, sometimes pronounced "*S1* cap *S2*") is the set of objects *x* such that *x* is an element of both *S1* and *S2*:
>
> ```
> { x : x ∈ S1 AND x ∈ S2 }
> ```

The set theory difference operator is surely familiar too:

> **Definition:** The **difference** between sets *S1* and *S2*, in that order (in symbols, *S1* − *S2*), is the set of objects *x* such that *x* is an element of *S1* and not of *S2*:
>
> ```
> { x : x ∈ S1 AND x ∉ S2 }
> ```

As you can see from the foregoing definitions, union and intersection are set theory counterparts to the logical operators, or *connectives*, OR and AND, respectively. By contrast, difference is *not* quite a set theory counterpart to the logical operator NOT. Rather, the operator that does constitute such a counterpart is *complement*, which can be defined thus:

---

[1] See Exercise 4.5 in Chapter 4.

Definition: The **complement** of set S (in symbols, $\sim S$, sometimes pronounced "not S") is the set of objects x such that x is not an element of S:

```
{ x : x ∉ S }
```

However, observe now that if U is the pertinent universal set, then the complement of S is just the difference $U - S$. Indeed, the difference $S1 - S2$ is sometimes called the *relative complement of S2 with respect to S1*, and the difference $U - S$ (which above I called just the complement of S) is sometimes called, more specifically, the *absolute* complement of S.

Another useful operator is *exclusive union*, also known as *symmetric difference*. It's the set theory counterpart to the logical operator XOR ("exclusive OR").

Definition: The **exclusive union** of sets $S1$ and $S2$ is the set of objects x such that x is an element of $S1$ or $S2$ but not both:

```
{ x : x ∈ S1 XOR x ∈ S2 }
```

Note: There doesn't seem to be any consensus in the literature on a symbol to represent the exclusive union operator. Partly for this reason (and partly just for clarity), throughout the remainder of this appendix I'll use keywords to denote the various operators, as follows: UNION, INTERSECT, MINUS (for difference or relative complement), COMP (for absolute complement), and XUNION (for exclusive union or symmetric difference).

Exercises

Let $S1$ and $S2$ be the sets $\{2,3,5,7\}$ and $\{1,3,5,7,9\}$, respectively. What do the following expressions evaluate to?

C.9   *S1* UNION *S2*

C.10 *S1* INTERSECT *S2*

C.11 *S1* MINUS *S2*

C.12 *S2* MINUS *S1*

C.13 *S1* XUNION *S2*

C.14 *S1* MINUS (*S1* MINUS S2)

C.15 (*S1* MINUS *S2*) UNION (*S2* MINUS *S1*)

C.16 COMP (*S1*)

Answers

C.9 {1,2,3,5,7,9}

C.10 {3,5,7}

C.11 {2}

C.12 {1,9}

C.13 {1,2,9}

C.14 {3,5,7} (same as C.10, necessarily).

C.15 {1,2,9} (same as C.13, necessarily).

C.16 The answer here depends on what the pertinent universal set is. For simplicity, suppose it's the set of integers from 1 to 9. Then COMP (*S1*) is {1,4,6,8,9}.

SOME IDENTITIES

All of the operators discussed in this appendix so far, except for "∈", take sets (only) as inputs and return a set as output; in other words, we're talking about a closed system again. Various further (and desirable) properties also apply, as follows:[2]

- *Commutativity:* The dyadic operator *Op* is commutative if and only if, for all *A* and *B*, *A Op B* ≡ *B Op A*.[3] The set theory operators UNION, INTERSECT, and XUNION are commutative.

---

[2] Most of these properties are easily verified by means of Venn diagrams (exercise for the reader). *Note:* If you're not familiar with the concept of Venn diagrams, you can find an explanation in any elementary book on logic; see, for example, *Set Theory and Logic,* by Robert R. Stoll (W. H. Freeman and Company, 1965; Dover Publications, 1979).

[3] I assume an infix syntactic style here and throughout this section for definiteness. Also, the symbol "≡" can be read as "is equivalent to."

- *Associativity:* The dyadic operator *Op* is associative if and only if, for all *A*, *B*, and *C*, *A Op* (*B Op C*) ≡ (*A Op B*) *Op C*. The set theory operators UNION, INTERSECT, and XUNION are associative.

- *Distributivity:* The dyadic operator *Opx* distributes over the dyadic operator *Opy* if and only if, for all *A*, *B*, and *C*, *A Opx* (*B Opy C*) ≡ (*A Opx B*) *Opy* (*A Opx C*). The set theory operators UNION and INTERSECT each distribute over the other.

- *Idempotence:* The dyadic operator *Op* is idempotent if and only if, for all *A*, *A Op A* ≡ *A*. The set theory operators UNION and INTERSECT are idempotent.

- *Absorption:* The dyadic operator *Opx* absorbs the dyadic operator *Opy* if and only if, for all *A* and *B*, *A Opx* (*A Opy B*) ≡ *A*. The set theory operators UNION and INTERSECT each absorb the other.

The following identities also hold:

- *De Morgan's Laws:*

```
COMP ( A UNION B ) ≡ ( COMP ( A ) ) INTERSECT ( COMP ( B ) )

COMP ( A INTERSECT B ) ≡ ( COMP ( A ) ) UNION ( COMP ( B ) )
```

- Let *U* be the pertinent universal set. Then the following identities hold:

```
A UNION U ≡ U

A INTERSECT U ≡ A

A UNION ∅ ≡ A

A INTERSECT ∅ ≡ ∅
```

Exercises

Either prove or disprove the following:

C.17 (A MINUS C) MINUS (B MINUS C) ≡ (A MINUS B) MINUS C

C.18 (A INTERSECT B) UNION C ≡ C INTERSECT (B UNION A)

C.19 A INTERSECT (B MINUS C) ≡ (A INTERSECT B) MINUS (A INTERSECT C)

Answers

I'll give an answer here to Exercise C.17 only, just to illustrate the kind of reasoning involved in such questions.[4]

C.17 The equivalence is valid. Proof:

```
x ∈ ( ( A MINUS C ) MINUS ( B MINUS C ) )   if and only if
x ∈ ( A MINUS C ) AND x ∉ ( B MINUS C )   if and only if
x ∈ A AND x ∉ C AND ( x ∉ B OR x ∈ C )   if and only if
x ∈ A AND ( x ∉ C AND ( x ∉ B OR x ∈ C ) )   if and only if
x ∈ A AND ( ( x ∉ C AND x ∉ B ) OR ( x ∉ C AND x ∈ C ) )   if and only if
x ∈ A AND ( x ∉ C AND x ∉ B )   if and only if
x ∈ A AND x ∉ B AND x ∉ C   if and only if
x ∈ ( A MINUS B ) AND x ∉ C   if and only if
x ∈ ( A MINUS B ) MINUS C
```

THE ALGEBRA OF SETS

The combination of (a) a set U, defined to be the power set $P(S)$ of some given set S, (b) the operators UNION, INTERSECT, and COMP on elements of U, and (c) the set inclusion operator "⊆" on elements of U, together constitute an *algebra of sets*, in which U plays the role of the universal set. Such an algebra obeys the following laws:

- *Closure* (applies to UNION, INTERSECT, and COMP)

- *Commutativity* (applies to UNION and INTERSECT)

- *Associativity* (applies to UNION and INTERSECT)

- *Distributivity* (applies to UNION and INTERSECT with respect to each other)

- *Identities* (UNION and INTERSECT have as identities Ø and U, respectively)

- *Idempotence* (applies to UNION and INTERSECT)

- *Absorption* (applies to UNION and INTERSECT with respect to each other)

---

[4] Again Venn diagrams can help.

■ *Involution:*

```
( COMP ( COMP( A ) ) ) ≡ A
```

■ *Complementarity:*

```
A UNION ( COMP( A ) ) ≡ U
```

```
A INTERSECT ( COMP( A ) ) ≡ Ø
```

■ *De Morgan's Laws* (see earlier)

■ *Consistency:* The following expressions are all equivalent:

```
A ⊆ B
```

```
A UNION B = B
```

```
A INTERSECT B = A
```

CARTESIAN PRODUCT

Now I can begin to explain how set theory leads up to relational theory (but only *begin* to do so—I deliberately don't want to do more than scratch the surface of the issue here).

> **Definition:** An **ordered pair** $<x,y>$ is a combination of exactly two elements x and y such that x is the first element of the pair and y the second. More precisely, $<x,y>$ is defined to be shorthand for the set $\{\{x\},\{x,y\}\}$; note that one of the elements in this set determines the elements that constitute the ordered pair and the other determines which of those elements comes first.[5]

Observe that it follows from this definition that the ordered pairs $<x1,y1>$ and $<x2,y2>$ are equal if and only if $x1 = x2$ and $y1 = y2$ (thus $<x,y> \neq <y,x>$, in general).

Now I can define the (set theory) cartesian product operator:[6]

---

[5] You might think this definition breaks down in the case where the elements x and y are equal (since the expression $\{\{x\},\{x,y\}\}$ reduces to just $\{\{x\}\}$ in that case). In fact it doesn't, but the details of exactly why it doesn't are beyond the scope of this appendix.

[6] The set theory cartesian product operator isn't quite the same as its relational model counterpart. Come to that, the set theory binary relation, to be defined in just a moment, isn't quite the same as its relational model counterpart, either. For further discussion of such matters, I refer you to Appendix A of *SQL and Relational Theory*.

Definition: The **cartesian product** of sets *S1* and *S2*, in that order, is the set of all ordered pairs <*x,y*> such that *x* is an element of *S1* and *y* is an element of *S2*.

Note that the cartesian product of *S1* and *S2* is in fact a (set theory) *binary relation*. More generally:

Definition: A **binary relation** on sets *S1* and *S2*, in that order, is a subset of the cartesian product of sets *S1* and *S2*, in that order.

By way of example, let *S1* and *S2* be the sets {1,3} and {2,3,5}, respectively. Here then are some binary relations on *S1* and *S2*, in that order (actually four such):[7]

```
{ <1,2> , <3,3> , <3,5> }
{ <1,2> , <1,3> , <1,5> , <3,2> , <3,3> , <3,5> }
{ <1,5> }
{ }
```

And one final definition, mainly just for the record:

Definition: A **function** is a binary relation in which no two elements have the same first component.

CONCLUDING REMARKS

This brings us to the end of this short tutorial on set theory. As you can see, we've covered quite a lot of territory, but of course there's much, much more to the subject than it would be possible (or appropriate) to cover here. But I hope I've said enough to pique your interest. If indeed you're motivated to read further, I suggest you take a look at the book mentioned earlier in this appendix (in footnote 2), *Set Theory and Logic*, by Robert R. Stoll (W. H. Freeman and Company, 1965; Dover Publications, 1979)—or, of course, any other book on such matters that you find to your taste.

---

[7] As an exercise, show tabular representations of these four relations.

Appendix D

Relational Calculus

"If it was so, it might be; and if it were so, it would be;
but as it isn't, it ain't. That's logic."
—Tweedledee, in Lewis Carroll:
Through the Looking-Glass and What Alice Found There (1871)

As noted in Chapter 7, the relational calculus is an alternative to, and is expressively equivalent to, the relational algebra. It's based on predicate calculus (also known as predicate logic); in fact, it can be seen as a version of predicate calculus that's tailored for dealing with relations specifically. And a knowledge of the relational model can't truly be said to be complete if it fails to include at least a basic understanding of the calculus; hence this appendix, which presents a brief tutorial on the subject.

The plan of the appendix is as follows. Following these introductory remarks, I'll show a fairly lengthy series of simple examples, involving both queries and constraints, in order to give some idea of what calculus expressions look like "in action" (as it were); then I'll give a simple grammar for such expressions. Do please note, however, that I'm not trying to describe any commercially available language in this appendix; nor will what I do describe be anything close to industrial strength. Instead, I'll just show, and use, a somewhat hypothetical syntax that should be sufficient for illustrative purposes.

Now, a fundamental feature of the calculus is the *range variable*. Briefly, a range variable is a variable that "ranges over" some specified relation (i.e., it's a variable whose permitted values are tuples of that relation).[1] The relation in question is, typically, the current value of some specified relvar. Thus, if range variable *RV* is defined to range over relvar *R*, then, at any given time, the expression—actually a *range variable reference*—*RV* denotes some tuple within the relation *r* that happens to be the value of that relvar *R* at the time in question. For example, consider the query "Get supplier numbers for suppliers in London." This query might be formulated in relational calculus as follows:

```
RANGEVAR SX RANGES OVER S ;

{ SX.SNO } WHERE SX.CITY = 'London'
```

---

[1] As you might remember, we've encountered range variables before, albeit only in the context of SQL (see the answer to Exercise 11.1d in Chapter 11). Recall in particular that range variables aren't variables in the usual programming language sense; rather, they're variables in the sense of logic.

The sole range variable here is SX, and it ranges over the relation that's the value of the suppliers relvar S at the time the relational calculus expression in the second line is evaluated. That expression can be read as follows (loosely, and in somewhat stilted English): "For each tuple that's a possible value of range variable SX—in other words, for each tuple currently appearing in relvar S—return the SNO component of that tuple, if and only if the CITY component of that tuple is London."

Terminology: I'll refer to the construct that precedes the WHERE clause, in a relational calculus expression like the one in the second line of the foregoing example, as a *proto tuple*, because it represents a prototype of the tuples that will appear in the result when the expression overall is evaluated.[2] So the general form of a relational calculus expression is this:

```
proto tuple WHERE bool exp
```

And such an expression evaluates to a relation containing just those tuples that are permitted values of the proto tuple for which the boolean expression *bool exp* in the WHERE clause evaluates to TRUE.

With the foregoing by way of introduction, let me now move on to present the promised series of examples (sample queries and sample constraints). *Note:* In what follows, for simplicity, I'll mostly omit the range variable definitions—i.e., RANGEVAR statements—that would be needed in practice. Instead, I'll just assume as necessary that range variables SX, SY, etc., have been defined to range over relvar S; range variables PX, PY, etc., have been defined to range over relvar P; and range variables SPX, SPY, etc., have been defined to range over relvar SP. Also, I'll provide prose commentary on the examples only when I think there's something to say about them that might not be immediately obvious.

SAMPLE QUERIES

1. Get supplier numbers and status for suppliers in Paris with status > 20.

```
{ SX.SNO , SX.STATUS } WHERE SX.CITY = 'Paris' AND SX.STATUS > 20
```

2. Get pairs of supplier numbers, *x* and *y* say, such that suppliers *x* and *y* are located in the same city.

```
{ XNO := SX.SNO , YNO := SY.SNO }
                    WHERE SX.CITY = SY.CITY AND SX.SNO < SY.SNO
```

---

[2] The term *proto tuple* is apt but nonstandard. In fact, there doesn't really seem to be a standard term for the construct.

3.   Get full supplier information for suppliers who supply part P2.

```
{ SX.SNO , SX.SNAME , SX.STATUS , SX.CITY }
        WHERE EXISTS SPX ( SPX.SNO = SX.SNO AND SPX.PNO = 'P2' )
```

Explanation: As you can see, the boolean expression—let's call it *bx1*—in the WHERE clause here takes the form:

```
EXISTS RV ( bx2 )
```

Here *RV* is a range variable name, EXISTS *RV* is a *quantifier* (specifically, an *existential* quantifier), and *bx2* is another boolean expression. The overall boolean expression *bx1* is defined to return TRUE if and only if there exists at least one tuple, out of the set of tuples that are possible values for *RV*, that makes the inner boolean expression *bx2* evaluate to TRUE. Thus, we can imagine the query in this example as being evaluated as follows:

■   The system examines the tuples in the current value of relvar S—relvar S, because the proto tuple involves range variable SX, which (by my initial assumptions) is defined to range over that relvar—one at a time in some arbitrary sequence.

■   Consider one such tuple, say the one for supplier S1. For that tuple, the boolean expression in the WHERE clause effectively reduces to the following:

```
EXISTS SPX ( SPX.SNO = 'S1' AND SPX.PNO = 'P2' )
```

And this expression clearly evaluates to TRUE if and only if relvar SP currently contains a tuple for supplier S1 and part P1—which, given our usual sample values, it does, and so the tuple from relvar S for supplier S1 becomes part of the overall result.

■   The system then moves on to look at another tuple from relvar S, and the process repeats until all such tuples have been examined.

Points arising from this example:

■   In the literature, EXISTS is often represented by a backward E, thus: ∃. But I'll stay with the keyword in this appendix.

■   *Terminology:* A range variable that's subject to quantification is said to be *bound* (within the overall calculus expression in which it appears) by the quantifier in question; a range variable that's not bound in this sense is said to be *free*. In the example, therefore, SPX is bound and SX is free.

■ The proto tuple in the example actually mentions all of the attributes of the pertinent relvar. To save a little writing, we allow such a proto tuple to be abbreviated as shown in this alternative version of the overall expression:

```
{ SX } WHERE EXISTS SPX ( SPX.SNO = SX.SNO AND SPX.PNO = 'P2' )
```

4.   Get supplier names for suppliers who supply at least one red part.

```
{ SX.SNAME } WHERE EXISTS SPX ( SX.SNO = SPX.SNO AND
                   EXISTS PX ( PX.PNO = SPX.PNO AND PX.COLOR = 'Red' ) )
```

Or equivalently (but in *prenex normal form*, in which all of the quantifiers appear at the front of the boolean expression in the WHERE clause):

```
{ SX.SNAME } WHERE EXISTS SPX ( EXISTS PX ( SX.SNO = SPX.SNO AND
                   PX.PNO = SPX.PNO AND PX.COLOR = 'Red' ) )
```

Either way, the point about this example is that, of course, the boolean expression *bx* in a quantified expression of the form EXISTS *RV* (*bx*) can itself involve further quantifiers in turn.

5.   Get supplier names for suppliers who supply at least one part supplied by supplier S2.

```
{ SX.SNAME } WHERE EXISTS SPX ( EXISTS SPY ( SX.SNO = SPX.SNO AND
                   SPX.PNO = SPY.PNO AND
                   SPY.SNO = 'S2' ) )
```

Observe that this expression involves two distinct range variables ranging over the same relvar. *Note:* In practice, we might want to add the following to the boolean expression in the WHERE clause in this example (why, exactly?):

```
AND SX.SNO ≠ 'S2'
```

6.   Get supplier names for suppliers who supply all parts.

```
{ SX.SNAME } WHERE FORALL PX ( EXISTS SPX ( SPX.SNO = SX.SNO AND
                   SPX.PNO = PX.PNO ) )
```

Explanation: As you can see, the boolean expression—let's call it *bx1*—in the WHERE clause here takes the form:

```
FORALL RV ( bx2 )
```

Like EXISTS *RV*, FORALL *RV* is a quantifier (specifically, a *universal* quantifier). The overall boolean expression *bx1* is defined to return TRUE if and only if every tuple in the set of tuples that are possible values for *RV* makes the inner boolean expression *bx2* evaluate to TRUE. Thus, we can imagine the query in this example being evaluated as follows:

- The system examines the tuples in the current value of relvar S one at a time in some arbitrary sequence.

- Consider one such tuple, say that for supplier S1. For that tuple, the boolean expression in the WHERE clause effectively reduces to the following:

```
FORALL PX ( EXISTS SPX ( SPX.SNO = 'S1' AND SPX.PNO = PX.PNO ) )
```

  And this expression evaluates to TRUE if and only if relvar SP currently contains a tuple for supplier S1 and part P*x* for every part number P*x* currently appearing in relvar P— which, given our usual sample values, it does, and so the supplier tuple from relvar S for supplier S1 becomes part of the overall result.

- The system then moves on to look at another tuple in that relvar, and the process repeats until all such tuples have been examined.

  Points arising from this example:

- In the literature, FORALL is often represented by an upside down A, thus: ∀. But I'll stay with the keyword in this appendix.

- Observe that a single "good" example suffices to make an existentially quantified expression evaluate to TRUE, while a single "bad" example (i.e., a single "good" counterexample) suffices to make a universally quantified expression evaluate to FALSE.

- Any boolean expression involving FORALL can always be transformed into one involving EXISTS instead,[3] thanks to the following identity:

```
FORALL X ( bx ) ≡ NOT EXISTS X ( NOT bx )
```

  Example 6 could thus alternatively have been expressed as follows:

```
{ SX.SNAME } WHERE NOT EXISTS PX ( NOT EXISTS SPX
                                  ( SPX.SNO = SX.SNO AND
                                    SPX.PNO = PX.PNO ) )
```

---

[3] Of course, the converse is true as well.

Aside: The foregoing observation is relevant to SQL in particular, because SQL, although it does support EXISTS,[4] doesn't support FORALL. One consequence of this state of affairs is that queries for which FORALL seems to be "naturally" suited tend to be quite awkward to express in SQL. See the answer to Exercise 11.1e in Chapter 11 for an illustration of this point. *End of aside.*

7.   Get supplier names for suppliers who do not supply part P2.

```
{ SX.SNAME } WHERE NOT EXISTS SPX
                        ( SPX.SNO = SX.SNO AND SPX.PNO = 'P2' )
```

8.   Get supplier numbers and cities for suppliers who supply at least all those parts supplied by supplier S2.

```
{ SX.SNO , SX.CITY } WHERE FORALL SPX ( SPX.SNO ≠ 'S2' OR
                                EXISTS SPY ( SPY.SNO = SX.SNO AND
                                        SPY.PNO = SPX.PNO ) )
```

Paraphrasing: "Get supplier numbers and cities for suppliers SX such that, for all shipments SPX, either that shipment is not from supplier S2, or if it is, then there exists a shipment SPY of the SPX part from supplier SX."

9.   Get part numbers for parts that either weigh more than 16 pounds or are supplied by supplier S2, or both.

```
RANGEVAR PV RANGES OVER  ( { PX.PNO } WHERE PX.WEIGHT > 16.0 ,
                           { SPX.PNO } WHERE SPX.SNO = 'S2' ) ;

{ PV.PNO } WHERE TRUE
```

Points arising:

- The range variable PV in this example is effectively defined to range over the union of the projections on PNO of relvars P and SP. Note that the definition of PV relies in turn on range variables PX and SPX.

- If no WHERE clause is specified, a WHERE clause of the form WHERE TRUE is assumed by default. The calculus expression in the example could thus be simplified to just:

```
{ PV.PNO }
```

---

[4] Well, sort of. Actually its support for EXISTS is logically flawed (see *SQL and Relational Theory*).

10.   For each part, get the part number and the weight in grams.

```
{ PX.PNO , GMWT := PX.WEIGHT * 454 }
```

11.   Get all suppliers and tag each one with the literal value "Supplier."

```
{ SX , TAG := 'Supplier' }
```

12.   For each shipment, get full shipment details, including total shipment weight.

```
{ SPX , SHIPWT := PX.WEIGHT * SPX.QTY } WHERE PX.PNO = SPX.PNO
```

13.   For each part, get the part number and the total shipment quantity.

```
{ PX.PNO , TQTY := SUM ( { SPX } WHERE SPX.PNO = PX.PNO , QTY ) }
```

The first argument to the SUM invocation here is a relation, of course, and it's denoted by another relational calculus expression.

14.   Get the total shipment quantity.

```
{ SUM ( { SPX } , QTY ) AS GRANDTOTAL }
```

15.   Get part cities that store more than five red parts.

```
{ PX.CITY } WHERE COUNT ( { PY } WHERE PY.CITY = PX.CITY
                                AND   PY.COLOR = 'Red' ) > 5
```

SAMPLE CONSTRAINTS

I consider the same five examples here—the same five "business rules"—that I used in Chapters 6 and 13.

1.   Supplier status values must be in the range 1 to 100 inclusive.

```
CONSTRAINT CX1 NOT EXISTS SX ( SX.STATUS < 1 OR SX.STATUS > 100 ) ;
```

Note that if relvar S happens to be empty when this constraint is checked, the constraint is satisfied trivially. In general (but a trifle loosely), we can say the quantified expression

```
EXISTS X ( bx )
```

necessarily evaluates to FALSE "if there aren't any *X*'s" (i.e., if the range variable *X* happens to range over an empty set), no matter what the boolean expression *bx* happens to be. Thus, the negated form

```
NOT EXISTS X ( bx )
```

necessarily evaluates to TRUE in those same circumstances.

Incidentally, it follows from the above that the expression FORALL *X* (*bx*) also necessarily evaluates to TRUE if there aren't any *X*'s—again, no matter what the boolean expression *bx* happens to be. Thus, another and arguably more user friendly possible formulation of the constraint in the example is as follows:

```
CONSTRAINT CX1 FORALL SX ( SX.STATUS ≥ 1 AND SX.STATUS ≤ 100 ) ;
```

2. Suppliers in London must have status 20.

```
CONSTRAINT CX2 FORALL SX ( SX.CITY ≠ 'London' OR SX.STATUS = 20 ) ;
```

3. Supplier numbers must be unique.

```
CONSTRAINT CX3 FORALL SX ( UNIQUE SY ( SX.SNO = SY.SNO ) ) ;
```

This example illustrates the use of another kind of quantifier (the third kind we've seen). In general, the quantified expression

```
UNIQUE X ( bx )
```

evaluates to TRUE if and only if there exists exactly one value, out of the set of values over which the variable *X* ranges, that makes the boolean expression *bx* evaluate to TRUE. In the example, therefore, the expression

```
FORALL SX ( UNIQUE SY ( SX.SNO = SY.SNO ) )
```

effectively means "For all suppliers SX, there's exactly one supplier SY with the same supplier number." For example, if SX denotes the S tuple for supplier S4, say, then SY must also denote the S tuple for supplier S4—in general, in other words, SX and SY must denote the very same tuple—in order for the constraint to be satisfied.

4.   Suppliers with status less than 20 mustn't supply part P6.

```
CONSTRAINT CX4
   FORALL SX ( SX.STATUS ≥ 20 OR
               NOT EXISTS PX ( PX.PNO = 'P6' AND
                               EXISTS SPX ( SPX.SNO = SX.SNO AND
                                            SPX.PNO = PX.PNO ) ) ) ;
```

For interest, let me also show a prenex normal form version of this constraint:

```
CONSTRAINT CX4
   FORALL SX ( FORALL SPX ( FORALL PX
      ( SX.STATUS ≥ 20 OR PX.PNO ≠ 'P6' OR
                     SX.SNO ≠ SPX.SNO OR SPX.PNO ≠ PX.PNO ) ) ) ;
```

5.   Every supplier number in SP must also appear in S.

```
CONSTRAINT CX5 FORALL SPX ( UNIQUE SX ( SX.SNO = SPX.SNO ) ) ;
```

A SIMPLIFIED GRAMMAR

In this section, then, I present as promised a simplified BNF grammar for relational calculus expressions. Note that many features that would be needed in a real language—e.g., the ability to write relation literals—are deliberately excluded here, in order to concentrate on the essence of the matter.

```
<range var def>
    ::=   RANGEVAR <range var name> RANGES OVER <range> ;

<range>
    ::=   <relvar name> | ( <relation exp commalist> )

<relation exp>
    ::=   <proto tuple> [ WHERE <bool exp> ]

<proto tuple>
    ::=   { <entry commalist> }

<entry>
    ::=   <range var name> | [ <attribute name> := ] <attribute exp>

<attribute exp>
    ::=   <exp>
```

Note: The *<exp>* is allowed to contain a *<range attribute ref>*—see below—wherever a literal of the appropriate type would normally be allowed to appear.

```
<range attribute ref>
    ::=   <range var name> . <attribute ref>
```

```
<bool exp>
    ::=    all the usual possibilities, together with:
         | <quantified bool exp>
```

Note: The *<bool exp>* is allowed to contain a *<range attribute ref>* wherever a literal of the appropriate type would normally be allowed to appear.

```
<quantified bool exp>
    ::=    <quantifier> ( <bool exp> )

<quantifier>
    ::=    <quantifier name> <range var name>

<quantifier name>
    ::=    EXISTS | FORALL | UNIQUE
```

EXERCISES

Write relational calculus expressions for the following queries and constraints:

D.1   Get all shipments.

D.2   Get part numbers for parts supplied by supplier S2.

D.3   Get suppliers with status in the range 15 to 25 inclusive.

D.4   Get supplier numbers for suppliers with status lower than that of supplier S2.

D.5   Get part numbers for parts supplied by all suppliers in Paris.

D.6   Get part numbers for parts supplied by a supplier in London.

D.7   Get part numbers for parts not supplied by any supplier in London.

D.8   Get all pairs of part numbers such that some supplier supplies both of the indicated parts.

D.9   All red parts must weigh less than 50 pounds.

D.10 No two suppliers can be located in the same city.

D.11 At most one supplier can be located in Athens at any one time.

D.12 There must be at least one London supplier.

D.13 Supplier S1 and part P1 must never be in different cities.

ANSWERS

As in the body of the appendix, I assume the availability of range variables SX, PX, SPX, and so on (as needed).

D.1 `{ SPX }`

D.2 `{ SPX.PNO } WHERE SPX.SNO = 'S2'`

D.3 `{ SX } WHERE SX.STATUS ≥ 15 AND SX.STATUS ≤ 25`

D.4 `{ SX.SNO } WHERE UNIQUE SY ( SY.SNO = 'S2' AND SX.STATUS < SY.STATUS )`

D.5 `{ SPX.PNO } WHERE FORALL SX ( SX.CITY ≠ 'Paris' OR`
`                        EXISTS SPY ( SPY.SNO = SX.SNO AND SPY.PNO = SPX.PNO ) )`

D.6 `{ SPX.PNO } WHERE UNIQUE SX ( SX.SNO = SPX.SNO AND SX.CITY = 'London' )`

D.7 `{ SPX.PNO } WHERE FORALL SX ( SX.SNO ≠ SPX.SNO OR SX.CITY ≠ 'London' )`

D.8 `{ XNO := SPX.PNO , YNO := SPY.PNO } WHERE SPX.SNO = SPY.SNO`

D.9 `CONSTRAINT DX9 FORALL PX ( PX.WEIGHT < 50 ) ;`

D.10 `CONSTRAINT DX10 FORALL SX ( UNIQUE SY ( SX.CITY = SY.CITY ) ) ;`

D.11 `CONSTRAINT DX11 COUNT ( { SX } WHERE CITY = 'Athens' ) < 2 ;`

D.12 `CONSTRAINT DX12 EXISTS SX ( SX.CITY = 'London' ) ;`

D.13 `CONSTRAINT DX13 NOT EXISTS SX ( NOT EXISTS PX`
`          ( SX.SNO = 'S1' AND PX.PNO = 'P1' AND SX.CITY ≠ PX.CITY ) ) ;`

Appendix E

A Guide to Further Reading

I don't mind your thinking slowly;
I mind your publishing faster than you think.

—Wolfgang Pauli (attrib.)

There's a vast literature on relational database technology, and another such on matters related to SQL. This appendix contains an annotated list of publications from these two sources (both books and individual papers or articles) that you might find interesting. *Note:* I apologize for the number of times my own name appears as either author or coauthor in this list, but given the nature of the material, such a state of affairs is—if you'll pardon me for saying so—more or less inevitable.

Papers by E. F. Codd

- "Derivability, Redundancy, and Consistency of Relations Stored in Large Data Banks," IBM Research Report RJ599 (August 19th, 1969); "A Relational Model of Data for Large Shared Data Banks," *CACM 13,* No. 6 (June 1970). *Note:* The first of these papers was reprinted in *ACM SIGMOD Record 38*, No. 1 (March 2009); the second was reprinted in *Milestones of Research—Selected Papers 1958–1982 (CACM 25th Anniversary Issue), CACM 26,* No. 1 (January 1983) and elsewhere.

  The 1969 paper was Codd's very first paper on the relational model; essentially, it's a preliminary version of the 1970 paper, with a few interesting differences, the main one being that the 1969 paper permitted relation valued attributes while the 1970 one didn't. That 1970 paper was the first of Codd's papers to become widely available. It's usually credited with being the seminal paper in the field, though that characterization is a little unfair to its 1969 predecessor. I'd like to suggest, politely, that every database professional should read at least one of these papers every year.

- "Relational Completeness of Data Base Sublanguages," in Randall J. Rustin (ed.), *Data Base Systems, Courant Computer Science Symposia Series 6*. Englewood Cliffs, NJ: Prentice Hall (1972).

This is the paper in which Codd first formally defined both the original relational algebra and the original relational calculus. Not an easy read, but it repays careful study.

■ "Further Normalization of the Data Base Relational Model," in Randall J. Rustin (ed.), *Data Base Systems, Courant Computer Science Symposia Series 6*. Englewood Cliffs, NJ: Prentice Hall (1972).

This is the paper in which Codd defined 2NF and 3NF, thereby laying the groundwork for the entire field of research into database design theory. The title is a little misleading—further normalization isn't something that's done to the relational model, it's something that's done to relvars, or rather to relvar designs. (In particular, as we saw in Chapter 9, the relational model as such doesn't care how the database happens to be designed, just so long as the design in question doesn't violate any of the precepts of the relational model.) Also, a caveat: The definition of 1NF in this paper differs from that given in the present book, and is in fact (I would argue) incorrect.

Books by C. J. Date

■ *An Introduction to Database Systems* (8th edition). Boston, MA: Addison-Wesley (2004).

A college level text on all aspects (not just relational aspects) of database management. SQL discussions are at the SQL:1999 level, with a few comments on SQL:2003; in particular, they include a detailed discussion of SQL's "object/relational" features (REF types, reference values, and so on), with a detailed explaining of why they violate relational principles. *Note:* Some other texts covering a similar range of topics are as follows:

- Raghu Ramakrishnan and Johannes Gehrke: *Database Management Systems* (3rd edition). New York, NY: McGraw-Hill (2003).

- Ramez Elmasri and Shamkant Navathe: *Fundamentals of Database Systems* (6th edition). Boston, MA: Addison-Wesley (2010).

- Avi Silberschatz, Henry F. Korth, and S. Sudarshan: *Database System Concepts* (6th edition). New York, NY: McGraw-Hill (2010).

■ *Go Faster! The TransRelational^{TM} Approach to DBMS Implementation.* Frederiksberg, Denmark: Ventus (2002, 2011). Free download available at *www.bookboon.com*.

This book describes a radically novel approach to implementing a relational DBMS, one that's significantly different in a variety of fundamental ways from that found in all of the mainstream SQL products currently available.

- *Date on Database: Writings 2000–2006.* Berkeley, CA: Apress (2006).

This book is a collection of essays on a variety of topics, several of which are directly relevant to the subject of this book. In particular, it includes many discussions of SQL's departures from the relational model and the negative effects of the departures in question. Relevant chapters include Chapter 8 ("What First Normal Form Really Means"); Chapter 9 ("A Sweet Disorder," on the issue of left to right column ordering); Chapter 10 ("Double Trouble, Double Trouble," on the problems caused by duplicates); and Chapter 18 ("Why Three- and Four-Valued Logic Don't Work," on—among other things—problems arising from the logic allegedly underpinning SQL's concept of nulls).

- *SQL and Relational Theory: How to Write Accurate SQL Code* (2nd edition). Cambridge, MA: O'Reilly (2012).

This is the book referred to repeatedly in the present text by its abbreviated title *SQL and Relational Theory.* Topics discussed in this book and not covered in detail (or at all) in the present book include: views and other derived relvars; further problems with duplicates; type theory; relation valued attributes; multiple assignment; an SQL grammar; recursive queries; the importance of tuple equality; selectors and THE_ operators; nulls and three-valued logic; how to handle "missing information"; "dimensional data"; optimization and expression transformation; "domain check override"; predicate logic; further relational operators; relation constants; and other topics. See the preface to the present book for further background.

- *Database Design and Relational Theory: Normal Forms and All That Jazz.* Cambridge, MA: O'Reilly (2012).

- *View Updating and Relational Theory: Solving the View Update Problem.* Cambridge, MA: O'Reilly (2013).

Books by C. J. Date and Hugh Darwen

- *A Guide to the SQL Standard* (4th edition). Boston, MA: Addison-Wesley (1997).

This book is concerned primarily with SQL:1992, though it does also contain details of the Call Level Interface feature CLI (1995), the Persistent Stored Modules feature PSM (1997), and a few features that became part of SQL:1999. Despite the fact that the standard is now in its 2011 edition, the book remains, in my not unbiased opinion, a reliable reference and tutorial as far as SQL's "relational" features are concerned.

■ *Databases, Types, and the Relational Model: The Third Manifesto* (3rd edition). Boston, MA: Addison-Wesley (2007).

This book introduces and explains *The Third Manifesto*, a precise though somewhat formal definition of the relational model and a supporting type theory (including a comprehensive model of type inheritance). Note that the *Manifesto* itself constitutes just one comparatively short chapter in the book (twelve pages, out of a total of well over 500).

■ *Database Explorations: Essays on The Third Manifesto and Related Topics.* Bloomington, IN: Trafford (2010).

Among other things, this book contains recent revisions to both *The Third Manifesto* as such and the **Tutorial D** language. (Please note in passing that **Tutorial D** is not part of the *Manifesto* as such but is merely one possible language that can be used to explain the ideas of the *Manifesto*.) The book also contains some proposals for upgrading **Tutorial D** to industrial strength. *Note:* The website *www.thethirdmanifesto.com* gives information regarding a variety of existing **Tutorial D** implementations, as well as other projects related to the *Manifesto*. See also *http://dbappbuilder.sourceforge.net/rel.html*, which provides access to downloadable code for *Rel*, a prototype implementation of (a dialect of) **Tutorial D**, by Dave Voorhis.

 Incidentally, an appendix to Chapter 27 of this book ("Is SQL's Three-Valued Logic Truth Functionally Complete?") contains a detailed, comprehensive, and careful description of SQL's nulls and nulls-related features.

Other Publications Related to SQL

■ Donald D. Chamberlin and Raymond F. Boyce: "SEQUEL: A Structured English Query Language," Proc. 1974 ACM SIGMOD Workshop on Data Description, Access, and Control, Ann Arbor, MI (May 1974).

As noted in Chapter 10, this is the paper that first introduced the SQL language (or SEQUEL—"Structured English QUEry Language"—as it was originally called). There are some interesting differences between SEQUEL as described in this paper and SQL as generally understood today. Here are some of them:

- There were no nulls.

- Although the SELECT clause was supported, the "SELECT *" form didn't exist. Thus, for example, to obtain all suppliers in London, you just wrote S WHERE CITY = 'London'—and to obtain all suppliers, you just wrote S.

- Duplicates were eliminated by default (though not in "set functions," which is the term used, rather inappropriately, in the SQL standard to refer to constructs such as SUM and AVG).

- The FROM clause always contained exactly one table name. In other words, SEQUEL had no way to do a join as such.

- The right comparand (only) in a comparison in a WHERE clause was allowed to be a subquery (though the term *subquery* didn't exist—the construct was called a *mapping* instead), in which case the comparison was in fact an ANY or ALL comparison (see *SQL and Relational Theory* for an explanation of these latter constructs). ANY was the default, and could be specified only implicitly. IN syntax as such was not supported; "=" (meaning, by default, "=ANY") was used instead.

- Set comparison operators (set inclusion, etc.) were supported.

- There was no GROUP BY clause as such; GROUP BY functionality did exist, but it was specified as an option on the FROM clause.

- There was no HAVING clause; "set functions" could be invoked in the WHERE clause instead.

- There were no *correlation names* (the original SEQUEL term for SQL's range variables). Instead, "blocks"—in this context, apparently another term for mappings in the sense explained above—could be labeled, and block labels could be used as dot qualifiers.

- Expressions such as QTY / AVG(QTY)—i.e., expressions involving "set function" invocations, as well as simple column references and the like—were legal in the SELECT clause, and presumably in the WHERE clause also.

- "Mappings" could be combined by means of intersection, union, and difference (and these operators were denoted by conventional mathematical symbols rather than keywords).

The paper also discusses several alleged differences between SEQUEL and the relational calculus, claiming in every case an advantage for SEQUEL over the calculus. However, the differences and claims in question don't really stand up to careful analysis.

- International Organization for Standardization (ISO): *Database Language SQL,* Document ISO/IEC 9075:2011 (2011).

The official SQL standard (2011 version). Note that it is indeed an international standard, not just (as so many seem to think) an American or "ANSI" standard. Note too that although SQL:2011 is the current version of the standard, essentially all of the SQL features discussed in the present book were already included in SQL:1992 or even earlier versions.

■ Jim Melton and Alan R. Simon: *SQL:1999—Understanding Relational Components;* Jim Melton: *Advanced SQL:1999—Understanding Object-Relational and Other Advanced Features.* San Francisco, CA: Morgan Kaufmann (2002 and 2003, respectively).

So far as I know, these two books are the only ones available that cover in detail, between them, any version of the standard later than SQL:1992. Melton was the editor of the standard for many years (and still is, at the time of writing).

■ Stéphane Faroult with Peter Robson: *The Art of SQL.* Cambridge, MA: O'Reilly (2006).

A practitioner's guide on how to use SQL to get good performance in currently available products. The following lightly edited list of subtitles from the book's twelve chapters gives some idea of its scope:

1. Designing Databases for Performance
2. Accessing Databases Efficiently
3. Indexing
4. Understanding SQL Statements
5. Understanding Physical Implementation
6. Classic SQL Patterns
7. Dealing with Hierarchic Data
8. Difficult Cases
9. Concurrency
10. Large Data Volumes
11. Response Times
12. Monitoring Performance

The book doesn't deviate much from relational principles in its suggestions and recommendations—in fact, it explicitly advocates adherence to those principles, for the most part. But it also recognizes that today's optimizers are less than perfect; thus, it gives guidance on how to choose the specific SQL formulation for a given problem, out of many logically equivalent formulations, that's likely to perform best (and it explains why).

Miscellaneous

■ Patrick Hall, Peter Hitchcock, and Stephen Todd: "An Algebra of Relations for Machine Computation," Conf. Record of the 2nd ACM Symposium on Principles of Programming Languages, Palo Alto, CA (January 1975).

This paper is perhaps a little "difficult," but I think it's important. **Tutorial D** and the version of the relational algebra I've been describing in this book both have their roots in this paper.

■ Jim Gray and Andreas Reuter: *Transaction Processing: Concepts and Techniques*. San Francisco, CA: Morgan Kaufmann (1993).

The standard text on transaction management (see Chapter 8 in the present book).

■ Lex de Haan and Toon Koppelaars: *Applied Mathematics for Database Professionals*. Berkeley, CA: Apress (2007).

Among other things, this book shows how to implement integrity constraints by means of procedural code (if necessary!—see Chapter 13 of the present book).

Index

For alphabetization purposes, (a) differences in fonts and case are ignored; (b) quotation marks are ignored; (c) other punctuation symbols—hyphens, underscores, parentheses, etc.—are treated as blanks; (d) numerals precede letters; (e) blanks precede everything else.

Have it your way.

Get even more for your money.

Join the O'Reilly Community, and register the O'Reilly books you own. It's free, and you'll get:

- $4.99 ebook upgrade offer
- 40% upgrade offer on O'Reilly print books
- Membership discounts on books and events
- Free lifetime updates to ebooks and videos
- Multiple ebook formats, DRM FREE
- Participation in the O'Reilly community
- Newsletters
- Account management
- 100% Satisfaction Guarantee

Signing up is easy:

1. **Go to: oreilly.com/go/register**
2. **Create an O'Reilly login.**
3. **Provide your address.**
4. **Register your books.**

Note: English-language books only

To order books online:

oreilly.com/store

For questions about products or an order:

orders@oreilly.com

To sign up to get topic-specific email announcements and/or news about upcoming books, conferences, special offers, and new technologies:

elists@oreilly.com

For technical questions about book content:

booktech@oreilly.com

To submit new book proposals to our editors:

proposals@oreilly.com

O'Reilly books are available in multiple DRM-free ebook formats. For more information:

oreilly.com/ebooks

O'REILLY®

Spreading the knowledge of innovators | oreilly.com

Ingram Content Group UK Ltd.
Milton Keynes UK
UKHW050932280623
424075UK00022B/539

9 781449 369439